D1479027

ETHIOPIA,
THE
UNITED STATES
AND THE
SOVIET UNION

DAVID A. KORN

Southern Illinois University Press
Carbondale and Edwardsville

Published in Great Britain by Croom Helm Ltd.,
Provident House, Burrell Row, Beckenham,
Kent BR3 1AT

Published in the United States and Canada
by Southern Illinois University Press,
P.O. Box 3697, Carbondale, IL 62902-3697

Library of Congress Cataloging-in-Publication Data

Korn, David A., 1930-
    Ethiopia, the United States, and the Soviet Union.

    Bibliography: p.
    Includes index.
    1. United States — Foreign relations — Ethiopia.
2. Ethiopia — Foreign relations — United States.
3. Ethiopia — Foreign relations — Soviet Union.
4. Soviet Union — Foreign relations — Ethiopia.
5. Ethiopia — Politics and government — 1974-
I. Title.
E183.8.E8K67   1986   327.73063   86-11921
ISBN 0-8093-1338-3

CONTENTS

To my wife Roberta Cohen who, despite the political odds and on her own initiative, reopened the American cultural, educational and information programs in Ethiopia.

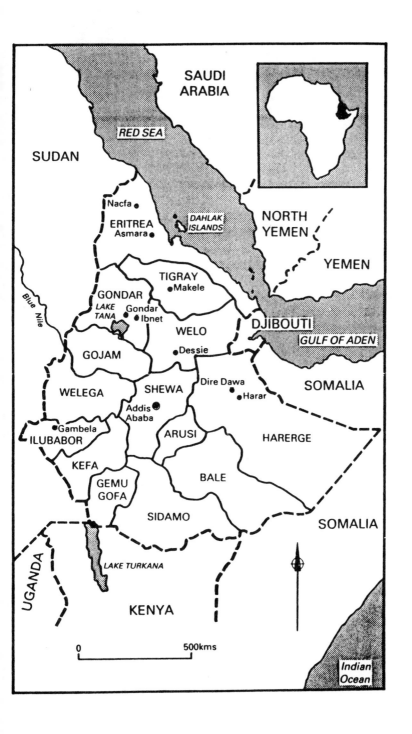

ABBREVIATIONS

ADB	African Development Bank
COPWE	Commission for the Organization of the Party of the Workers of Ethiopia
CRS	Catholic Relief Service
EDU	Ethiopian Democratic Union
EEC	European Economic Community
ELF	Eritrean Liberation Front
EPLF	Eritrean People's Liberation Front
EPRP	Ethiopian People's Revolutionary Party
ERA	Eritrean Relief Association
FAO	Food and Agriculture Organization
IBRD	International Bank for Reconstruction and Development
MEISON	[All Ethiopian Socialist movement]
MSF	Médecins Sans Frontières
NAMRU	[US Navy's Medical research center]
NSC	National Security Council
OAU	Organization of African Unity
OLF	Oromo Liberation Front
PDRE	People's Democratic Republic of Ethiopia
PMAC	Provisional Military Administrative Council
REST	Relief Society of Tigray
RRC	Relief and Rehabilitation Commission
SNM	Somali National Movement
SPLA	Sudanese People's Liberation Army
SSDF	Somali Salvation Democratic Front
TPLF	Tigrean People's Liberation Front
UNECA	United Nations Economic Commission for Africa
USAID	United States Agency for International Development
USIS	United States Information Service
WPE	Workers Party of Ethiopia
WSLF	Western Somali Liberation Front

PREFACE

In the pages that follow I have tried to trace the history of relations between the United States and Ethiopia and the Soviet Union and that country from 1974 to 1985. The former is of course the year of the Ethiopian revolution and the latter the second year of the terrible famine that brought the ancient African nation once again to the forefront of world attention. The focus of this account is the period from mid-1982 to mid-1985, the time of my service as officer in charge of the American Embassy in Addis Ababa. Given the background from which I write, I naturally have a great deal more to say about the United States' dealings with Ethiopia than about the Soviet Union's. The one is viewed from the inside, the other from the outside. If this disparity is a flaw, it is an unavoidable one. The impossibility of presenting a matching inside view of Soviet–Ethiopian relations would not be good cause for limiting the account strictly to the American side. The role played by the Soviet Union in Ethiopia since 1974 is too big for that. It is simply not possible to deal with the history of this period without discussing, albeit necessarily incompletely, the Soviet side of things. This book does, I believe, have some new material to offer even on that aspect of the problem. The Soviet Embassy in Addis Ababa held itself very much aloof from Western embassies. In Third World countries where Western influence is predominant, Soviet diplomatic personnel make themselves accessible and within limits do their best to mix with their Western colleagues. In Ethiopia they stayed coldly apart. They obviously considered it their territory and saw no reason to give Westerners, particularly Americans, any openings. Still, some very limited contacts did take place, and the doings of the Soviet Embassy were the object of keen scrutiny by Western embassies.

Some words of explanation may be in order. Diplomats sometimes make history themselves and often witness much more at first hand. But they seldom write about it. When they do come forward to help fill out the public record, it is usually many years later. When I arrived in Addis Ababa at the beginning of June 1982 to take charge of the American Embassy I knew that I had come to a very unusual place at a quite extraordinary time. Here was an

ancient Christian empire that only eight years earlier had
undergone a revolution that ranked with history's most bloody and
most thorough. It had emerged with a government that proclaimed
itself Marxist–Leninist, dedicated to the establishment of a new
society and the creation of a new 'socialist man'. From the time that
it began to open itself up to the outside world early in this century,
Ethiopia had looked westward. Since the Second World War it had
had the closest relations with the United States. Now, suddenly, it
was allied with the Soviet Union and embarked on remaking its
economy and its society on the Soviet model. I knew that I was
taking part in quite an exceptional piece of history. As time passed I
became persuaded that what I was witnessing should be made part
of the public record.

What I did not know at the beginning was just how firmly
anchored Ethiopia's new alliance was. Newly arrived diplomats
almost always carry in their mental baggage the belief that, thanks
to their own especially keen understanding and unique talents,
unfavorable situations can be made right. Even if unburdened by
such illusions, the head of the diplomatic mission, the person most
immediately responsible for relations between his and a foreign
government, must never stop looking for ways to make relations
better, no matter how unpromising the prospects may seem. At the
same time he must reach a realistic appraisal of the foreign
government in question, an appraisal that will be a trustworthy
guide for his and his government's actions. Management of the
tension between these two basically contradictory requirements is
one of the most difficult problems faced by a chief of a diplomatic
mission, as much in a friendly country as in one that is hostile.

I struggled with this problem each day of the 37 months that I
spent in Ethiopia. I am sure I did not always achieve a perfect
balance. Ethiopia in the first half of the 1980s had pronounced
aspects of unreality. What one saw depended to a considerable
extent on what mirror one looked into. The Ethiopians that the
foreign diplomat or visitor were likely to meet were almost all
Western-educated. Almost all had fond memories of their student
days in the United States, Great Britain or other Western countries
and regretted the gulf that had developed between their
government and the West. One way or another, with greater or
lesser degrees of caution, many would make known their desire for
a return to closer ties with the West. Taken in isolation, these
contacts with Ethiopians could only leave Westerners wondering

why there should be any serious or unsurmountable problem between the West and Ethiopia. Unfortunately, the Ethiopians one most frequently encountered were not the ones who made the decisions; even those who held ministerial rank were for the most part no more than implementors and technicians. All matters of any significance touching on relations with East and West, in fact all matters of importance in any area, were decided by 'Chairman' — later 'General Secretary' — Mengistu Haile Mariam and his coterie. If actions spoke louder than words — though in Mengistu's case words usually spoke quite loudly enough — then all but the most deluded optimist would after a time have to conclude that Mengistu and those closest to him had chosen the Soviet side and were not about to reconsider or stray even a short distance from that choice. There were, I have to say, a few wishful thinkers among my Western diplomatic colleagues in Addis Ababa.

One of my main purposes in writing this book was to present for public consideration the record of the United States' efforts to reach a better understanding with the government of Ethiopia. It is, as will be seen, an extensive one. No such undertaking is ever perfect. Critics might argue that this one should have been conducted with different emphasis or in different ways. But the record does show that the United States made repeated attempts to come to grips with the problems that becloud its relations with Ethiopia and that Mengistu's government showed no serious interest in joining that effort, though at times for tactical purposes it feigned an interest. Evidently, it feared that better understanding with the United States would mean — or would be taken by the Soviets to mean — a slackening in Ethiopia's ties with the Soviet Union.

Another purpose of the book is to make available to the public a factual account of why and how relations between the United States and Ethiopia broke down in the mid-1970s following the revolution and why and how the regime that emerged from the revolution allied itself with the Soviet Union. In the service of its own political objectives, the Ethiopian government has distorted and obscured the history of its relations with the United States and the Soviet Union during the years 1974 to 1977, so as to make it seem that Ethiopia had no choice but to break with the United States and turn to the Soviet Union. The truth is very different. But even among Westerners who should know enough to be skeptical, and among Ethiopians who oppose Mengistu's regime, this story has found remarkably broad acceptance. At least in part this is because so little has been written about the subject in the West; there has been no solid widely accessible historical record. The definitive history of the period remains to be written. The account offered herein makes no claim to being exhaustive but I do not believe that more detailed research and publication — which it is to be hoped will come one day — will change the essential thrust of the story told in Chapters 1 and 2. I hope it is sufficient to give the reader a sense of the course that Ethiopia's relations with West and East took during the critical formative years of 1974 through 1977.

Finally, I wanted to tell the story, as my colleagues and I at the American Embassy in Addis Ababa saw it, of the great drought and famine of 1984 and 1985. It brought an enormous outpouring of sympathy from people around the world and substantial contributions from the pockets of private citizens in the United States and Western Europe, to say nothing of the very large sums appropriated by their governments. Yet the callousness and dereliction of the Ethiopian government in the face of massive suffering by its citizens makes a sad and shocking tale, one that deserves to be more widely known than the international press has so far made it. The same is true of the Ethiopian government's resettlement program, though by the time the manuscript for this book was completed it was beginning to get more attention. Everybody would agree that resettlement can be a useful tool for development and for alleviating problems associated with drought and soil exhaustion. But it matters a great deal just how it is carried out. Proper planning and execution are essential. They have been conspicuously absent from the Ethiopian government's program, and so has for the most part even elementary concern for human life. The book is, of course, not closed on the Ethiopian government's program, but there is reason to doubt whether it will eventually bring the large increases in food production that the authorities in Addis Ababa claim to expect from it. Certainly these cannot be counted on soon. And unfortunately, as the reader will see, it cannot be expected that the last has been heard of famine in Ethiopia. The politically inspired agricultural policies pursued by the Ethiopian government virtually guarantee that its people will remain dependent on food hand-outs from the West for a long time to come.

None of these subjects would be intelligible without some broader background, in particular on the fascinating figure of Mengistu Haile Mariam and on the civil wars in Eritrea and Tigray. Chapters dealing with both are offered herein. The civil wars

remain Ethiopia's main problem, though drought and famine —
with which they interlock — have momentarily overshadowed them
in the public mind. Mengistu is the central figure in Ethiopia. No
understanding of the course of Ethiopia's history since 1974, and no
evaluation of its likely future course, is possible without some
insight into the character of this extraordinary man. What I am able
to offer here is admittedly limited, owing to the secrecy in which
Mengistu shrouds himself. Still, I think it is enough to permit the
reader to make the essential judgments.

For fairness sake, I want to add here a word about the role of
Dawit Wolde Giorgis, the Chief Commissioner of the Ethiopian
Government's Relief and Rehabilitation Commission, the agency
responsible for famine relief programs and for part of the resettlement program. Commissioner Dawit and most of his staff
genuinely cared about the plight of the starving and made real
efforts to rescue them. Their dilemma was the classic one of officials
who try to do good in a system and under a leadership that is
inherently bad: one pays for one's license to do some good work by
making painful compromises with the system and by accepting
identification with, and even responsibility for, its more disre-
putable practices. The shortcomings of the RRC recorded herein
derived from this source and from the paucity of resources accorded
it by the Ethiopian government. I admired the RRC for what it
accomplished in saving lives. I do not believe that Commissioner
Dawit ever truly supported Mengistu's resettlement program, and I
suspect that he argued against its continuation once the terrible toll
it would take became evident. I was not at all surprised when, a few
months after my departure from Ethiopia, he found the
compromises required of his position too heavy a burden and chose
to seek refuge in the West, as so many outstanding Ethiopians have
done since 1974.

Sources and Acknowledgements

A list of the main works consulted, books and articles or pamphlets,
will be found in the bibliography at the back of this volume. My
firsthand account of the happenings of the period from June 1982 to
July 1985 is based on my own notes and recollections from that time.

The many Ethiopians who in one way or another contributed to my education about their country, its government and its recent and not so recent history must necessarily remain nameless, but I am deeply indebted to them. I owe particular thanks to Paul B. Henze of the Rand Corporation for having given me so generously of his time and of his insights into Ethiopia and relations between Ethiopia and the United States, for his having made available to me his unpublished as well as his many published writings on that country, and for the many helpful suggestions he made on the manuscript. Among others who read the manuscript I also want to thank Dr James Piscatori, currently of the Australian National University, for his helpful comments. I am grateful to my State Department colleague Donald K. Petterson, American Ambassador to Somalia from 1978 to 1982, for his having so generously made available to me his published and unpublished writings on Somalia and Ethiopia; I drew extensively on his material for Chapter 1. Of course, any errors or omissions anywhere in the book are entirely my own.

The manuscript was written during a year's assignment to the Royal Institute of International Affairs in London beginning in September 1985. I want to thank the entire staff of Chatham House for their helpfulness, courtesy and patience, in particular the Director, Admiral Sir James Eberle, the Director of Studies, Dr William Wallace, the Publications Manager, Ms Pauline Wickham, and the staff of the press library and the library. The Center for the Study of Foreign Affairs of the Department of State's Foreign Service Institute was my sponsor during this year, and I want to thank its Director, Dr Hans Binnendijk, and its Research Director, Mr Joseph V. Montville, for the support they gave me for my project.

For those who may wonder, I should make clear in advance that the book was entirely my own idea and neither it nor anything in it was suggested to me by the Department of State, though the Department of course had to and did approve my request for authorization to publish what I had written. The views expressed herein are, also, entirely my own.

1 THE TURN FROM WEST TO EAST

For those who were watching — and not everyone was — the Horn of Africa was the scene of astonishing political acrobatics in the mid-1970s. Ethiopia plunged into turmoil early in 1974 and in September of that year Emperor Haile Selassie was deposed. With his fall, Ethiopia's ties with the United States were called into question. By 1977 a reversal of alliances had taken place. The United States, for over 30 years Ethiopia's main foreign friend and purveyor of economic and military assistance, was shorn of its presence and influence and its place was seized by the Soviet Union. Somalia, since 1969 a faithful friend and protégé of the Soviet Union, cut its ties with Moscow and turned toward Washington.

Haile Selassie's troubles started a decade and a half earlier and they were, at least in part, the outgrowth of his successes. After the British set him back on his throne in 1941, the Emperor schemed and politicked tirelessly to assure the return of the Ogaden — the British had thoughts of detaching it and keeping it for their Somalia protectorate — to Ethiopian sovereignty, and to bring Eritrea back under Ethiopia's wing. In the former he succeeded easily, but the latter proved a more difficult task. Eritrea had been under Italian colonial rule since the mid-1880s, and, while the Ethiopian government vociferously asserted that it was historically an integral part of the empire, others were not so sure. The British wanted to pare off the northern part and give it to Sudan but were willing to leave the rest to Ethiopia. The Soviets at times favored making it an independent state. The Italians would have liked to have had it back as a trust territory, in the same way that they got former Italian Somaliland. The United States understood that Haile Selassie would regard its position on Eritrea as a critical test of friendship. It did not think Eritrea would be a viable entity on its own, and it was concerned that it might not be able to keep its military communications station in Asmara if Eritrea were to become independent. So it eventually decided to support handing the former Italian colony over to Ethiopia, albeit under a statute of federation. This was done in 1952. It was one of the strangest marriages of convenience ever spawned by international politics: a territory with a democratically elected parliament and executive federated with an absolute

1

monarchy responsible for defense, foreign affairs and money that regarded federation as an anomoly to be corrected at the earliest opportunity.

Haile Selassie must have felt satisfied with himself, for he had not only preserved the gains of his predecessor, Menelik II, in the south but secured the outlet to the sea in the north that Menelik had been obliged to forfeit. But in the 1960s these achievements became nightmares. Britain's Somaliland protectorate and the Italian UN trust territory became one independent state with an openly declared policy of irredentism that called for the incorporation of the Ogaden region of Ethiopia, the French port of Djibouti, and a part of northern Kenya, all territories inhabited in part or in whole by ethnic Somalis. Somalia immediately set about finding a foreign sponsor that would equip it with an army to enable it to accomplish these aims. Though for the first nine years of its existence Somalia practised Western-style parliamentary democracy, the West was not interested in promoting its military ambitions or sponsoring its territorial fantasies. The United States was solidly entrenched in Ethiopia, whose army it was building and equipping under an agreement signed in 1953; it had no desire to jeopardize its position in Ethiopia or to assume the contradictory obligation of arming the only neighbor that entertained a territorial claim against Ethiopia. Inevitably, along came the Soviets, first in a relatively modest way in 1963 and then in a very big way after General Mohammed Siad Barre threw out the politicians and made himself dictator in 1969. In between time, in 1964, Ethiopia had to fight a small war with Somalia to hold on to the Ogaden. After 1969, when the Soviets got seriously to work on the business of arming Somalia, the Ethiopians turned frantically to the United States. It was not the ideal moment. The United States was mired in Vietnam and had neither the resources nor the desire to build bigger armies for small clients in remote places. It responded with soothing words, assuring the Ethiopians that Somalia was not really that much of a threat, and with a plan for a modest build-up of the Ethiopian army over the 1970s, a $200 m. program to provide M-60 tanks, patrol boats, F-5E fighter aircraft and a variety of lesser equipment.

But Haile Selassie and his generals wanted more, and they wanted it faster. In the spring of 1973 the Emperor flew to Washington, assuring his army and government that he would make the Americans understand. He gave the Nixon administration a request for $450 m. in military equipment. This caused him to get a decidedly cool reception, though he was promised that F–5E fighter aircraft would be provided. The administration was already locked in its struggle with the Watergate scandals and was not able or inclined to give the Emperor's visit a great deal of attention; little public fanfare attended it. In Ethiopia the trip was seen to be a failure. This was a great blow to the Emperor's prestige, which was not repaired thereafter by a visit to Moscow that brought no promise of arms.

Meanwhile, in 1962 the Emperor abolished the federation and put Eritrea under his direct rule. This wholly predictable step had a largely predictable result: by the mid-1960s there was armed rebellion in the hills of the northern province. The 1967 Arab–Israeli war compounded Ethiopia's woes: the closure of the Suez Canal dealt Eritrea's economy a massive blow and sent a chill through the entire Ethiopian economy. In the frustration of their defeat, the Arabs turned to helping the Eritrean rebels against the United States' and Israel's friend, Haile Selassie. So did Cuba, Communist China and, surreptitiously, the Soviet Union. Haile Selassie responded to this challenge with two brilliant diplomatic maneuvers. In 1971 he flew to Peking and, in exchange for recognition of the People's Republic of China, got the government of that country to sever its ties with the Eritrean insurgents and pledge $100 m. in economic aid. In 1972 he came to terms with President Nimeiri of Sudan, who had just had a close call at the hands of the small Sudanese Communist party. Sudanese tolerance of the Eritrean rebels, for whom safe haven in Sudan was very near to essential, began to wane. The government regained the upper hand in Eritrea. Still, the Ethiopians saw themselves caught in a vice, between insurgents assisted by the Arabs and the Soviet bloc in the north and Somalis armed to the teeth by the Soviets and Cubans in the south and east. They imagined their situation to be desperate and considered themselves deeply wronged by the United States' apparent inability to comprehend their predicament.

Then came natural disaster. In 1972 and 1973 cyclical drought struck the north-central provinces of Welo and Tigray. Widespread famine followed. Characteristically, the Ethiopian government's first reaction was to ignore what was happening, even to deny that thousands were dying. Drought and famine were not unusual in Ethiopia, particularly in Welo and Tigray where over-use of the land and massacre of forests by a too numerous peasantry in desperate search for fuel had caused serious erosion. In earlier

times there had not been much to be done about famine. There were
no roads and very little surplus food to distribute; inattention was
the traditional response. What Haile Selassie and those around him
failed to appreciate was that traditional responses were inadequate
in the age of television, thanks to which the world had developed a
conscience about the suffering of peoples in far off places. It had
also developed the agricultural surpluses and the means of deliv-
ering them to starving populations. The imperial government's
slowness to act caused it to be viewed as callous, irresponsible and
incompetent. In the United States, there was much embarrassment
at being associated with a regime universally judged derelict in its
duty to its citizens. In Ethiopia, the government's authority was
undermined and radicals used the famine to discredit it. A picture
was put about of the Emperor feeding hunks of meat to his dogs,
juxtaposed with another of starving peasants in Welo.

Then there was the Emperor himself, still in the 1970s an absolute
monarch governing with methods that had worked brilliantly in the
1920s and 1930s. Haile Selassie wanted to develop his country, but
social justice was not a concept that made a great impression on
him. Opinions differ substantially over the degree to which
Ethiopia's backwardness in the early 1970s was to be attributed to
his policies. Unquestionably, however, the flaunting of the wealth
of the aristocracy and the business class, many of them foreigners,
made the poverty of the masses seem all the more terrible. The state
provided few if any services; literacy at the time of the revolution
was estimated at between 6 and 9 per cent. There was, nevertheless,
a young educated elite and it regarded Haile Selassie's rule as
antiquated and ineffectual. Dissatisfaction on the part of those who
wanted more modern and progressive government led to an attempt
to overthrow Haile Selassie in December 1960 while he was out of
the country on a visit to Brazil. It failed, but the very fact that it had
occurred, and might in different circumstances have succeeded,
dimmed the aura of invulnerability that had surrounded the
Emperor. Radical students began to coalesce and conspire, and the
educated public, even those with a substantial stake in the system,
sensed that the moment for change was coming. In 1972 Haile
Selassie celebrated his eightieth birthday; he was commonly
believed to be even a few years older. Since the late 1960s he had
begun to experience moments of senility. His ministers complained
of having constantly to repeat themselves to him. Since they
continued to have to consult him on all but the most trivial business,

the work of government was much impeded by this imperial failing. John Spencer, an American who served for many years as an advisor on foreign affairs to the Ethiopian government, recounts that, at a state dinner in honor of President Mobutu of Zaire, Haile Selassie summoned an aide to ask who was the guest of honor sitting opposite him.[1] The Emperor's senility was not evident in his public appearances, but it was well known. It created a general sense that change was imminent.

For some this translated into the feeling that power was up for grabs, particularly since, like most absolute rulers, Haile Selassie had not prepared a strong succession. Crown Prince Asfa Wossen was intelligent and well disposed towards liberalization but he was not a man of his father's calibre. Moreover, he was in poor health; he suffered a stroke in 1973 and was out of Ethiopia during much of 1974. Faced with an impending vacuum, some among the aristocracy hoped for at least a partial restoration of the power shorn from them by Haile Selassie decades earlier. The growing middle class and some intellectuals dreamed of an uneventful transition to at least a limited form of democracy. Many of the young were attracted to more radical doctrines, to Marxism in its Chinese or Soviet embodiment. Very few, however, foresaw the upheaval that was about to occur.

Even taken all together, these converging elements — pressure from Somalia and from Eritrea, discontent among educated elites, drought and famine, and the inevitable physical decline of an aged monarch — do not fully explain the cataclysm that struck Ethiopia, the destruction of a system and a society that was overripe for change but that almost no one thought could simply be swept away. Contrary to the impression given in writings of Soviet bloc commentators and Western Marxists, the Ethiopian revolution was not brought about by a spontaneous uprising of the masses. The peasantry, 90 per cent of the population, was not involved at all during the first year. The troubles began with mutinies in the military, in January and February of 1974, over living conditions and pay. When the regime did not move to crush these but rather to propitiate, agitation erupted in Addis Ababa. An ill-timed increase in gasoline prices brought a strike by taxi drivers. Students demonstrated, and finally there was a general strike in Addis Ababa. In April, Haile Selassie allowed his Prime Minister of sixteen years, Aklilu Habte Wold, to step down. He appointed an ambitious nobleman, Endalkatchew Makonnen, and promised changes in the constitution to make the Prime Minister responsible to Parliament. This concession seems merely to have whetted appetites. The army's junior officers and non-commissioned officers formed committees and effectively took control of their units. They became the only force that could assure order. The government gradually ceased to exercise authority. The new Prime Minister tried to manipulate the army and secure its backing by offering up to the military committees, for imprisonment, the main figures of the imperial regime; he may also have hoped thereby to rid himself of people he thought were potential rivals. But the more concessions Endalkatchew made, the more his government came under attack. By June, when he could no longer govern — and by which time he had handed over for imprisonment all the members of the previous cabinet and many of his own — the mutineers took him away too. At the end of June they formed themselves into a committee that took the name, coined from Geez, of 'the Derg'. This body, composed of some 120 middle grade and junior officers and NCOs — there was a rule that no member could be higher in grade than Major at the time of the Derg's formation — was supposedly elected from the various units. As it disposed of military force, and the regular organs of state had no further authority, it was in a position to dictate its wishes. This it proceeded to do, albeit cautiously at first. It proposed, and Haile Selassie accepted, a new Prime Minister, a Fabian socialist nobleman known for his malleability, Michael Imru, and a new Defense Minister, General Aman Andom. General Aman, an Eritrean, had led Ethiopian forces to victory over Somalia in 1964. His success was recompensed by removal from the army and placement in the Senate created by the constitution that Haile Selassie had promulgated in 1955. There he waited for his day of revenge. For him, and for others who wanted Haile Selassie out of the way, it came on 12 September when, after a violent campaign of vilification against the monarch, the Derg declared him deposed and, in calculated humiliation, took the former Emperor from his palace in the back seat of a Volkswagen Beetle.

In all this remarkable chain of events, the thing that testifies most persuasively to Haile Selassie's senility is that at no point did he make a determined effort to protect his throne or seriously try to prevent the imprisonment of those who had long served him. In June he passed up what was probably his last opportunity to save himself when he vetoed a proposal by the commander of his bodyguard, a unit of division size, to attack and crush the mutineers. The operation would almost certainly have succeeded, but there would have been bloodshed. Evidently Haile Selassie, like Endalkatchew, thought he could manipulate the young officers. He had no idea of the violence of the forces that had been unleashed. Perhaps, naïvely, he also expected that the United States, his friend and protector for so many years, would somehow save his throne for him.

For the United States, the crisis in Ethiopia could hardly have come at a worse time. Richard Nixon's struggle with the Watergate scandals ran a parallel course to Haile Selassie's slow political agony in Addis Ababa, and the American President resigned only a month before Haile Selassie was deposed. The American Embassy in Addis Ababa continued to go about its business during the eventful months of 1974, working to keep up with and report latest developments. Officers in the State Department followed reports from Addis Ababa closely. But at the top of the US administration there was evidently very little time to be concerned over what was happening in Ethiopia.

One wonders whether it would have been greatly different if the upheaval in Ethiopia had occurred at a moment of less distraction in Washington. The passing of Haile Selassie's rule had been expected for some years, and few in Washington were moved to sorrow by the prospect. The Ethiopian monarch was generally thought to have outlived his time; change was considered inevitable. Though the troubles in Ethiopia were accompanied by much radical rhetoric, there was no bloodshed before November. The Derg was largely a mystery to the Americans, as it was to others. The officers of the US military mission in the Ethiopian capital knew few of its members, and those that could be identified and approached shied away from contact with the Americans. This was worrisome, but the Derg's first pronouncement, issued at the time of its formation at the end of June, was unexceptionable: it proclaimed the motto 'Ethiopia Tikdem', meaning 'Ethiopia First', which to all appearances was simply intended to express the group's strong feelings of nationalism. Also on the reassuring side, the new Minister of Defense, General Aman, was regarded as a moderate and a friend of the United States. Aman visited Washington in August and held talks at the Departments of State and Defense. After Haile Selassie's removal in September, Aman was named Chairman of the Provisional Military Administrative Council, the body set up to direct the affairs of state.

The State Department, therefore, counseled patience. The specific issue facing the United States was whether to continue to supply arms to Ethiopia. The United States' first reaction to the troubles in Ethiopia in 1974 was to increase arms supplies, as a measure to strengthen the government and friendly elements in the military. In previous years, despite Haile Selassie's urgent appeals, US military assistance to Ethiopia had been held to about $10 m. a year. Now, in the early summer of 1974, Washington approved a new program of credits and cash sales that would allow Ethiopia to obtain about $100 m. in American military equipment during 1974 and 1975.' As Gerald Ford assumed the Presidency in mid-August, the State Department urged that the supply of military hardware to Ethiopia be continued. In a memorandum sent to the National Security Council on 29 August for briefing the new President, the Department wrote:

> As long as there exists a distinct possibility that the present situation will result in a strengthened, more moderate state, and in a continuation of the traditional Ethiopian ties with the west, we should continue to carry out our program of military aid and sales as agreed. Suspension of these shipments would only strengthen the hands of radical elements among the military and further frustrate the moderates, perhaps leading them to concur in more radical initiatives.[2]

The memorandum nonetheless noted that the amount of military assistance the United States could provide was 'severely limited'. It advised encouraging 'appropriate third countries, namely Iran and Saudi Arabia, to provide any assistance they can to Ethiopia . . .' An approach to the Soviet Union — these were the days of *détente* — was also suggested, to discuss tensions between Ethiopia and Somalia. And it urged that an American ambassador be appointed to Addis Ababa, 'to increase our limited ability to influence events'. The last American ambassador before the revolution was Ross Adair, a former Republican congressman defeated in the 1970 elections and sent to Ethiopia by the Nixon administration in consolation. By the testimony of his subordinates, he was a kind man who considered his staff his new constituency and was undemanding of them and of Washington. He became ill and had to leave Ethiopia in January 1974, just a few weeks before the outbreak of the troubles that precipitated the monarchy's downfall. For reasons presumably connected with the unsettled state of affairs in Washington, no immediate move was made to replace him. To his career deputy fell the uncertain charge of the Embassy for the rest of 1974 and the early part of 1975 and, unfairly or not, the subsequent blame for the failure of US policy during that time. G. McMurtrie Godley, a career officer with a fierce reputation — earned in Zaire and Laos — for dealing with troublesome Third World radicals, was proposed in the fall of 1974 but was rejected by the government of Ethiopia. After that a less controversial but very highly respected career officer, Arthur Hummel, was appointed, but by the time he arrived in Addis Ababa in the late spring of 1975 relations were so poor that he was unable to play a significant role.

The State Department's memorandum concluded, with characteristic high mindedness, that it was in the US interest to 'assist Ethiopia to remain an independent, cohesive, moderately inclined and responsible nation'. Interestingly, the US military communications station at Asmara did not figure at all in this document as a rationale for US assistance. The Kagnew station, as it was called,[3] grew to a staff of several thousand during the 1950s and 1960s, in which years it was repeatedly cited as the main American interest in Ethiopia. Had presidents been obliged to make a choice, the United States' political interest in a friendly and stable Ethiopia would certainly always have come first. But Kagnew was an ideal lever for getting the Pentagon and the Congress on board for military and economic aid programs. Its frequent invocation in official testimony and in memoranda caused its importance for US policy toward Ethiopia to be exaggerated by journalists and other writers on current affairs. By the early 1970s Kagnew had in fact ceased to be of prime importance for US military communications, owing to the development of satellites and the establishment of a large American military communications center on the Indian Ocean island of Diego Garcia.

Whatever hopes Washington may have placed on General Aman, and on the new regime's adopting a course of moderation, were shattered in late November. Aman sought to use his position first as Defense Minister and then as Chairman of the PMAC to bring about a solution to the war in Eritrea. As an Eritrean himself, he was uniquely suited to do this. He engineered the appointment of a Christian Eritrean, Amanuel Amde-Michael, as governor of the province. He traveled extensively in Eritrea, conferred with notables and returned to Addis Ababa with proposals for steps to conciliate the population and restore a degree of autonomy. Aman's proposals found some support in the Derg. Though not formally a member of that body,[4] the General had a certain personal following there. But he met with very determined opposition from a small group of officers opposed to any compromise in Eritrea. First among this group was a young officer named Mengistu Haile Mariam, of whom we shall hear much more in the course of this narrative. Aman's clash with Mengistu was not solely over Eritrea. Mengistu and others wanted to execute a number of the top figures of the former regime imprisoned earlier in the year with the assurance that they would receive a fair trial. Aman opposed this move; he belonged to the same social class as these people and was on friendly terms with many of them and their families. Aman was also showing signs of ambition. He was talking of a republic and wanted to diminish the authority of the Derg in favor of a smaller group of more senior officers.

The showdown came in mid-November. After refusing to agree to proposals put forward by Mengistu and Atnafu Abate (another senior figure in the Derg) to send additional forces to Eritrea and to execute prisoners, Aman resigned. This proved a fatal mistake. From his home in the days that followed he tried to rally supporters in the military. But Mengistu discovered this and denounced Aman in speeches to the Derg. On the night of 22 November soldiers were sent to Aman's home to arrest him. When he resisted, fire from anti-tank weapons was directed against the house and Aman was killed. The same night 57 other top figures of the imperial regime were taken from their prison and executed. Mengistu is generally credited with having, on his own, ordered Aman's arrest and in fact his execution. He is believed to have pushed hard for the executions of the notables carried out the same evening, but these were approved by the Derg in its entirety. In the Derg's meeting on 22 November in which the executions were decided, the name of each of the prisoners was called out and anyone who did not think the man should be shot was asked to speak up. Few did.

The killing of General Aman and of the old regime notables was the turning-point for the Ethiopian revolution. To that moment events in Ethiopia had unfolded without bloodshed; thereafter blood flowed freely. Aman's proposals for Eritrea had not found universal acceptance, either there or in Addis Ababa, but they offered a good prospect for getting steps toward reconciliation and a settlement under way; and the very fact that he was an Eritrean boded well for success. The rejection of Aman's proposals by Mengistu and other hardliners in the Derg, and his death at their hands, cast the die for both Ethiopians and Eritreans. The Ethiopian government from that moment on was propelled in search of a military solution in Eritrea that more than ten years later still eludes it. For Eritreans, Aman's death was tantamount to a declaration of war. The insurgency, quiet for most of the late summer and fall of 1974, quickly took on much greater proportions. It grew throughout 1975 and 1976, to the point where in early 1977 it had all of rural Eritrea under its control, had seized most of the towns outside Asmara and Massawa, and was on the verge of taking Asmara. The war in Eritrea became the regime's biggest problem until the Somalis struck in the summer of 1977, and it can fairly be said that it was a self-inflicted wound. Even the ordeal that Ethiopia suffered from the Somali invasion can be attributed in large part to the choice that Mengistu forced upon Ethiopia in late November of 1974. The Somalis had been preparing to seize the Ogaden for years, almost since the moment Somalia became an independent state, but they timed their invasion of Ethiopia to take advantage of the difficulties that the Ethiopian army was experiencing in Eritrea. It can be argued that they might have invaded anyway, but it cannot be posited that under other circumstances they would have met with the same degree of success.

The killings of 22 November also launched Ethiopia on the path of internal revolution. The first step was the promulgation, on 20 December, of what was called the 'ten-point program'. It decreed that 'Ethiopia Tikdem', originally only a nationalistic slogan, was henceforth 'to be based on a specifically Ethiopian socialism'. Accordingly, it provided that 'the entire economy shall be in the hands of the state' and that 'industry will be managed by the state'. And it called for the creation of 'a great political party based on the revolutionary philosophy of Ethiopia Tikdem . . .' The party was not to materialize until a decade later, but the other steps came very quickly. On 1 January 1975 three banks, three other financial institutions, and fourteen insurance agencies were nationalized. On 3 February some one hundred industrial and commercial companies were seized. On 4 March, in the most sweeping action to that time, all rural land was nationalized. The decree of 4 March became known, not entirely accurately, as the land reform act. It did indeed eliminate large private holdings and free peasants from debt and traditional tenancy practices that were a heavy burden for them. But it placed the ownership of land not in the hands of the tiller but in those of the state. The peasant was given the right to cultivate land, up to a maximum holding of 10 hectares. But he was not allowed ownership and was forbidden to sell or exchange his plot or to hire labor to help him farm it. The Soviets and Cubans are said to have counseled the Ethiopians against the land nationalization decree, on the grounds that it was too sweeping and carried the revolution along too far too fast, and was thus dangerous to it. The PMAC evidently had two immediate aims in putting it through: to deprive the remnants of the old order of their sole remaining source of wealth, and thus of power; and to gain the support of the peasantry, the overwhelming majority of the population. Both of these objectives, however, could have been accomplished by expropriating the holdings of large landowners, canceling debts and putting ownership in the hands of the small tillers. That in fact was what was called for in the ten-point program, when it specified that 'the right to own land shall be restricted to those who work the land'. Between 20 December, 1974, when the ten-point program was issued, and 4 March, 1975, when the land nationalization decree came out, thinking in the Derg had obviously altered to the point where, not far down the road, a much more radical step was envisaged: collectivization.

To one degree or another, the executions of the night of 22 November and the consequences that flowed from them brought the United States and Ethiopia into collision. First of all, the bloodshed, by its sheer scale, caused anger and dismay in the United States and Western Europe. Up to that time, public opinion in the United States had been largely inclined to take a sympathetic view of what was happening in Ethiopia. Now, Ethiopia's revolution took on an entirely different coloration. Many of the people who were executed were internationally known. *The New York Times*, in an editorial on 27 November, declared that the executions had 'shocked the world' and asked what had driven the PMAC to mass slaughter 'in flagrant violation of their promise of a fair trial for all political prisoners'. More stridently, the *Chicago Tribune* wrote that 'if the old regime of Emperor Haile Selassie was corrupt, Ethiopia's ruling military council has shown after some months that the new regime is murderous beyond belief'.[5] From that moment on, as purges and executions succeeded one another in Ethiopia, human rights were to become a subject of increasing friction between Washington and Addis Ababa.

At the outset at least the nationalizations did not raise problems. By the mid-1970s Washington had shed, albeit momentarily, its doctrinary aversion to socialism in the Third World. The State Department was unperturbed by the prospect of 'Ethiopian socialism' and prepared even to put the most favorable possible interpretation on it. In a comment sent to Under-Secretary of State for Political Affairs Joseph Sisco on 24 January, 1975, the Department's Policy Planning Staff had this to say: 'The PMAC's publication of its "ideology" of "Ethiopian Socialism" manifests another African trait, closer to Nyerere's African Socialism than to Marxism–Leninism-Maoism.'[6] Both the Ford and the Carter administrations tried to convey to the Ethiopians that the US government had no quarrel with the social aims of the revolution. During a visit to Addis Ababa in June 1975, Assistant Secretary of State for African Affairs Nathaniel Davis told PMAC Second Vice-Chairman Atnafu Abate that the United States was in no way unhappy with the Ethiopian government's efforts to improve the welfare of the Ethiopian people and had no objections to the social reforms that were being implemented. Davis and others told the Ethiopians that the United States regarded nationalization as a matter for decision by the Ethiopian government; all the United States asked was that compensation be accorded American citizens, as required by international law.[7] To the extent that these statements were based on the assumption that Ethiopia was headed toward some kind of benign African socialism, they were truly and genuinely felt. The Ethiopian leadership seemed inclined to dismiss them as so much diplomatic palaver. Perhaps rightly so, for it knew that it was moving in an entirely different direction from the one that some in Washington supposed. Even then, however, the clash eventually came not over socialism versus Marxism–Leninism but over compensation. The holdings of American citizens in pre-revolutionary Ethiopia were not large. Even by the estimate of the claimants, the value of nationalized properties came only to about $30m. But as years passed and no compensation was paid, the claims of American citizens became a contentious and even emotional issue.

The consequences of the Derg's rejection of Aman's policy of compromise and conciliation in Eritrea were felt very quickly both on the scene in Eritrea and in US–Ethiopian relations. Fighting intensified in Eritrea early in 1975. In January the rebels launched an attack on Asmara. This led to a request by the Ethiopian regime for an American airlift of $30m. in small arms and ammunition. It confronted the Ford administration with a dilemma. Platitudinous ruminations about willingness to live with Ethiopian socialism were one thing. Furnishing arms to help the Ethiopian regime carry out a military solution in Eritrea was quite another. The large military supply commitment of 1974 was rationalized at the time as needed to offset stepped-up Soviet arms deliveries to Somalia. Washington did not believe that the Eritrean insurgency could be brought to heel by arms alone, and it was reluctant to be seen to be endorsing what it regarded as the Derg's mistaken policy. Yet it feared the consequences for relations with the Derg if it refused outright. The United States had a big investment in Ethiopia, dating back over 30 years; several hundred millions of dollars in military and economic assistance and decades of hard work had gone into it. So it was not something to be abandoned lightly. The radical rhetoric and the vituperation directed by the Ethiopian press, radio and television against 'imperialism' in general, and the United States in particular, were worrisome. But Washington still hoped that the few moderate and friendly people in the Derg might eventually gain the upper hand. Things were obviously in flux in Ethiopia. Conventional wisdom both in Washington and among foreign observers in Addis Ababa at the time was that the regime brought into being by the Derg was too monstrous and unpopular to last very long. So it seemed that the better part of valour was to hang on and hope for a change, if not for miracles.

Trapped between these conflicting impulses, Washington chose the course of delay. And delay, naturally, caused the Ethiopian request to become known publicly and public pressure to build against it. The ever-watchful *Chicago Tribune*, in an editorial on 12 March 1975, advocated refusing further military deliveries to Ethiopia on the grounds that 'the army officers who recently seized control of the central government at Addis Ababa have proved bloodthirsty and despotic . . .' On 17 March, a month after the Ethiopian request was made, the State Department announced that the United States would sell Ethiopia up to $7m. in ammunition. The Department's spokesman expressed the hope that 'the two sides' — the Ethiopian government and the insurgents — would soon start negotiations. He added that the United States was 'working on a parallel track' to get negotiations going.[8] This was a reference to an approach made by the State Department to Egypt,

Saudi Arabia, Sudan and Lebanon suggesting that they encourage the Eritrean Liberation Front — the moslem-led rebel organization — to talk with the Ethiopian government. Nothing seems to have come of this initiative. Neither the Eritreans nor the Ethiopians were at the time interested.

If the Administration's decision disappointed American critics of Ethiopia, it outraged Ethiopian authorities. They were at pains to make clear that they saw it as a sign that the United States was opposed to the revolution and was reneging on a long-term commitment to supply Ethiopia with arms. The Ethiopian government immediately told Washington that it considered the decision to supply only $7m. in ammunition out of a total request of $30m. to be only an interim response; Ethiopia expected the United States to come forward with additional supplies. At the time, there was still much sentiment in the Department's Bureau of African Affairs for keeping the military supply pipeline to Ethiopia open. The Bureau's report to the White House understated the Ethiopian reaction: 'The Derg has indicated disappointment at the limited nature of our response and the fact that it took so much time for us to reach a decision.'[9] Despite this effort by the State Department to put a good face on things, overall the administration was beginning to view Ethiopia with considerable reserve. The Ethiopian government was clearly no longer an ally or even a friend of the United States. The shipment of large amounts of ammunition could lead, it was feared, to more involvement than the US Congress or public would tolerate at a time when the lesson being drawn from the United States' experience in Vietnam was that all foreign military involvement was to be avoided. And there were also fears that Americans in Eritrea might be imperiled — the Kagnew station was still in operation — and US access to Eritrea and its strategic coastline jeopardized in the event that the insurgents succeeded in establishing an independent state. As the year wore on, the arguments in favor of maintaining a military assistance tie with Ethiopia came to look increasingly threadbare. The 'distinct possibility' of August 1974 that Ethiopia would become a more moderate state maintaining traditionally close ties with the West began to sound like a very bad joke. Vituperation against the United States in the government-owned and directed Ethiopian media became commonplace. The regime turned increasingly violent and repressive. On 30 September 1975 it declared a state of emergency and carried out a wave of arrests of suspected opponents. Report after report of violence in Ethiopia reached the outside world. On 21 October *The New York Times*'s correspondent Henry Kamm wrote from Addis Ababa that, 'while fulfillment of the junta's radical but vague socialist aims remains largely a matter of the future, repression, mass arrests and brutal civil warfare in many regions are the present reality . . . The regime rules through secrecy and fear.'

Nonetheless, the Ford administration, stung by the fall of Angola to a pro-Soviet faction and by the criticism that this engendered in conservative circles in the United States, made one last effort to protect ties with Ethiopia. In the spring of 1976 Secretary of State Henry Kissinger approved the provision to Ethiopia of two squadrons of F–5E fighter bombers and agreed to take under consideration a request from the Ethiopian government for approximately one hundred million dollars in additional military supplies. The decision was taken after extensive review and with considerable reluctance; Kissinger is said to have regarded it as 'taking a chance'. Very soon afterward, the United States got word from alarmed Ethiopian diplomats in Western European capitals that the Derg was developing a plan for recruiting a huge peasant militia from the center and south of Ethiopia to send to Eritrea to push out or kill recalcitrant Eritreans; for their services members of the militia would be rewarded by being given the land thus vacated. This was a time-honored stratagem for Ethiopian emperors short on resources, but in the second half of the twentieth century it sounded simply barbaric. The Derg's military operations in Eritrea in 1975 had been a failure. They left more of the region in insurgent hands than before and the rebellion continued to gain strength in 1976, despite growing rivalry between the ELF and the Eritrean People's Liberation Front, the two main armed groups. The 'peasants' march', as it came to be known, was considered the brain-child of Mengistu, now risen from Major to Lieutenant-Colonel and First Vice-Chairman of the PMAC. Kissinger sent Mengistu a message that amounted to an ultimatum: if the plan were carried out, the ability of the United States to continue providing military assistance would be called into question. The threat was not an idle one, for Ethiopia was still almost entirely dependent on the United States for arms and was still receiving a substantial amount of economic assistance from the United States; and the F–5Es had not yet been delivered.[10] After Ambassador Hummel handed over Kissinger's missive and made other approaches, the march was 'inexplicably halted' in May.[11] It resumed in June, albeit on a smaller scale.

Mengistu would have done well to heed Kissinger's advice unreservedly and cancel it altogether, for it became a rout: Tigrean guerrillas gunned down the marchers well before they could reach Eritrea.

It might be argued that Kissinger's blunt message to Mengistu was the last straw for the Ethiopians. But the thesis that it pushed Mengistu over the brink and into the arms of the Soviets would not be sustainable for the simple reason that no pushing was needed. Soviet arms were what Mengistu and many others in the Derg wanted from the very beginning. According to an account quite sympathetic to the revolutionary regime, the PMAC decided in September of 1974 to seek arms from the Soviets.[12] This is confirmed by another account, according to which members of the Derg approached the Soviets soon after Haile Selassie was deposed.[13] The Soviet ambassador in Addis Ababa, Anatoly Ratonov, is said to have let the PMAC know that the Soviet Union would be amenable to requests for military purchases. This initiative apparently took him beyond his authority, for when requests were made he was unable to respond. In the spring of 1975, presumably after it had received the disappointing American response, the Ethiopian regime secretly sent a delegation to Moscow to sound out possibilities for military assistance.[14] The Soviets were ready to talk but did not seem enthusiastic; they expressed concern about the future direction of the revolution and hinted that the presence of a number of pro-Western people in government made it difficult for them to provide many weapons. They agreed to send a military delegation to Ethiopia but it did not arrive until September, and its only immediate comment on the arms request presented it by the Ethiopians was that 'it is on the big side'.[15] The Soviets made no formal reply until early 1976 and then offered only what has come to be called, in military jargon, non-lethal equipment. All this was deeply disappointing to those in the Derg who hoped to get arms from the Soviets. Mengistu was reportedly confronted in the summer of 1976 by angry airforce officers at Debre Zeit airbase who wanted to know why Ethiopia had remained dependent on American supplies; he is said to have replied that he preferred Soviet help and had asked for it, but that the Russians were not responding.[16]

There were two reasons why Mengistu and others in the Derg wanted Soviet arms. First, they came to power as revolutionaries with a radical program. They regularly denounced imperialism, yet they remained dependent on the bulwark of what they called imperialism, the United States, for the most critical of all commodities, weaponry for their army. Could they be true revolutionaries and socialists and still have such a vital link to the United States? It was very embarrassing. But it was more than that. For the second and equally powerful motive that pushed them toward the Soviets was that they wanted a much bigger army than Ethiopia had at the outbreak of the revolution. The decision to go for a military solution in Eritrea made this absolutely essential, and there was also growing concern over the threat from Somalia. Clashes with Somali guerrillas, or regular army troops — they were pretty much one and the same — became increasingly commonplace in 1975 and 1976, and, thanks to large-scale Soviet aid, the Somali army was growing to worrisome proportions. Mengistu and others knew that, whatever satisfaction they might get from the Americans, they were not going to be given weaponry on anything like the scale to which they aspired. If they wanted a truly big army, they could get the wherewithal to equip it only from Moscow.

That the Soviets were at first the reluctant party in this courtship is not at all surprising. Somalia had become the first African nation to pledge itself to scientific socialism and to proclaim its readiness to establish a Marxist–Leninist party. In 1974 Soviet President Podgorny visited Mogadishu and a treaty of friendship was signed. After that the Soviets lavished weapons on Somalia; it is estimated that from 1974 to 1977, during the time that Mengistu and others in the Derg were trying to interest them in Ethiopia, they sent more than $300m. in arms to Somalia.[17] The Soviets got the use of naval and air facilities at Berbera and Mogadishu, and they, the Cubans and the Eastern Europeans had thousands of technicians and advisors in Somalia. In short, they had a major stake in Somalia and did not want to put it in jeopardy; Gromyko is reported to have alluded, in a conversation with the Ethiopian ambassador in the summer of 1975, to the problems that supplying arms would create for the Soviet Union in Somalia.[18] While the overthrow of the Emperor and the radical measures that followed gave the Soviets much encouragement, it was not clear for quite some time just where things were headed in Ethiopia. Several powerful figures in the Derg were considered to be friendly to the West. Even on the Left the Soviets had no monopoly, for radical students and some in the military first looked to the Chinese. Their brief flirtation with

China ended quickly, however, after the Chinese made clear that they were ready to give moral support to the revolution but little in the way of money or arms. Beijing was simply not interested in competing with the Soviets in Ethiopia.

Gradually, however, Soviet reserve began to melt. It must have become clear to the Soviets very early on that in Mengistu they had a loyal and very capable and ruthless friend. Late in 1975 Mengistu moved to establish ties with a Marxist–Leninist student group, the All Ethiopia Socialist movement, known as MEISON, and to make its leader, Haile Fida, his advisor on ideological matters. On 20 April 1976 Mengistu made an unusual public appearance in Addis Ababa to deliver a speech announcing a program of National Democratic Revolution. In the Marxist–Leninist historiography of the Ethiopian revolution, this is depicted as a pivotal step. It evidently persuaded the Soviets that Ethiopia was launched in the right direction and was worth a few risks. An Ethiopian delegation visited Moscow in early July 1976 and was warmly received, though evidently there was no extensive discussion of military assistance.[19] In mid-July one of Mengistu's most prominent rivals in the Derg, Major Sisay Habte, was purged and executed along with 18 others. Sisay was a graduate of an American university and was suspect of pro-Western sympathies; he and his accomplices had evidently aimed to get rid of Mengistu.[20] Just what happened after that in Ethiopian–Soviet relations is not known. But in December an Ethiopian military delegation went secretly to Moscow where it signed an agreement with the Soviets for some $100m. in military equipment, mainly T–34 tanks and artillery. Some sources say Mengistu was a member of the delegation, but that is not known for a fact. Neither is what conditions the Soviets may have required for their aid, but it is generally believed that they sought and were given assurance that Ethiopia would sever its military assistance tie with the United States.[21]

As for the United States, the State Department gave its approval in principle to the $100m. Ethiopian request of the spring of 1976, but after the delivery of the squadron of F–5Es in the summer of that year deliveries proceeded slowly. It was the last Ethiopian request for military equipment to be approved. By the summer of 1976 there was deep pessimism in Washington over prospects for relations with Ethiopia. Even before the execution of Sisay Habte, Bernard Weintraub commented in *The New York Times* that the military supply relationship between the United States and Ethiopia had become an embarrassment to both parties.[22] Weintraub observed that 'it is a situation tinged with irony — the United States supporting a radical military regime that condemns "western imperialists", "bureaucratic capitalists" and "right wing reactionaries"'. In Washington, the Ford administration was coming under increasing pressure from Congress and the media, aroused by the continuing political killings and arrests in Ethiopia as well as the Ethiopian regime's evident hostility toward the United States, to stop supplying arms to Ethiopia. This the State Department was reluctant to do. The military supply relationship was all the United States had left with Ethiopia; severing it would mean the end of the US position there. It was not a step the Department wanted to rush into. The Senate Foreign Relations Subcommittee for Africa held hearings on Ethiopia in August. Assistant Secretary of State for African Affairs William Schaufele defended continuation of military assistance to Ethiopia. Asked by the Subcommittee Chairman, Senator Dick Clark, if it were true that the Ethiopian government was "Marxist, socialist-oriented or strongly anti-United States', Schaufele replied that 'to the extent that some kind of cohesive doctrine' existed within the PMAC, the internal policies of the government were socialist in nature. But Schaufele declared that, despite Ethiopian press attacks on the United States, he would not call the Ethiopian government anti-American; it was 'not symstematically or instinctively anti-United States'.

Schaufele's remarks met with much skepticism. It was, after all, an election year, and Gerald Ford was being sorely challenged for the Republican nomination by Ronald Reagan, whose conservative wing of the party was bitterly critical of the fall of Angola to a pro-Soviet faction. The administration was not eager to announce that yet another African state had been given up as lost to the Soviets. The feeling in the State Department was that Schaufele had put the best possible face on a bad situation. In fact, relations between the United States and Ethiopia continued to deteriorate through the fall of 1976. On the American side, the administration continued to be pressed by members of Congress, the media and human rights organizations. In Ethiopia, the press, radio and television continued to attack the United States, and official Americans found it more and more difficult to live and work in the growing atmosphere of suspicion and hostility. In October the American Defense Attaché was detained for several hours and Ethiopian policemen entered an office of the United States Information Service three times to arrest Eritrean employees. Schaufele's statement to the Senate Africa Subcommittee in August 1976 was the last time that a spokesman for an American administration would defend arms deliveries to Ethiopia or speak with even restrained optimism about the attitude of the Ethiopian regime toward the United States.

Still, the United States was not ready to abandon its long-standing ties with Ethiopia. A major effort had been made to preserve the United States' stake in that country. Altogether from 1974 to 1977 the United States supplied Ethiopia with approximately $180m. in arms, in dollar value approximately one and a half times more than everything it had furnished up to 1974.[1] In retrospect, one might ask whether it was worth it. Was it not a mistake to try to use the supply of arms to bind Ethiopia to the United States when the dominant element among those who had seized power so clearly intended to sever the political relationship? As 1976 closed, the die was not yet finally cast in Ethiopia. It was still not implausible to hope that something could be salvaged. But, increasingly, approvals of arms for Ethiopia had taken on the aspect of a gamble; that was the way Kissinger regarded his decision of the spring of 1976. Neither the Ford administration nor its successor could continue to gamble without some encouragement from the Ethiopian side.

Notes

1. *Ethiopia at Bay, A Personal Account of the Haile Selassie Years* (Reference Publications, Algonac, Michigan, 1984), p. 335.
2. Quoted in Donald K. Petterson, 'Ethiopia Abandoned? An American Perspective', unpublished article.
3. After the Ethiopian brigade that fought alongside US forces in the Korean war.
4. Aman held the title of 'spokesman' for the Derg.
5. Quoted in Petterson, 'Ethiopia Abandoned?'.
6. Ibid.
7. Ibid.
8. Ibid.
9. Issues Paper on Ethiopia for the President's Briefing, Department of State, 29 March 1975, quoted in Petterson, 'Ethiopia Abandoned?'.
10. One squadron was delivered in stages during the spring and summer of 1976. A second was to have been provided beginning in 1978 but was cancelled when the United States cut off deliveries of military equipment to Ethiopia after Mengistu denounced the US–Ethiopian military assistance agreement and expelled the American military assistance group in April 1977.
11. David B. Ottaway, 'US Said to Oppose Ethiopian Mass March', *International Herald Tribune*, 14 June 1976.

12. Fred Halliday and Maxine Molyneux, *The Ethiopian Revolution* (Verso Editions, London, 1981), p. 244.

13. Bruce, D. Porter, *The USSR in Third World Conflicts* (Cambridge University Press, 1984), p. 192.

14. Ibid., p. 192.

15. Ibid., p. 193.

16. Paul Henze, 'Getting a Grip on the Horn' in Walter Laqueur (ed.), *The Pattern of Soviet Conduct in the Third World*(Praeger, New York, 1983), p. 167.

17. Ibid., p. 168. Henze points out that during the same period the United States provided Ethiopia with approximately $180m. in military equipment, and that the $300m. given Somalia by the Soviets from 1974 to 1977 was, in dollar value, more than the United States provided Ethiopia during the entire period of its military supply relationship, which in a span of 24 years came to $287m.

18. Porter, *The USSR in Third World Conflicts* p. 193.

19. Ibid., p. 194.

20. Rene Lefort, *Ethiopia, An Heretical Revolution?* (Zed Press, London 1983), p. 179.

21. See, notably, Henze, 'Getting a Grip on the Horn' and David and Marina Ottaway, *Ethiopia, Empire in Revolution* (Africana, New York, 1978).

22. On 6 June, 1976.

2 1977: YEAR OF REALIGNMENT

The Carter administration, in its initial policy review on the Horn of Africa, concluded that US assistance programs in Ethiopia 'should be tailored to fit the reality of the deterioration of relations'.[1] What this meant was that, barely two weeks after the new administration took office, there occurred an event that caused already bad relations to take a sharp turn for the worse.

The execution of Major Sisay Habte and 18 others in July 1976 had seemed a serious blow to prospects that Ethiopia would adopt anything like a position of non-alignment. One after another, it appeared, those who wanted to keep some balance in Ethiopia's relations with East and West were being eliminated. Not by coincidence, these were the same people who on one issue or another had found themselves on opposite sides of an argument from the Derg's Vice-Chairman, Lieutenant-Colonel Mengistu Haile Mariam.[2] But the July executions seemed to spark a reaction within the Derg. Mengistu's readiness, if not eagerness, to shoot down opponents was beginning to cause a good deal of unease. Sisay's execution provoked serious unrest in the military. Many concluded that the time had come to rein Mengistu in. According to one account the following scene took place in a plenary meeting of the Derg on 16 July, three days after Sisay and the members of his group were shot:

> A voice was raised in the Assembly demanding that its First Vice Chairman render his accounts: by what right had he alone decided the execution of Aman Andom and probably that of Sisay Habte? Mengistu demanded the immediate arrest of the questioner. His motion was put to the vote — and defeated.[3]

After this confrontation a reorganization of the PMAC was set in motion. As one might imagine, the outcome was longly and hotly contested, so much so that it was not until 29 December that the new structure was announced. Brigadier General Teferi Bante, chosen as a colorless, unambitious and therefore unthreatening figure to be Chairman of the PMAC after Aman's execution in November 1974, emerged with broad powers: Chairman of the PMAC, Head of State (to that time he had been provisional head of state), Chairman

23

of the Standing and Central Committees — the decision-making bodies — and, most important of all, Commander-in-Chief of the armed forces. Two of Mengistu's main opponents, Captains Alemayehu Haile and Mogus Wolde Michael, took key positions, those of Secretary-General of the PMAC and Chairman of the Political Affairs Committee respectively. Many of Mengistu's supporters were removed from the Derg and sent to the provinces or for assignment outside Ethiopia. Mengistu retained his post as Vice-Chairman of the Derg, and was given the Chairmanship of the Council of Ministers, which put him in charge of the day-to-day operations of the various governmental departments. But this was considered a poisoned gift, one that would set him up as scapegoat in case of failures. In theory, Mengistu remained the regime's second ranking officer, but Teferi Bante's position as Chairman was much strengthened, and the broad powers implicitly conferred on the Secretary-General, a new post, in fact put Alemayehu Haile ahead of the Vice-Chairman.

The new structure was meant to put restraints on Mengistu but it was also an important step toward the centralization of power. Given the mounting troubles the regime was facing, this was urgently needed. Opposition to the Derg was on the upsurge both in Addis Ababa and in the provinces. In Addis, the Ethiopian People's Revolutionary Party, after — predictably — failing in its effort to get the Derg to dissolve itself and make way for a civilian government, went underground late in 1976 and launched a campaign of assassinations against members of the Derg and of MEISON, a rival civilian left-wing organization that had allied itself with the Derg. In Eritrea each of the Ethiopian army's offensives seemed to leave less of the province in the hands of the government than before. Most of Tigray was beyond the control of the government and Gondar region[4] seemed also to be slipping away. In the east the Afars had risen against the Derg and were harrassing road traffic between Assab, Ethiopia's main port, and Addis Ababa. In the south-east and south the Western Somali Liberation Front was becoming increasingly aggressive; it obviously enjoyed the sympathy and support of ethnic Somalis in the Ogaden. The Somali Abdo Liberation Front, with substantial encouragement from Mogadishu, was also stepping up guerrilla attacks in Bale and in Sidamo. This worsening situation caused many in the Derg to advocate measures to rally the EPRP and to conciliate the population of Eritrea. The means proposed for accomplishing the former was the creation of a broadly based political party embracing all elements that supported the revolution.

Mengistu had declared himself opposed to both these steps. On 29 January Teferi Bante broadcast a speech over the radio and repeated it in public before a large crowd in Revolution Square the next day. Alemayehu Haile and Mogus Wolde stood beside the PMAC Chairman but Mengistu was not there. General Teferi called for national unity and the formation of a party 'to channel the energy of progressive forces in a single direction and to hold the reins of government'. He did not attack the EPRP or the EPLF. In the gathering at Revolution Square, EPRP partisans applauded Teferi's speech, while MEISON — allied with Mengistu — hissed and booed. Altercations broke out between the two groups.

To this Mengistu responded by accusing General Teferi and his associates of being 'capitulationists' and demanding a discussion of their proposals in the Derg. The meeting began at 7 in the morning on 3 February, at first in the absence of Teferi Bante. Exactly what happened is in dispute and may never be known with certainty. What is reasonably sure is that there was a shoot-out and that Mengistu and his followers succeeded in killing Teferi Bante, Alemayehu Haile, Mogus Wolde and the other main figures associated with them. (The official version of events is that the 'capitulationists' were arrested and, on a vote of the Derg, condemned to death and executed on the spot.) The next day, the population of Addis Ababa was convoked to Revolution Square to rally in support of the victor. There Mengistu delivered a violent speech denouncing Teferi Bante and his group, accusing the CIA and the United States of supporting them and of complicity with Ethiopia's enemies domestic and foreign, and calling for all-out war on the EPRP.

It is legitimate at this point to ask whether Mengistu's putsch of 3 February was a spur of the moment reaction to the challenge laid down by Teferi Bante and his group just a few days earlier or simply a convenient pretext for carrying out a prearranged plot to put them out of the way and seize power? The speeches of 29 and 30 January faced Mengistu with the choice of acting immediately or being stripped of much of his power and possibly purged himself. But the reorganization of 29 December posed the same threat, if less immediately and acutely. Would Mengistu not have moved against his opponents anyway, as soon as the opportunity presented itself? It seems very likely that he would. Support is lent to this hypothesis, and to the suspicion that Mengistu sought and received Soviet endorsement for his plans to eliminate those who stood between him and absolute power, and who threatened his position, by the fact that the next day the Soviet and Cuban ambassadors called on Mengistu to congratulate him and assure him of their governments' backing. What is more surprising is that Teferi, Alemayehu and Mogus failed to take precautions. They more than anyone else knew that everything they were doing was aimed at shunting Mengistu aside. Did they think he would simply sit by and let it happen? Perhaps after the reorganization of 29 December they thought their position too strong to be seriously challenged. But probably the best explanation is that, even at that late date, they simply underestimated both Mengistu's abilities and his ruthlessness.[5]

The Carter administration came to office with a program that called for more emphasis on human rights in the formulation of American foreign policy but also for steps to improve the United States' relations with radical Third World regimes. In Ethiopia's case these two aims stood in stark contradiction to one another, a contradiction that was not readily susceptible to resolution. No sooner had Mengistu seized power than he unleashed an orgy of killing. Arms were given out to the Kebelles ('Urban Dwellers Associations') and a 'people's militia' was formed. Mengistu publicly urged it and the army to 'dispense revolutionary justice' and 'liquidate counter revolutionaries'.[6] Revolutionary justice meant summary killing, without trial, of suspected enemies of the regime. Mengistu's aim was to break the back of the EPRP, a group that had attracted large numbers of university and high school students. Large-scale arrests and killings of students followed. The worst of the bloodletting took place at the end of April. On 29 April about five hundred youths, some demonstrating against the regime and distributing pamphlets, were shot dead by the people's militia and the army. The killings continued in the days that followed. The regime denied reports of the massacre, which it dismissed as 'imperialist propaganda'. But on 16 May the Secretary-General of the Swedish Save the Children Fund declared that 'about one thousand children have been massacred in Addis Ababa and their bodies, lying in the streets, are ravaged by roving hyenas'.[7] The new Chairman also reinstated public execution.

Mengistu's diatribe against the United States in his speech of 4 February gave the Carter administration no incentive to overlook any of this; it simply confirmed for Washington his already well-established reputation as the man in the Ethiopian government who wanted to put the Americans out of Ethiopia and bring the Soviets in. In mid-February PMAC Vice-Chairman Atnafu Abate announced publicly that Ethiopia would turn to the Soviet Union for arms. Atnafu made no mention of the fact that an arms deal with the Soviets had already been secretly arranged in December.

With prospects equally bleak on the political and human rights fronts, Washington decided to make a public move. The budget proposal submitted by the Ford administration in its waning days had carried no provision for grant military assistance for Ethiopia for the coming US fiscal year. Deputy Assistant Secretary of State for African Affairs Talcott Seelye was dispatched to Addis Ababa to inform the Ethiopian regime that there would be no further money for the supply of military equipment on a grant basis after the end of the 1977 US fiscal year. Grant money for training was excepted from this cut-off, as were cash sales. Human rights violations were cited as the rationale for the decision. Seelye was instructed to tell the Ethiopians that the United States wanted to improve its relations with Ethiopia and would be prepared to do so if Ethiopia would show more respect for the rights of its citizens and if public attacks on the United States were restrained. He arrived in Addis Ababa on 23 February. Whether the Ethiopians already knew of or suspected the content of his message is not clear, but Seelye was deliberately given a cold reception. He was able to meet only with the Ethiopian Acting Foreign Minister. He conveyed his message just a few hours before Washington announced that aid to Argentina, Uruguay and Ethiopia would be reduced because of human rights violations. Being lumped with Latin American military regimes added insult to injury so far as the Ethiopian government — with its pretensions of revolutionary socialism — was concerned. In Washington, particularly to officials of the State Department's Human Rights Bureau, the company seemed entirely fitting. The governments of each of the three countries had launched programs of mass killings of political opponents.

The first Soviet arms shipments arrived in Ethiopia in March; 30 tanks were hastily sent over from South Yemen. By mid-April more than one hundred more tanks and armored personnel carriers were delivered directly from the Soviet Union. Media attacks on the United States, and now on China, were stepped up, to the point where they amounted to incitation: on 20 March three fire bombs were thrown at USIS installations in Addis Ababa. On 17 April, at a large rally at Revolution Square, Mengistu repeated earlier appeals to the Ethiopian people to heed the 'call of the motherland' and he again denounced the United States. This time he declared that the 'blood of American imperialism will be spilled'; to emphasize his point Mengistu smashed on the pavement at that moment a Coca Cola bottle filled with blood.

On 21 April the US Embassy in Addis Ababa advised the Ethiopian government that the United States was prepared to begin negotiations for the closure of the Kagnew station scheduled for 30 September of that year. The Embassy considered this a more or less routine notification. The US decision to phase out Kagnew was made in 1971 and reductions in personnel were begun that same year. By the time of the revolution, the station's American staff had dropped from two thousand to only a few dozen. The Ethiopian government had earlier been told that Kagnew was to be closed, though it is not clear whether the date of 30 September had been communicated to them.

Mengistu, however, seized upon this American notification to make a series of dramatic moves. On 23 April the Ethiopian government announced that it was ordering the immediate closure of the Kagnew station, the American consulate in Asmara, USIS offices throughout Ethiopia, the US Military Assistance Advisory Group office and the US Navy's medical research center, known as NAMRU. At one swoop an official American presence of several hundred was reduced to only a few dozen. Personnel of these units were given four days to leave Ethiopia, though at the Embassy's request the deadline was extended another three days. On 27 April three Western reporters, including David Ottaway of the *Washington Post*, were expelled on 48 hours' notice. On 30 April the Ethiopian government terminated its 1953 Mutual Defense Assistance Agreement with the United States, one year ahead of scheduled expiration.[8] A few weeks later, on 28 May, Mengistu called in US Chargé d'Affaires Arthur Tienken and ordered a 50 per cent reduction in the staff of the American Embassy. Mengistu himself set the ceiling for the US official presence in Ethiopia henceforth at 28, including clerical personnel and a small contingent of Marine guards.

Having thus formally severed Ethiopia's last important ties with the United States, Mengistu flew off to Moscow to make a dramatic show of alignment with the Soviet Union. During a week's stay there, he made a speech in which he declared that the goal of the

Ethiopian revolution was to 'lay a firm foundation for transition to Socialism' and for 'the establishment of the People's Democratic Republic' in Ethiopia. The Ethiopian leader got from the Soviets a second very large arms pledge, for between $350m. and $450m. according to one source.[9] He also signed agreements on 'principles of friendly relations' and on economic, scientific and cultural co-operation.

As the Soviets publicly embraced Mengistu and Ethiopia, they began to consider what to do about the dilemma that this step posed for their relations with Somalia. Since 1969 Somalia had been their close friend and, increasingly, their ally. Between 1974, when the treaty of friendship and co-operation between the Soviet Union and Somalia was signed, and 1977, the Soviets poured some $300m. worth of arms into Somalia. They built up the Somali army to a force of thirty thousand, equipped with hundreds of tanks and dozens of modern fighter aircraft, and with all the other paraphenalia of a modern army preparing for war. Their political investment was equally impressive and must have been considered in Moscow to be even more valuable than the military facilities accorded the Soviet Union at Berbera and Mogadishu. Until Angola and Mozambique became independent and allied themselves with Moscow, Somalia was the only state on the African continent to profess Marxism–Leninism. In December 1976, as Ethiopia and the Soviet Union were secretly concluding their first arms deal, Somalia's Marxist–Leninist vanguard party was declared officially formed.

Ethiopia, with its population of more than thirty million — outstripping Somalia by a factor of ten — its larger territory and its position as seat of the headquarters of the Organization of African Unity and United Nations Economic Commission for Africa, no doubt impressed the Soviets as the bigger prize. But there is no indication, at least at first, that the Soviets were ready to accept the proposition that gaining Ethiopia inevitably meant losing Somalia. After the decision to link up with Ethiopia was made, the Soviets focused their energies on finding ways to preserve their ties with Somalia.

This produced, in mid-March of 1977, surprise visits to Ethiopia and Somalia by Fidel Castro and a secret meeting between Castro, Mengistu and Siad Barre in Aden. There the Cuban proposed to the Ethiopian and Somali leaders that they should bury the differences between their countries in a federation together with South Yemen, in which the Ogaden and Eritrea would enjoy a status of autonomy.

This bizarre scheme deserves closer scrutiny than it has ordinarily won from writers on the Horn of Africa. The logic invoked on its behalf was sheer Marxist sophistry: Somalia and Ethiopia had been at loggerheads because of the reactionary character of the regimes that had previously governed them; now that both had dedicated themselves to the path of socialism, they should be able to live together in peace and harmony. The Cubans attributed the idea to Mengistu. On 16 March, while Castro was in Addis Ababa, the official Cuban newspaper *Granma* reported that Mengistu had advocated an alliance between Somalia, South Yemen and Ethiopia, which would form, together with an independent government in the French territory of Afars and Issas, 'a common anti-imperialist front'.[10] This appears to be the only official Cuban statement made on the proposal. Journalists did their best to fill in the blank spaces, whether accurately or not cannot be known. According to one, the proposal provided for a federation in which Eritrea would have a status within Ethiopia comparable to Ukraine or Byelorussia in the Soviet Union.[11] Another described it as follows: Ethiopia would give up the Ogaden part of Hararghe province, which was shown on an accompanying map as a narrow strip running parallel to Ethiopia's eastern border with Somalia; Ethiopia and Somalia would guarantee to respect Djibouti's independence; and, for Eritrea, the Soviet Union would give aid to the Marxist EPLF against its two non-Marxist rivals if EPLF leaders would agree to retain links between a 'Marxist Republic of Eritrea' and Ethiopia.[12] These two accounts and others say that Mengistu accepted Castro's proposal and that Siad Barre rejected it. The Somali leader later publicly confirmed his rejection but did not explain it other than to say that Mengistu had shown himself, during their meeting in Aden, to be no revolutionary but a Fascist. Mengistu did not disown the proposal; in fact he is not known to have made any public comment about it. If he did actually embrace it, his doing so would seem a sharp departure from positions he had taken previously. He had adamantly rejected autonomy for Eritrea; that was the reason — or was it only the pretext? — for his clash with General Aman that cost the General his life. So far as is known, autonomy for the Ogaden had never been discussed or even considered in Ethiopian government councils, but Mengistu could not have been in favor of it while opposing autonomy for Eritrea. Was agreement to Castro's proposal the price that the Soviets extracted from Mengistu in return for their promise of arms? Did Mengistu agree to it on the assumption that all that would be required of him was a meaningless gesture? Such hypotheses seem reasonable, and doubt about Mengistu's sincerity would have contributed to Siad Barre's rejection of Castro's proposal. Still, the leap of principle that the Ethiopian leader was evidently prepared to take, at the behest of his patrons in Moscow and Havana, is nothing short of breathtaking. Even after the unsuccessful meeting in Aden, the Soviets did not drop the federation idea. Podgorny visited Addis Ababa and Mogadishu early in April and pursued discussion of it, albeit to no avail as Siad Barre remained opposed.

By the spring of 1977, Siad wanted — and evidently felt he could get — more than Mengistu or any other Ethiopian could offer and still hope to stay in power. Ethiopia seemed literally to be coming apart at the seams. The rebels controlled all of Eritrea except Asmara and Massawa — even the important city of Keren fell in April — and seemed headed for complete victory there. The Ethiopian Democratic Union[13] was pressing down from the north; with Sudanese assistance its forces took Metemma, near the Sudanese border, Humera, some distance further in, and threatened Gondar city itself. The Afars and the Oromos were stepping up their activities and Somalia's own WSLF was on the warpath. Somalia had been armed by the Soviets as fully and as heavily as it could hope to be. Ever since it had started seriously building an army, in 1963 with Soviet help, it had been planning its war to grab the Ogaden from Ethiopia; and by the Ogaden it meant the entire south-eastern part of Ethiopia and perhaps more, not a narrow strip along the border. Should it now stand down and let slip its golden opportunity, in return for promises of autonomy for a truncated Ogaden that might never be kept? And all the while watch the Soviets arm Ethiopia to the point where any Somali hope of victory in a war would be lost?

Siad watched with growing disgust as the Ethiopians and Soviets came together, but he thought, or at least hoped, that he had an alternative. For quite some time the Saudis, joined by Sadat and the Shah, had been courting him with promises of support if he would break with the Soviets. There was talk of a big arms package whose purchase from the United States the Saudis would finance. Sadat and Prince Fahd visited Washington in the spring of 1977 to meet the new American president. Both evidently urged Carter to take advantage of the rift developing between Somalia and the Soviet Union to establish a position for the United States in Somalia. This advice fell on attentive ears.

The loss of Ethiopia was very upsetting for the Carter administration. Although, as has been seen, the breach between the United States and Ethiopia developed much earlier, the final scenes of rupture played themselves out in the third month of Carter's presidency, in April 1977. The administration's notification to Ethiopia of the termination of grant aid and the closing of the Kagnew station, along with its human rights report published in February, gave Mengistu pretexts for severing what remained of the formal tie, but if he had not had these he would have found others. The Carter administration could not reasonably be blamed for what had happened, but it was sorely embarrassed by it and uncertain how to react. It responded to Mengistu's expulsion of the military assistance group and denunciation of the mutual defense assistance treaty by suspending delivery of military equipment on order by Ethiopia, some of which the Ethiopian government had already paid for.[14] But it did not know what to do beyond that. After Angola, the Soviet Union's establishing itself in yet another African country, one so important and so long taken for granted as securely in the Western camp, was bound to raise a hue and cry in the United States that could threaten the new administration's hopes for a useful working relationship with Moscow and for SALT II. Since Washington had no power to reverse the course of events in Ethiopia, it first tried to make adversity look like advantage. Administration spokesmen put word out to the media that the American explusion from Ethiopia was in fact a blessing. 'The United States is so far showing little concern and some relief over the anti-American action taken by Ethiopia's military leaders,' the London *Daily Telegraph* reported on 26 August. That same day *The New York Times* reported that 'administration officials believe Soviet gains could be of short duration'. On 3 May the *International Herald Tribune* in a piece by Graham Hovey reported that 'in more than one department of the government the concern about the deterioration in relations was tempered by relief that the United States was now out from under commitments that the Soviet Union has begun to assume . . .' The Soviets, it was put about, had bought a pig in a poke; they were 'riding for a fall' and would soon regret their adventure into Ethiopia.

This kind of facile rationalization offered only very meager consolation. What was needed was some American gain to offset the US loss and the Soviet gain in Ethiopia. Somalia seemed to present a ready recourse. The Somalis had already put out feelers to Washington. After Mengistu's visit to Moscow at the beginning of May, during which the Soviets committed themselves to a large new arms package for Ethiopia, the Somalis and those pleading their case — the Saudis, Sadat and the Shah — became much more insistent. As early as March 1977 Vice-President Mondale sent Carter a memorandum advocating *rapprochement* with Somalia. In reply to this, NSC staffer Paul Henze sent the President and the Vice-President a paper in which he warned of the dangers of becoming involved with Somalia. But Carter apparently had become persuaded that Somalia offered his administration the possibility of an early and easy success. The Somalis continued to press for a meeting with him, and on 16 June he received Somali Ambassador Addou. The Somali envoy delivered a message from President Siad that was blatantly dishonest: Siad feared the Ethiopians were getting ready to attack and he needed arms to defend himself. If he got them he would be ready to shift his allegiance from the Soviets to the United States. Carter was not taken in by this. But according to an American official who was present at the meeting, the President replied that the United States would be ready to help Somalia if it were genuinely threatened but could in no case provide anything other than defensive weaponry.[15] Addou distorted the import of Carter's words in reporting them back to Siad and Siad evidently gave it a further wishful twist. On 9 July the Somali Embassy in Washington presented a long list of military equipment that was desired from the United States. On 15 July Carter approved a decision 'in principle' to help meet Somalia's 'defensive requirements' in co-operation with other countries. The Somalis were notified of this on 25 July and the next day a public announcement was made by Washington. Barely a week later, however, the State Department's Assistant Secretary for African Affairs, Richard Moose, called in the Somali ambassador and told him that Somali military operations in the Ogaden precluded implementation of the agreement in principle. The United States had learned that regular Somali forces were in the Ogaden, Moose advised the ambassador. If would not itself supply arms to Somalia or agree to others transferring American equipment until Somalia withdrew its forces. The British and French governments, which simultaneously with the American announcement had also declared themselves ready to sell 'modest quantities' of arms to Somalia for 'defensive purposes', likewise did an about face.

With these few lurching steps the Carter administration earned itself the worst of both worlds. The administration's announcement of its decision to supply arms to Somalia in fact coincided with the full-scale launching of the Somali offensive in the Ogaden. The Ethiopians were outraged. They accused the United States both of providing arms to the Somalis and of encouraging them to attack Ethiopia. The administration's turnabout in early August came as Somali forces were sweeping across south-eastern Ethiopia. The Somalis accused the United States of betraying them at a critical moment and complained bitterly that the United States was turning a blind eye to Soviet expansionism. In truth, neither side had so much to complain about as it pretended. The United States provided no arms to Somalia in 1977 or thereafter until 1982, and it refused permission to the Saudis, Iranians and others to transfer to Somalia US weapons in their arsenals. The charge that the US announcement encouraged Somalia to invade Ethiopia is more serious. Washington's promise of arms may in fact have entered into Siad's decision, if only through his own and his ambassador's distorted interpretations of it. The Somalis were not given a blank check in Washington in July, only a promise in principle to supply defensive weapons. As Assistant Secretary Moose later said, this was not a basis on which a 'prudent man' would have taken action. It may, of course, be objected that the Somalis were not prudent men and that the United States should have taken this into account in its dealings with them. In any event, the operation was a major blunder. It contributed to the reputation that the administration later developed for bumbling and indecisiveness.

How did it happen? The protagonists have remarkably little to say on the subject in their memoires. Carter is silent about the whole matter.[16] Brzezinski recounts in detail his row with Vance over the handling of the matter of Cuban troops in Ethiopia but says nothing about what position he took earlier. Vance alone relates the circumstances and the debate that led up to the decision of 15 July, but his account is very brief. One learns only that he 'recommended to the president that we refuse to supply even defensive military equipment or to permit our allies and friends to transfer US arms to Somalia until the Ogaden affair was settled', and that the decision in principle to provide defensive weapons was taken 'after considerable discussion' within the administration.[17]

Carter himself was unquestionably the driving force behind the opening to Somalia. The President is quoted as having issued an order in the presence of reporters on 6 April to 'tell Cy and Zbig that I want them to move in every way possible to get Somalia to be our friend'. According to another journalistic source, the US initiative in agreeing to provide weapons to Somalia was 'a result of the personal involvement of President Carter, who has spent many hours in governmental briefings and diplomatic discussions about the maneuverings in the Horn of Africa . . . Within a few weeks of taking office, Mr. Carter was reading voluminous studies he had ordered on the area . . .'[18] The new President was looking for ways to make his mark, 'to challenge the Soviet Union in a strategically important part of the world and thereby avoid giving the impression that [the US] was passively watching the Russians make inroads there . . .' He wanted to 'show . . . that if they [i.e. governments] break with the Russians they can count on help from the United States'.[19] In pursuit of this objective, Carter and Vance — the latter presumably at the President's direction and after having been overruled on his recommendation to supply no arms to Somalia — made a series of public statements. On 10 June, in an interview, Carter spoke of challenging the Soviet Union in its own sphere and in this connection specifically mentioned Somalia.[20] In a speech on 1 July, Vance warned the Soviets against 'pouring substantial quantities of arms and military personnel into Africa'. He added that 'we will consider sympathetically appeals for assistance from states which are threatened by a buildup of foreign military equipment and advisers on their borders, in the Horn and elsewhere in Africa'.[21] On 28 July Carter commented at a news conference that, while the United States did not want to compete with the Soviet Union in supplying arms, in the case of Somalia 'we are trying to work not on a unilateral basis but in conjunction with other nations like the Saudis'.[22] The next day Vance disclosed at a news conference that the administration's decision came after the Somalis had 'indicated that they wished to have an alternate source of supply to meet their defensive needs . . .'[23]

What emerges from all this is a picture of a new and still inexperienced President and administration tempted by the hope of pulling off a success against the Soviets into a poorly thought-out scheme that quickly backfired. Carter wanted to offset the loss of Ethiopia and, more broadly, was eager for some gain that would give his administration the reputation of being tough and effective with the Soviets so that SALT could be pursued. He was warned by his NSC staff, and evidently by Vance, against involving himself with the

Somalis. US intelligence on the Somali invasion of Ethiopia was very good. When the Somalis invaded, the United States knew almost exactly where they were, when, and how they got there. If Carter was advised of this intelligence, he ignored it. He failed to appreciate, until it was too late, the complexity and the pitfalls of the situation in the Horn of Africa. He was encouraged by hawks in his administration on both sides of the political spectrum — liberals as well as conservatives — who thirsted to chalk up a cheap victory over the Soviets. And he was impelled by his own instincts. As a member of his NSC staff put it: 'He loved to be in direct touch with foreign leaders. He had a naïve but at that point essentially boundless faith in his own ability to convince any leader of his and his country's good and peaceful intentions everywhere in the world. So he was tempted to play with the Somalis.'

The case that the administration deliberately encouraged the Somalis to attack Ethiopia seems to rest on the testimony of Dr Kevin Cahill, a US citizen and President Siad's personal physician. Dr Cahill alleged that he was told in the spring of 1977 by a State Department official that the United States was 'not averse to further guerrilla pressure in the Ogaden'.[24] In the spring and summer of 1977 Dr Cahill was a frequent caller at the offices of the White House domestic staff, and there he may have gleaned encouragement — deliberate or inadvertent — for his advocacy of Somalia. But he meticulously avoided officials of the NSC and the State Department who had responsibility for the Horn of Africa. His reports, together with hints from various others that the United States would be ready to supplant the Soviets as a massive supplier of arms if Somalia severed its ties with Moscow, no doubt encouraged fanciful thinking in Mogadishu.

This offers a classic example of the kind of error into which foreign governments, especially those of an oriental or Machiavellian bent, frequently fall in their dealings with Washington. These governments operate on the basis of declared and real policies, the latter often being quite different from the former. It is accepted practice to convey the real policy through a carefully placed hint or a clever insinuation. Those who seek in this way to fathom the views of an American administration — and they are regrettably many — frequently come to grief. So vast and chaotic is the United States government that any reasonably diligent representative of a foreign power can be sure of finding someone with supposed connections to high places who will say something susceptible of interpretation in ways desired by his government. But this is not how policy is made or conveyed, except in rare instances, in Washington. The charge that the Carter administration deliberately led the Somalis to believe that the United States would supply arms, in the aim of encouraging Somalia to attack Ethiopia, assumes a truly breathtaking degree of recklessness and irresponsibility on the part of the President, the Secretary of State and other members of his administration that nothing in their other actions corroborates. An equal or even greater measure of paranoia is required to believe — as some Ethiopian government officials profess to — that even when Carter made his commitment to Somalia he deliberately intended to withdraw it so as to escape blame for the Somali invasion. The plausible explanation is simply that the administration acted impulsively. When the full realization of what Somalia was doing dawned upon it, it moved quickly to disassociate the United States from it. Overall, it was a sad and embarrassing episode for the administration.

The charge that the Soviets incited Somalia to attack Ethiopia, so that they could come to Ethiopia's rescue and thereby consolidate their position in that country, stands up no better under scrutiny. The Soviets do bear a heavy responsibility for arming Somalia, after 1974, far beyond any imaginable requirement for internal security or defense against invasion. One can only wonder what the Soviets thought they were up to or whether they ever had secret qualms about providing so much weaponry to a government that they knew to be unabashedly irredentist. The invasion of Ethiopia would have been far less likely — and this is a point that Ethiopian leaders ignored and continue to ignore when they lay responsibility at the US doorstep — had the Soviets exercised some modicum of restraint in arming Somalia. Yet the record is reasonably clear that, even after Siad's rejection of the federation proposal, the Soviets hoped to hold on to their position in Somalia while continuing to establish themselves in Ethiopia, and that they recognized that a war would make this impossible.

In May, after Mengistu's visit to Moscow and the signing of the second arms agreement, the Somalis began issuing increasingly clamorous warnings to the Soviets. In a statement to the press in mid-May, Siad denounced Soviet involvement in Ethiopia as a 'danger' to Somalia and hinted that, if continued, it would affect relations between Mogadishu and Moscow. His Vice-President, General Mohammed Ali Samantar, called in East bloc ambassadors at this same time and warned that Somalia would review its relations with the Soviet Union if the latter persisted in supplying arms to Ethiopia; according to other reports, Siad sent Samantar to Moscow to deliver this notice to the Soviet leadership in person. Colin Legum reported that the Soviets responded to these warnings by holding up further large-scale direct shipments of military equipment to Ethiopia and channeling supplies through Libya and Cuba.[25] After the full-scale Somali invasion was launched in the second half of July, the Soviets reportedly pressed the Somalis for a cease-fire.[26] Madagascar, a Soviet friend, began a vigorous but ultimately fruitless mediation effort. Soviet ambassadors were reported to be pressing African governments to step in and arrange a cessation of hostilities. The Soviet ambassador in Kampala is said to have called on Idi Amin, then Chairman of the OAU, to urge that the OAU intervene to stop the fighting. Amin reportedly replied, with a cynicism that must have stunned even the Soviets, with the advice that the Soviet Union should 'supply as many weapons as possible to both sides'.[27]

The initial reaction of the Soviet media to the Somali army's invasion of the Ogaden was to castigate 'American imperialists'. The first Soviet statement, issued by the Soviet Union's Afro-Asian Solidarity Committee on 6 August (two weeks after the Ethiopian government, on 23 July, announced invasion by regular Somali units), named 'imperialist forces' as the culprit and tried to strike a stance of impartiality. It spoke of the 'special sympathy' felt by the Soviet public for the peoples of Somalia and Ethiopia and called for an immediate end to hostilities.[28] Not until a week later, on 14 August, was there a noticeable shift in tone. The Soviet Foreign Ministry statement issued that day called on the leaders of Somalia and Ethiopia to 'display statesmanship' and put an end to the fighting. But blame was apportioned this time, albeit without Somalia's being named: 'The invasion of the territory of one country by the armed forces of the other does damage to the cause of peace and security of the peoples in Africa and all over the world.'[29] The Soviets signed an economic and technical co-operation agreement with the Somalis on 19 August and the international press reported Soviet vessels to be unloading arms at Mogadishu's port at the end of that month. But, from mid-August on, Soviet Press and official statements were increasingly critical of Somalia. By the second week of September the Soviets were expressing 'solidarity with the courageous struggle of the progressive forces of Socialist Ethiopia . . .'[30] Siad Barre made a quick visit to Moscow at the end of August, evidently to have a last try at patching things up with the Soviets. He returned to Mogadishu disappointed and without having seen Brezhnev. From there on, Somali statements turned increasingly hostile to the Soviet Union.

For the Ethiopian regime, August and September were months of terrible crisis. They must also have been a time of some friction with the Soviet Union. The Soviet arms shipments that arrived in Ethiopia in the spring of 1977 were immediately sent north to strengthen Ethiopian forces reeling under the blows of Eritrean and Tigrean insurgents and the offensive of the Ethiopian Democratic Union. There do not seem to have been any substantial deliveries from the Soviet Union in the midsummer months. The Ethiopian regime greeted the first stage of the Somali offensive with announcements that it had scored heroic victories and had crushed the invaders. The Somalis responded by denying that they had any forces in the Ogaden. It was a strange war: fictitious Ethiopian victories over an allegedly non-existent Somali army. But by mid-August the extent of the Somali conquest had become too great to be hidden. Both Ethiopia and Mengistu's rule were in serious danger. On 20 August Mengistu went on radio and television to tell the Ethiopian people that they faced a 'life and death struggle' and to call for mass mobilization. Marxism–Leninism was relegated to silence and historical and nationalistic themes were emphasized; at a rally in Revolution Square on 24 August, the Patriarch of the Ethiopian Orthodox Church appeared at Mengistu's side. Early in September, Mengistu was reported personally to be leading Ethiopian troops in a battle in the Ogaden in which, according to an official statement, 'decisive victories were scored'. Nonetheless, things continued to go badly for the Ethiopians. On 12 September, the third anniversary of the revolution, the key town of Jigjiga fell to the Somalis, evidently after the unit responsible for its defense mutinied and fled.[31] The way was open for the Somalis to attack Harar and Dire Dawa, major cities that had to be held; if they were to fall, Ethiopia's defense would be at serious risk of collapse, and its regime as well. By this time the Soviets had abandoned their balancing act and had clearly put themselves on Ethiopia's side, but the flow of Soviet arms needed to halt and reverse the Somali progress had not yet begun. The squadron of F–5Es, delivered to Ethiopia the previous summer, proved indispensable at this critical juncture. The American aircraft performed extremely well against Somali MIGs. Thanks to them, the Ethiopians quickly came to control the skies and were able to inflict heavy damage on Somali ground units, slowing the Somali advance.

In this desperate moment, some in the Ethiopian government argued for an appeal to the United States, perhaps even for a shift in policies that would make it possible for Ethiopia again to get large amounts of military equipment from the United States. Mengistu was not ready to go so far, but in mid-September he did call in the American Chargé to ask for spare parts for the F–5Es and for other items that were embargoed after the expulsion of the US military assistance group and the denunciation of the mutual defense assistance agreement in April. The Ethiopian leader held a press conference on 18 September in which he mentioned his request to the United States and delivered a rebuke to the Soviets: 'If Socialist countries are still supplying arms to Somalia, this is not only violating one's principles, but also tantamount to complicity with the reactionary Mogadishu regime.'[32]

It seems questionable that Mengistu seriously thought the United States could be persuaded to help him. The Carter administration was still smarting from the brutal manner in which the United States had been expelled from Ethiopia and was not inclined to rush to the rescue of the regime that had thrown it out. The President had sent NSC-Staff Officer Paul Henze and State Department East Africa Office Director Richard Post to Ethiopia and Somalia in the first half of September. Their assessment was that, although a substantial number of experienced Ethiopians desperately hoped for a return to good working relations with the United States, the pro-Soviet group in the regime was very much in the ascendancy. Those desiring a shift toward the United States were not strong enough to influence the overall pro-Soviet tilt of the dominant group. And in any case a resumption of military supply by the United States would not have any decisive effect on Ethiopia's eventual course. Mengistu's request was taken under consideration in Washington but was not acted upon. When Soviet jet fighter aircraft began to arrive in Ethiopia early in October, it was deemed to have been overtaken by events. In any case the Carter administration was by that time moving toward a decision to embargo arms shipments to both sides so long as the fighting in the Ogaden continued. The Somalis and their Saudi and Egyptian friends continued to implore Washington to relent and open its arsenal to

Somalia, or at least to permit the Saudis and others to transfer American-made weapons to Mogadishu. To each of these entreaties, the administration replied that it would be ready to provide defensive arms for Somalia as soon as Somali troops left the Ogaden.

The Soviets made substantial deliveries to Ethiopia of tanks and aircraft at the end of September and early in October. Soviet and Cuban military advisors and technicians began arriving in large numbers at that time also. Thanks to this East bloc assistance, the Ethiopians were able to halt the Somali offensive against Harar and Dire Dawa and to push the Somalis back a short distance. On 19 October, the Soviet ambassador in Addis Ababa issued a statement, quickly broadcast by the Ethiopian radio, announcing 'officially and formally' that 'the Soviet Union has stopped arms supplies to Somalia'. He added that the Soviet Union was providing Ethiopia with 'defensive weapons to protect her revolution'. If the Somalis were disappointed over the United States' refusal to give them arms, they were outraged by these Soviet statements. A wave of anger against the Soviet Union and Cuba swept through Somalia. On 13 November, after very long deliberations by the assembled Somali leadership,[33] Siad Barre announced that his government had decided to break relations with Cuba, expel all Soviet and Cuban military personnel and close down the naval and air stations operated by the Soviets at Berbera and Mogadishu. The preponderance of journalistic opinion at the time was that Siad was gambling on American support. He may have hoped that a break with the Soviets would make Washington change its mind about supplying arms, but he had no reason to expect it. The Carter administration had by then made it quite clear that Somali troops would have to leave Ethiopia before US arms would begin to flow. The Somali break with the Soviets and Cubans seems to have been less a gamble on a change in American policy than an emotional gesture. Siad's announcement of the decision was hailed by thousands of chanting demonstrators in Mogadishu.

Despite the moral and material backing they gave Ethiopia, and their cut-off of supplies to Somalia, the Soviets kept their personnel in Somalia right up to the moment of the rupture. There were rumors in July that Soviet and other East bloc personnel were leaving Mogadishu, but they turned out to be untrue. When the break came in November, the Somalis invited the Western media in to film the Soviets' expulsion, which they made as humiliating as possible. Western television crews sent back films of Russians being jeered in the streets by children and waiting in sweaty discomfort at the airport while Somali customs inspectors meticulously dug through the contents of their suitcases.

Many of these Soviets went straightaway to Ethiopia, where they played key roles in the next act in the drama, the Soviet Union's mammoth air and sea lift to Ethiopia of Soviet military equipment and Cuban troops beginning in mid-December in preparation for an offensive to drive the Somalis out of Ethiopian territory in February. Quite clearly, the Soviets did not easily reach their decision to intervene massively to rescue Mengistu. Once they did so, however, they spared no effort.

The sudden build-up of Cuban troops and Soviet arms in Ethiopia caused much alarm in Washington. The immediate concern in Washington was that, duly armed by the Soviet Union, the Ethiopians and the Cubans would recapture Somalia for the East bloc by pursuing the Somali army to Mogadishu and setting up a new government there. Brzezinski says that on 14 December he pressed Soviet Ambassador Anatoly Dobrynin for assurance that the Ethiopians would not cross the Somali border once they began to recapture the Ogaden, and Dobrynin gave it on the spot.[34] Since the Soviet air lift and Cuban troop build-up were just beginning at that time, Dobrynin's ready assurance suggests that the Soviets had already arranged this particular detail with Mengistu, probably as a condition for their help to him in expelling the Somalis. Both the Ethiopians and the Soviets had many compelling reasons for stopping at the Somali border. The situation in Eritrea was desperate; Ethiopian forces there held only Asmara and Massawa at the end of 1977, and in December the EPLF launched a drive to take Massawa that nearly succeeded. There was urgent need for the Ethiopian army to turn its attention to Eritrea as soon as the Ogaden had been dealt with. But beyond this there were reasons of international politics. So long as they were defending Ethiopia's territorial integrity from Somali invasion, the Ethiopians and the Soviets had the moral and political high ground. Early in August, Ethiopia had brought the Somali invasion before the OAU and that body had rejected Somalia's claim and endorsed Ethiopia's position. The Americans could complain about Soviet arms and Cuban troops, but so long as the Ethiopians stayed on their side of the border there was not much the United States could do to rally even other Western governments. Once they crossed into Somalia, it would be a wholly different story. The OAU, the UN and even the Arab League could be brought into play against them.[35] Conservative Arab states and the United States might intervene on Somalia's side. Mengistu must have been sorely tempted to seek revenge against Siad Barre, but invasion of Somalia was more of a risk than the Soviets, and probably the Ethiopian leader as well, cared to take.

More generally, however, even if Soviet-backed Ethiopian and Cuban forces did not enter Somalia, Washington was alarmed about the way the Soviets were throwing their weight around in Africa. What would the Soviets do next? Might they not even send Cuban troops to Rhodesia? Brzezinski says nothing that would suggest that he did not believe Dobrynin's assurance that the Ethiopians would not cross the Somali border. Yet he pressed strongly for steps to confront the Soviets by deploying a US aircraft carrier task force near Ethiopia. His arguments had more to do with global politics than with the immediate situation in Ethiopia and Somalia. The Soviets, he said, must not be led to calculate 'that the US will simply again adjust to the consolidation of Soviet presence in yet another African country'.[36] If Ethiopia and South Yemen became Soviet associates, 'not only will access to Suez be threatened . . . but there will be a serious and direct political threat to Saudi Arabia'.[37] And it was 'important that regional powers not see the United States as passive in the face of Soviet and Cuban intervention . . . even if our support was, in the final analysis, only for the record'. Brzezinski wanted to establish a link between Soviet actions in Ethiopia and the major issues on the US–Soviet agenda, notably the SALT II negotiations. He and many outside the administration considered that a broad and highly visible response was required so as to show both the Soviets and the rest of the world that the United States would not accept more of the same elsewhere.

In sum, Brzezinski wanted to enlarge the ramifications of Soviet and Cuban intervention in Ethiopia. Vance wanted to circumscribe them. He was concerned more about the specific situation in the Horn of Africa and he wanted to limit damage to US–Soviet relations in other areas. As he wrote later,

Our interest lay in preventing the resumption of Soviet influence in Somalia either by force or by a new Somali turnabout . . . with the limited diplomatic means at our disposal. We could not in the short run expect a break between the Soviets and the Marxist regime in Addis Ababa. To allow that to be regarded as a realistic objective by the public and Congress ensured that the outcome would be seen as administration weakness in the face of Soviet challenge'.[38]

Brzezinski continued to press his carrier task force idea even after Vance had got from Dobrynin, on 10 February, and Deputy National Security Advisor David Aaron had got directly from Mengistu, on 17 February, renewed and unequivocal assurances that Ethiopian and Cuban troops would not cross the Somali border. Vance and Defense Secretary Harold Brown opposed it and nothing was done. As Brzezinski noted in his memoirs, 'In the end I did not carry the day.'

The Ethiopian–Cuban offensive was launched in mid-February under the direction of General Vasily Petrov, commander of Soviet ground forces, assisted by three other Soviet generals, one of them the former head of the Soviet military mission to Somalia. It made quick progress. The Somalis, now outnumbered and unable to secure adequate resupply, were driven out of their conquests in the Ogaden in a matter of weeks. On 9 March Siad Barre made a virtue of necessity by announcing withdrawal of Somali forces.

The war was over even though skirmishing persisted for years thereafter and Ethiopia and Somalia continued to exchange accusations. Long before the Somalis struck their flag, however, the Ethiopian regime had invented its own version of events, aimed at justifying its reversal of alliance, almost as if it felt guilt over what it had done and needed a good alibi. The whole story of US-Ethiopian relations after the overthrow of Haile Selassie, indeed the whole complex and eventful history of the years 1974 through 1977, was reduced to one simple formula: the United States had abandoned Ethiopia in its hour of need and had sided with Somalia. Ethiopia had, therefore, turned to the Soviet Union. This fable has been peddled with surprising success over the years to Westerners visiting Ethiopia, to naïvely credulous Western parliamentarians and government officials to journalists and to prominent private citizens. Its simplicity appeals even to many Ethiopians who have no brief for the regime but have had no opportunity to inform themselves of the history of relations between their country and the United States and the Soviet Union in these critical years.

Like all stories invented to serve a political purpose, it has a grain of truth to it. As we have seen, the United States, in its headlong lurch to try to offset Soviet gains in Ethiopia through a concommitant American gain in Somalia, did announce that it was ready 'in principle' to offer Somalia 'defensive arms'. By this action it may have given unintended encouragement to Somalia's aggression, but it quickly drew back when its error became apparent. Somalia got no American arms in 1977 or in any of the succeeding years until 1982. The rest of the story has not a leg to stand on. The regime that seized power after Haile Selassie was deposed and General Aman was killed embarked on policies that brought it into collision with the United States. It did nothing to moderate these policies in the interest of preserving ties with the United States. It made no effort to cultivate a good atmosphere between it and the United States. It showed no interest in good relations with the United States and at times seemed actually to be trying to spoil relations. It wanted ties with the Soviet Union, and it courted the Soviets with such determination that finally they had no choice but to yield and put their investment in Somalia at risk.

The United States wanted to preserve its position in Ethiopia. It did not give as much attention to doing so as it might have done, but it made a substantial effort; given the constraints of the time and of the American political system, it probably could not have gone a lot further than it did. It came only very gradually and reluctantly to recognize that the aims and methods of the regime that took shape in Ethiopia, as purge followed purge, as pro-Western elements disappeared and pro-Soviet figures won out and repression and killing intensified, were too incompatible with those of the United States to permit continuation of a serious working relationship. By the end of 1976, US–Ethiopian relations had reached a point very near to deadlock. Mengistu's seizure of power at the beginning of February 1977 was the last turn of the screw. Mengistu himself carried out the formal rupture, in April, three months to the day before his government — on 23 July — announced that Somalia had invaded Ethiopia with its regular forces.

Ethiopia suffered invasion and immense loss of life and destruction in 1977, not because the United States abandoned it but because the Soviet Union recklessly armed Somalia in the years before, and because Mengistu miscalculated in his gamble on the Soviets. As the Soviet Union struggled to preserve its stake in Somalia while establishing its position in Ethiopia, it at first continued to supply arms to its old client while evidently slowing — or certainly not hastening to make — deliveries to its new one. This at a time when the war in Eritrea, the war that the Derg ordained when it rejected Aman's proposals for conciliation, was going so badly that it could only be a sore temptation to any aggressor. Even when the Ethiopians publicly announced themselves invaded by the Somalis, the Soviets did not immediately declare in Ethiopia's favor. They dallied for three weeks, quite clearly in the hope that things could be patched up and a rupture with Somalia avoided. Not until 14 August did they publicly begin to take Ethiopia's side. And it was over a month after that before they could make deliveries of weapons in sufficient quantities to halt the advance of the Somali army. If these facts are considered, the United States makes a very unlikely scapegoat for Ethiopia's brush with defeat and dismemberment in the summer of 1977.

Notes

1. Donald K. Petterson, 'Ethiopia Abandoned? An American Perspective', unpublished article.
2. Promoted to that grade in November 1976.
3. Rene Lefort, *Ethiopia, An Heretical Revolution?* (Zed Press, London, 1983), p. 180.
4. Called Begemder until the revolution and now renamed after its administrative capital, the city of Gondar.
5. Lefort, *Ethiopia, An Heretical Revolution?*, p. 197, puts it this way: 'Mengistu won primarily because his opponents had underestimated or even despised him.'
6. Amnesty International Report, 1977, p. 71.
7. Ibid., pp. 71–2.
8. The agreement had a term of 25 years if not renewed.
9. Bruce D. Porter, *The USSR in Third World Conflicts* (Cambridge University Press, 1984), p. 196.
10. According to a Reuters report carried in the *Guardian*, 17 March 1977.
11. David B. Ottaway, *International Herald Tribune*, 1 March 1977.
12. Colin Legum, *Observer*, 8 May 1977.
13. A movement that brought together a number of figures from the imperial regime and former generals; it advocated liberal democracy for Ethiopia.
14. The Ethiopian government had stopped payment on loans for earlier purchases of American weapons. Ethiopia's outstanding debt was greater than the nominal value of arms for which payment had already been made. The Defense Department eventually auctioned this equipment and applied the proceeds to the Ethiopian debt.
15. Former Secretary of State Cyrus Vance, *Hard Choices* (Simon and Schuster, New York, 1983), p. 73, says Carter told the Somali Ambassador that 'it would be difficult for us to provide military assistance but we would see whether our allies could help Somalia maintain defensive strength'. Vance adds that the Somalis considered Carter's reply to reflect a 'forthcoming attitude'.
16. Jimmy Carter, *Keeping Faith* (Bantam Books, 1982).
17. Vance, *Hard Choices*, p. 73.

18. *International Herald Tribune*, 27 July 1977.

19. An anonymous State Department official quoted in *The New York Times*, 28 July 1977.

20. Raymond L. Garthoff, *Detente and Confrontation — American–Soviet Relations from Nixon to Reagan* (Brookings, 1985), p. 633.

21. State Department Bulletin, Vol. 77, 8 August 1977, pp. 169–70.

22. State Department Bulletin, Vol. 77, 22 August 1977, p. 222.

23. State Department Bulletin, Vol. 77, 22 August 1977, p. 229.

24. *Newsweek*, 26 September 1977, pp. 43–4.

25. *Observer Foreign News Service*, No. 36069, 24 May 1977.

26. *International Herald Tribune*, 4 August 1977.

27. Colin Legum, *The Observer*, 25 September 1977.

28. *Soviet News*, 9 August 1977.

29. *Soviet News*, 16 August 1977.

30. Afro-Asian Solidarity Committee statement, reported in *Soviet News*, 13 September 1977.

31. The Ethiopian government steadfastly refused to acknowledge Jigjiga's fall even after Western correspondents confirmed it by visiting the town as guests of the Somali army.

32. *Washington Post*, 27 September 1977.

33. Some reports say the session lasted 10 hours, others that it went on for 19 hours.

34. Zbigniew Brzezinski, *Power and Principle* (Farrar Straus Giroux, New York, 1983), p. 179.

35. Somalia, though not ethnically Arab, had managed to gain membership in the Arab League.

36. Brzezinski, *Power and Principle*, p. 181.

37. *Ibid.*, p. 181.

38. Vance, *Hard Choices*, p. 88.

3 THE UNITED STATES TRIES TO RECOUP

The massive Soviet air lift of arms to Ethiopia and the entry on the scene of Cuban combat troops generated heated calls in the United States for the Carter administration to 'do something' to 'stop the Russians'. By itself, the administration's decision, taken in November 1977, to embargo arms shipments to both Ethiopia and Somalia so long as fighting continued in the Ogaden, risked giving an appearance of passivity. To counter this, Carter and Vance made a series of public statements in December and January calling for negotiations between Ethiopia and Somalia and mediation by the OAU. When the administration's appeal for negotiations went unheeded, it added a new twist: withdrawal of Somali forces from Ethiopia in return for evacuation of Cuban and Soviet military personnel, and the sending of neutral observers to monitor the cease-fire and the border. Various European governments gave their endorsement to this idea, but it met with no greater success than the call for negotiations. Neither the Soviets nor the Ethiopians were interested. They neither wanted nor saw the need to bargain for the Somalis' departure; they were in a position to drive them out and looked forward to doing so. The Somali President purported to play Washington's game when he advised Carter on 9 March that he was withdrawing his forces from the Ogaden, but it was an empty gesture. By then his army was broken and routed.

The administration saw Somalia's withdrawal as opening up attractive new prospects for American diplomacy in the Horn of Africa. The United States could proceed now to develop its relations with Somalia and to re-establish links with Ethiopia. And now that the stated reason for the presence of Cuban troops in Ethiopia, that is the Somali invasion, no longer existed, it hoped to press more effectively for their withdrawal.

Ethiopia was simply too big and important to write off, no matter what gains might be anticipated from Somalia. No one in the administration seriously thought that the United States stood any chance of regaining the position it had occupied in Ethiopia before the revolution. But it was hoped that the United States could re-establish some measure of influence and presence in Ethiopia. Once Mengistu achieved victory over the Somalis and made headway in

Eritrea, it was reasoned, he would be more free to pursue a course of independence in international affairs. It was noted that Mengistu had purged his pro-Soviet Marxist–Leninist ideologues — his MEISON supporters — in September 1977. It was hoped that this might be an indication that he intended to take some distance, at least ideologically, from Moscow. What seems to have been overlooked was that the Soviet Union's massive assistance in expelling the Somalis had in fact considerably strengthened and consolidated its position in Ethiopia.

The first weeks of 1978 were not auspicious ones for relations between Ethiopia and the West. In response to Carter's and Vance's statements on Cuban and Soviet military personnel in Ethiopia, and to US hints that, if Somalia were invaded, the United States would reconsider its refusal to provide arms to that country, the Ethiopian Foreign Ministry, in a statement issued on 14 January, made a veiled threat to break relations with the United States. On 30 January Mengistu delivered an address over radio and television in which he strongly criticized President Carter and accused the United States of orchestrating conspiracies against Ethiopia. At a press conference early in February Mengistu reiterated the Foreign Ministry's threat to break relations. Early in January the Ethiopian government seized the West German School and the next day asked the FRG military attaché to leave. When the German ambassador protested too loudly, he too was expelled. Nonetheless, when Carter proposed at the beginning of February to send his deputy national security advisor, David Aaron, to Addis Ababa, Mengistu agreed.

Though it had the broader aim of improving relations between the United States and Ethiopia, the Aaron mission's most immediate objective was to keep them from being broken off altogether. The newly arrived Ethiopian ambassador, Ayalew Mandefro, was able to confirm to officials in Washington that the public threats to break relations that were being made in Addis Ababa were by no means idle. Ambassador Ayalew, who had been Minister of Defense until September 1977, confided to State Department and NSC officials that a powerful faction within the ruling group wanted to break off entirely with the United States. Ayalew was seriously out of sympathy with his government, and at the beginning of February he was to resign his post and seek political asylum in the United States. Nominally, his appointment to Washington at the end of 1977 was intended as a move to improve ties; in fact he knew the mood in Addis Ababa to be just the opposite. He narrowly escaped assassination before leaving the Ethiopian capital for the United States; his car was blown up while parked in front of the Foreign Ministry. NSC-staffer Paul Henze proposed to Brzezinski that a presidential emissary be sent to Addis Ababa for direct talks with Mengistu. Brzezinski relayed the idea to Carter and Carter promptly approved. The President had by this time become deeply immersed in the affairs of the Horn of Africa and he immediately appreciated the value of a dramatic move. When discussion turned to who should head the mission, Carter ruled out a State Department officer. He wanted a specific White House label on the emissary. Brzezinski himself wanted to go, but Carter would not spare him for the job. David Aaron was the next logical choice, though he had had very little to do up to that time with the crisis between Ethiopia and Somalia. To emphasize the high level of the mission and Carter's personal commitment to it, Aaron was sent off in a presidential aircraft.

Aaron arrived in the Ethiopian capital on 16 February and met Mengistu that same evening. He sought and Mengistu readily gave assurance that Ethiopian troops would not cross into Somalia. But Mengistu quickly took Aaron to task over US support for Somalia and did not accept his assurance that no American weapons had been authorized for delivery to Somalia. Why, Mengistu asked, had the United States not publicly condemned Somalia's invasion? Aaron said Washington had not wanted to do anything that might work against its effort to persuade Siad Barre to withdraw his forces from Ethiopia; the reply left the Ethiopian leader unpersuaded. Aaron stressed that the United States wanted better relations with Ethiopia. He assured Mengistu that Washington did not oppose the economic and social aims of the revolution and that it intended to be impartial in its policies toward the countries of the Horn of Africa. He spoke of the possibility of increased economic assistance and reminded Mengistu that neighboring countries with which Ethiopia had problems — notably Egypt and Saudi Arabia — were friends of the United States and susceptible to influence from the United States. And he pointed out that the United States had never supported the insurgencies in Eritrea and had no reservation about endorsing, as it always had, Ethiopia's territorial integrity. When Aaron, Henze and State Department officer William Harrop left the meeting with Mengistu, they felt they had given the Ethiopian leader every possible assurance of the United States' good intentions. On leaving Addis Ababa on 18 February, Aaron characterized his meeting with Mengistu as 'frank and correct', a description that probably understated his feeling of satisfaction about his mission.

For some weeks after Aaron's visit the atmosphere in relations between the United States and Ethiopia improved. At the end of February the United States, in a minor exception to its 1977 embargo, released 23 military trucks and trailers and a consignment of spare parts for delivery to the Ethiopian army. Criticism of the United States by the Ethiopian media slackened off. The United States proposed, and the Ethiopian government gave agreement for, the appointment of an ambassador, Frederick Chapin, a career officer with a long background in Latin American affairs. Chapin arrived in Addis Ababa in July 1978 with a strong mandate to improve relations between the United States and Ethiopia. Soon afterwards he sent Washington a long cable recommending a program of $20m. in development assistance, a sum he reasoned would be a good start toward putting the United States back on the political map in Ethiopia.

These good intentions quickly ran up against an obstacle that in retrospect may seem strange, that of American citizen claims for compensation for holdings nationalized by the Ethiopian regime at the beginning of 1975. United States law required that the President terminate assistance to any country whose government failed to move promptly and in good faith to compensate for expropriated properties of American citizens. These claims were not large by ordinary standards: they amounted by the estimates of the claimants themselves to some $30m. There were 25 claimants, most of them small. The largest was Kalamazoo Spice, a firm with headquarters in the Michigan city of the same name, but others were people who had owned light aircraft, small businesses or shares in industrial or commercial companies that had been nationalized. Chapin made clear, when he met Chairman Mengistu on 21 July to present his credentials, that the United States was ready to provide economic aid but needed the help of the Ethiopian government in moving toward settlement of claims.

Compensation was one of those issues on which the gap in understanding between the United States and a Third World country would have been large under the best of circumstances. For the US side, the matter was clear-cut. Three and a half years had passed since expropriation and not a single claim had been settled. During this time, the Ethiopian government had shown no interest in and taken no step toward settling the claims of American citizens. The law, called the Hickenlooper amendment (to the Foreign Assistance Act of 1961) after the late Senator Burke Hickenlooper, required of aid recipient governments prompt steps to negotiate in good faith for settlement. The word prompt offered some leeway in interpretation, but only with great difficulty could it be made to stretch over a period of years. The claimants, though few in numbers, had senators and congressmen who did not hesitate to remind the administration both of their constituents' distress and of the terms of the law. Furthermore, the administration seems to have viewed the issue as a test of the Ethiopian government's interest in building better ties with the United States. After all, the amounts claimed were not large, even for Ethiopia, and both sides understood that international claims are never settled for 100 cents on the dollar. There was not even an immediate need to pay; the claimants would have been happy to have a promise to pay and a schedule of installments.

But what looked entirely reasonable to the Americans, the Ethiopians professed to see as almost sinister. Why should the Americans raise this untoward issue at this time? Was it not intended as a diktat to Ethiopia, an unacceptable condition? These reactions — partly contrived and partly genuine — produced a stiffening on the Ethiopian side. Chapin realized that, if the Ethiopians could not be persuaded to take some action on compensation, there would be no way to avoid a cut-off of American development assistance. So he kept plugging away. He raised compensation again with Mengistu on 1 October and with Foreign Minister Feleke a month later, but the Ethiopians did not budge. As the issue continued to fester, on 1 March 1979, Chapin on instructions from Washington proposed government-to-government negotiations for the settlement of claims. This proposal was intended to speed and simplify the process of disposing of US citizen claims by relieving the government of Ethiopia of the burden of having to negotiate individually with some two dozen claimants, some with so little money at stake that they had no incentive to come to Addis Ababa or even to hire an Ethiopian lawyer to represent them there.

Chapin also let the Ethiopians know that, if progress were not made on claims, the United States would soon have to move toward application of the various laws that required cut-off of development assistance and made it obligatory for the United States to oppose

International Bank for Reconstruction and Development and African Development Bank loans to Ethiopia. In fact, on 22 March 1979, the United States for the first time voted against an ADB loan to Ethiopia.[1] On 26 March the Ethiopian government sent the American Embassy an *aide-mémoire* in which it alleged that lack of progress on compensation was due to the claimants' failure to pursue their claims seriously. On 28 March Feleke called Chapin in and accused him of 'terrorizing' the Ethiopian government on this issue. He charged that the United States was using compensation as a 'political weapon' against Ethiopia. A claims attorney sent by the State Department to Addis Ababa for talks on government-to-government negotiations was given no appointment and left after a week's fruitless wait. At the beginning of May the Senate Foreign Relations Committee voted to recommend ending development assistance to Ethiopia. The Ethiopian government still refused to budge. On 5 July 1979 the American development assistance program was formally declared terminated.[2]

Before this happened, there occurred a bizarre but not unique episode that made the Americans wonder what forces were at work inside the Ethiopian government. By the spring of 1979 it was clear that the American initiative of the previous year had not brought the results hoped from it. Not only were relations with Ethiopia not improving, they had gone seriously downhill. Termination of the aid program would inevitably make things much worse. Chapin was recalled to Washington at the end of April for consultations. After he returned to Addis Ababa in mid-May he presented to Acting Foreign Minister Dawit Wolde Giorgis an invitation from Vance to send a delegation to Washington to discuss the state of relations overall and claims in particular. Dawit welcomed this American proposal and so did Foreign Minister Feleke, who called Chapin in the following week to express satisfaction over it. Yet hardly more than three weeks later, on 19 June, Feleke sent a vitriolic letter to Vance rejecting the proposal.

In addition to the claims issue, which the Ethiopians complained was being pressed too hard by the United States, a series of events contributed to the souring of relations during 1978 and 1979. At the end of July 1978, as a gesture of good faith, the United States made a $4m. aid grant to Ethiopia. Three days later one of the three aid officers stationed at the Embassy in Addis Ababa was arrested on flimsy charges; he was released and declared cleared of the allegations made against him, but was required to leave Ethiopia. In his speech on the fourth anniversary of the revolution, on 12 September, Mengistu attacked the United States and China and accused the latter of co-operating with the CIA in conspiracies against Ethiopia. Human rights emerged again as an issue between the two governments. Though the mass killings of late 1977 and early 1978 had subsided, arbitrary arrest and execution were still commonplace. For the Carter administration, with its declared emphasis on human rights, there could be no easy partnership with Ethiopia without some improvement in this area. At the beginning of November, on specific instructions from Washington, Chapin made a strong *démarche* on human rights. The Ethiopians were outraged; three days later the Foreign Ministry's Americas' Department head telephoned Chapin to protest about his 'unwarranted interference in Ethiopia's domestic affairs'. In mid-November Mengistu left Addis Ababa for an extended tour of African and East European capitals, and in Moscow on 20 November he signed a 20-year treaty of friendship and co-operation with the Soviet Union. The agreement was the standard document used to formalize relations between the Soviet Union and governments newly come into its orbit. It caused much concern in Washington. Hopes of earlier in the year, that the Ethiopian leader was in fact a nationalist with whom the West could work, faded. The trend toward strengthening Ethiopia's ties with the Soviet Union continued during 1979. Soviet Premier Kosygin attended the ceremonies celebrating the fifth anniversary of the Ethiopian revolution on 12 September. On 17 December Mengistu announced the creation of a Commission for the Organization of the Party of the Workers of Ethiopia, immediately to become known as COPWE. This was the political party that the Soviets had been pressing Mengistu to set up for so long, and in making his announcement he declared that it would be a 'Marxist–Leninist vanguard party'. Not everybody in the West, or even in Washington, was immediately persuaded that Mengistu was serious about establishing a party, but his action raised new and stronger questions about his political orientation. These were reinforced when, at the beginning of January 1980, after a brief news black-out on the Soviet invasion of Afghanistan, the Ethiopian media began to report events in that country in terms identical to those being used by the Soviet media. A few days later the Ethiopian Foreign Ministry issued a statement openly supporting Soviet intervention in Afghanistan. Locally, frictions between the Embassy and the

Ethiopian government were exacerbated when two Cuban soldiers climbed over the wall of the Embassy compound and asked for asylum and the Embassy rejected Ethiopian demands that they be turned out.

These events were a bitter disappointment to Washington and to the Embassy, but there was more to come. On 29 July 1980 the Ethiopian Foreign Ministry officially requested Chapin's recall, blaming him for the poor state of relations between the United States and Ethiopia.

The Carter administration was by that time already resigned to the failure of its early 1978 opening to Ethiopia. It had even considered recalling Chapin early in 1980. His expulsion marked a clear-cut end to the 1978 initiative and put relations in a very deep freeze. Increasingly preoccupied with the Iran hostage crisis and facing a difficult re-election campaign, the administration had little time and even less inclination to try to retrieve what by now seemed a hopelessly lost position in Ethiopia.

But early in January 1981, just two weeks before the inauguration of the Reagan administration, the Ethiopian side abruptly took an initiative that surprised Washington and recalled the events of May and June of 1979. On 5 January the American Chargé in Addis Ababa was called to the Foreign Ministry and told that Ethiopia desired better relations. The Ethiopian Chargé in Washington conveyed the same message to the State Department a day later. The way the opening was worded made clear that it was intended for the new administration, even though it had not yet taken office. It aroused considerable interest, but, as the new administration was considering how to respond, Mengistu, on 9 February in an address to the second plenary of COPWE, made a bitter attack on the West and the United States in particular. As an officer serving at the American Embassy in Addis Ababa at the time put it, after that the Ethiopian Foreign Ministry's interest in discussing improvements in US–Ethiopian relations 'waned'. What was one to make of this second Ethiopian somersault? Clearly, the Foreign Ministry wanted to restore at least a semblance of civil discourse in relations between Ethiopia and the United States. But this inclination either met with no approval at the top level of the Ethiopian government, or the top level was unable to pursue it. The latter implied, of course, that the Soviets had gained in Ethiopia a position so pre-eminent that they could enforce a veto over Ethiopian government actions. The former was equally disquieting. And one wondered how the

Foreign Ministry could fail to seek the approval of the leadership
before taking such a potentially important initiative, or how it could
be so apparently ignorant of the leadership's views?

The Ethiopian Foreign Ministry's turnabout confirmed Reagan
administration officials in their view of Ethiopia. The new administration came to office with no particular brief, in any event, for
radical Third World regimes. But Ethiopia seemed a model of
everything it disliked: its government professed Marxism–
Leninism, it gave military facilities to the Soviets, and a large
contingent of Cuban troops sojourned on its territory. To make
matters worse, it had long common borders with three states that
the United States counted among its best and most important
friends in Africa: Sudan, Somalia and Kenya. The Reagan
administration regarded the Ethiopian government with a very cold
eye. It rated prospects for an improvement in relations between the
United States and Ethiopia very low, too low to warrant unilateral
American gestures. What it wanted mainly was a policy for dealing
with and containing the threat that Ethiopia was presumed to pose
to its neighbors and, more broadly, to American interests
throughout Africa. But beneath these generally shared attitudes,
there were important differences of view. Some inclined toward
a tough approach: economic sanctions against Ethiopia, large-scale
rearmament of Somalia, even assistance to Ethiopian insurgents.
Others advocated a more cautious line, albeit a strongly
behavioralistic one: the Ethiopian regime should be made to see
that its comportment did not pay, but it should be given due encouragement and opportunity to mend its ways. The United States
should let the Ethiopian government know very plainly that it was
not pleased with Ethiopia's conduct, but it should not go so far as to
alienate Ethiopia outright.

These views did not immediately find expression in a single co-
ordinated and coherent policy document. The policy review that
each new administration traditionally holds for the Horn of Africa
was tardy in coming, partly because of differences of views and
partly because of preoccupation in the Department's Bureau of
African Affairs with other issues, in particular southern Africa. A
few preliminary policy review meetings were held in mid-1981 but
no conclusions were reached. Perversely, Ethiopia's leaders
seemed almost determined to take advantage of the new administration's inattention to earn for themselves an ever less favorable
reputation in Washington. At the end of February 1981, Mengistu

attended the congress of the Communist party of the Soviet Union and there made what was viewed in Washington as a slavishly pro-Soviet speech. As the year wore on, ties between Ethiopia and Libya, the administration's supreme *bête noire*, grew closer, and in August a 'tripartite pact', bringing together Libya, Ethiopia and the People's Democratic Republic of Yemen, was signed. Soon thereafter Qadhafi visited Addis Ababa where he was greeted by a mass public turnout organized by the Ethiopian regime. Reports circulated that Qadhafi had pledged $1.5b. in aid to Ethiopia.

Policy review for the Horn of Africa was resumed in the spring of 1982 and agreement was reached in July. The more extreme proposals, in particular those that called for aid to Ethiopian rebel groups, were eschewed. The new policy called for strong support for the United States' friends in the area, Sudan, Somalia and Kenya, but struck a moderate stance on the matter of arms for Somalia. It advocated greater co-ordination of policy toward Ethiopia and other area states on the part of the NATO allies. And it proposed to try to establish a 'dialogue' between the United States and Ethiopia in the aim of reaching a better understanding of one another's views and, it was hoped, an improvement in relations between them. What this meant was that the United States would make a try at talking with the Ethiopian government. It was not, in the early stage at least, prepared to offer the Ethiopian government any particular rewards — beyond the intrinsic value of better ties with the United States — for changing its policies.

Allied policies toward Ethiopia, from Washington's perspective in the summer of 1982, presented a panorama of troublesome diversity. In common they shared a more conciliatory view of the Ethiopian regime than that held by the United States, but beyond that they varied widely. The British were closest to the American view, but they were skeptical of the value of punitive measures; the UK's bilateral assistance program for Ethiopia was very small, so no impact could be made by cutting it back. The French were pessimistic about Ethiopia but for the most part uninvolved; they cared about Djibouti and the Djibouti–Addis Ababa railway that they had built early in the century but otherwise their resources were earmarked for the Francophone African states. The West Germans, typically, were divided and undecided. Some in Bonn thought the Ethiopian regime could be wooed while others considered its leadership irredeemably lost to the Soviets. Though they declared their aid program for Ethiopia stalled as a result of the Ethiopian government's seizure of their school, the West Germans were in fact prepared to hand out fairly substantial sums to build and maintain a position for themselves. The Japanese were not sure quite what they wanted out of Ethiopia besides a market for their goods, in which respect the country held very little promise; but they thought it prudent not to be entirely absent from the aid donor rolls. The European Economic Community vied with the IBRD for the position of largest multilateral aid donor. The EEC mission in Addis Ababa managed a program of about $100m. a year in development credits extended under the Lomé II convention of 1981. The EEC program seemed less a product of thought than one of bureaucratic momentum and badly oversimplified logic: the EEC had a fund to aid needy Third World countries, Ethiopia was a large and exceptionally needy Third World country, ergo the EEC program for Ethiopia. Those charged with administering it went about their task uneasily, haunted by a sense that the community's money was frequently wasted in a setting where Marxist–Leninist ideology, rather than pragmatic economic choice, predominated. Consequently a mixture of Euro-pessimism and Euro-cynicism enveloped the program. Not so the IBRD, which as a matter of principle preferred to ignore political considerations and had a kind of Scandinavian tolerant indulgence for radical Third World regimes. Ethiopia met all of the Bank's major criteria: it was very poor, on a per capita basis it received very little foreign assistance, and it had a capable bureaucracy and little corruption. The Bank pressed — because its policy compelled it to, but not very hard — for the Ethiopian government to pay off foreign claimants. Its officials wore a demeanor of perpetual surprise and puzzlement over the Ethiopian government's failure to move to settle American citizen claims.

And then there were the Italians, in principle the biggest donor of all and in fact the Western government with the best access to the Ethiopian government. This may seem strange in the light of past events. The Italian conquest and occupation of Ethiopia was brutal in the extreme, and Mussolini's government followed unabashedly racist policies. Yet when the war was over the Ethiopians took no retribution against the large Italian community that stayed on. In fact Haile Selassie urged them to remain and help build the country. The events of 1974 and afterwards caused a great many Italians to leave Ethiopia, but even then they continued to be the largest single

private foreign community. By virtue of its colonial past, Italy considered both Ethiopia and Somalia to be areas of special influence,
almost spheres of influence. The Ethiopians and Somalis, jealously
monogamous in their relations with the Americans and Soviets,
tolerantly countenanced duality where Italy was concerned. There
was, it seemed, always a struggle going on in Rome as to which of
the two former colonies should have favored status; always, it was
somehow connected, in unfathomable ways, with Italian domestic
politics. The vehicle for Italian influence was of course money, and
the Italians handed it — or at least promises of it — out in the grand
manner. For a time the Italian aid program for Ethiopia seemed a
sly trickery, a kind of Neapolitan sleight of hand. Italian politicians
descended upon Addis Ababa and promised enormous sums, yet
nothing materialized. The Italian Foreign Minister came to Addis
Ababa in 1981 and promised $80m. for development projects. In
August of 1982 Vice-Minister Palleschi, in charge of foreign aid
programs, announced another $280m.; it turned out, however, that
Palleschi had made these commitments without proper authority,
so they became null and void. The Ethiopians complained loudly,
though not publicly, and the Italian ambassador fretted. Finally, in
July 1984, the new Italian Vice-Minister in charge of external assistance, Rafaelli, came to Addis Ababa and pledged $275m. in
development loans and grants and another $100m. in commercial
credits, this time in earnest. Implementation of the first projects
began early in 1985. The Italians listened politely and patiently to
American lectures on the misdeeds of the regime in Addis Ababa
and the inadvisability of giving large amounts of aid. They then went
ahead and made their pledges regardless.

I arrived in Addis Ababa at the beginning of June 1982, as the
policy review was wending its way toward completion. Early in
August I was instructed to sound out Ethiopian officials about the
possibility of Chairman Mengistu's receiving a senior State
Department official who would come to Addis Ababa to present
Washington's views. After a few discreet probes at the Foreign
Ministry, I put the proposal directly to Foreign Minister Feleke
Gedle Giorgis. Feleke, a man of considerable intelligence and
charm though at times brooding and erratic, seemed disinclined to
raise our proposal with Mengistu. Several weeks passed without an
answer from him. Finally, through a circuitous route, our message
was got directly to Mengistu. In mid-December he replied that he
was not only ready to meet and talk but wanted the dialogue

between Ethiopia and the United States to be publicly announced. For it to be held secretly, he said, would 'confirm the mistaken perception that Ethiopia is not independent in foreign policy'. But no sooner did the US side reply that this was entirely agreeable than Mengistu changed his mind. A visit by an official from Washington, the Ethiopian leader advised, would 'raise expectations to an unduly high level' and be a 'media extravaganza'. Instead, he preferred to meet privately and without publicity with the American Chargé d'Affaires. If this first meeting turned out to be promising, someone could come later from Washington for further talks. Clearly, Mengistu wanted to avoid alarming his Soviet friends.

This reply, which overall seemed encouraging, was followed by a blistering attack on the United States by Mengistu in a speech delivered at the beginning of January at the third COPWE congress. The speech caused consternation in Washington. Officials there momentarily questioned whether it would be useful to go ahead with the planned meeting. These doubts were put aside after a few weeks and late in January I was given instructions on points to make to Mengistu and told to proceed. My dealings with the Foreign Minister had already accustomed me to Ethiopian government practices in the matter of receiving callers: you were not to expect to be given a day and an hour for an appointment but simply to wait to be convoked (this I eventually learned was a carry-over from imperial days, and it was a practice used only by Mengistu and other top officials). My summons came at a few minutes past 8 on the morning of 15 February. The voice at the other end of the line urgently instructed me to 'come immediately' to the Chairman's office in the Menelik palace. As this was my first meeting with Mengistu, I was eager to get a closer look at this man who had made so much history. I was escorted to his office and, after the customary wait, was introduced along a narrow strip of red carpet at the end of which the Ethiopian Head of State and his Foreign Minister, the latter looking very dour, stood as though at attention in a military reviewing line. Mengistu was a short man of medium build, and a good deal darker than shown in his portraits. He wore a dark Western business suit with a white shirt and dark tie together with a pair of heavy black military boots polished to a brilliant shine. As we sat down he brought out a packet of American cigarettes and smoked throughout the meeting. His manner combined graciousness with a heavy dose of authority. Following Haile Selassie's practice, he spoke in Amharic but required no translation from English. We proceeded very quickly to business. I explained Washington's concern over the poor state into which relations between the United States and Ethiopia had fallen in recent years and its proposal to send a senior representative from Washington to hold high level talks aimed at clearing up misunderstandings and setting a new course in our dealings with one another. I assured Mengistu that we had no hostile intentions toward Ethiopia but pointed out that we were concerned about Ethiopian government activities directed against Somalia and Sudan. Mengistu responded politely with a long discourse on the perfidy of Somalia and the danger caused to Ethiopia by the United States in supplying arms to Somalia. He said Ethiopia shared the United States' desire for better relations; it had no hostile intentions toward the United States but was concerned over American military activities in the area which it considered threatening. Ethiopia wanted no trouble with the United States or anyone else; it wanted only to develop its country and improve the life of its people. It was non-aligned, Mengistu insisted, and not a pawn or proxy for any great power. He said he did not think the time yet right for the United States to send a special emissary but assured that he welcomed the 'positive step' from the American side in proposing talks. He wanted to pursue it, but cautiously so as 'not to give the wrong interpretation' or arouse 'exaggerated expectations'. He would be in touch with us about next steps. Then, changing demeanor entirely, Mengistu closed by declaring with great fervor, 'I am a revolutionary; my life is dedicated to freeing the people'.

After this on the whole encouraging start, cautious optimism seemed to be in order. We waited for the next step, which Mengistu had said would come from the Ethiopian side. On 14 March the Ethiopian Chargé in Washington, Tesfaye Demeke, called on Assistant Secretary of State, Chester Crocker, to deliver a rambling and aggressive message from Mengistu. The Ethiopian leader accused the United States of being hostile to Ethiopia and to him personally. He professed to see no fundamental reason why the interests of the two countries should clash, but asked whether the United States objected to his presence in power? After handing over this somewhat disconcerting diatribe, Tesfaye informed Crocker that Mengistu would be ready to receive an emissary from Washington. Three weeks later Crocker called Tesfaye in and gave him a written message for Mengistu assuring that the United States had no hostility either toward Ethiopia or its Head of State, and that it desired better understanding with Ethiopia. Crocker proposed to send Deputy Assistant Secretary Princeton Lyman to Addis Ababa and suggested that talks between the two sides address first of all tensions between Ethiopia and Somalia, specifically the situation following Ethiopia's occupation in July and August of 1982 of the border towns of Balenbale and Goldogob. Having in mind Mengistu's desire to conduct his dealings with us discreetly, Crocker said Lyman would travel to Addis Ababa in late April as the US representative to the twenty-fifth anniversary ceremonies of the UNECA, headquartered in Addis Ababa.

From this point on, nothing went right. Tesfaye urged that I pass word of Lyman's coming directly to Mengistu's private secretary, Mengistu Gemechu. But when I telephoned Mengistu Gemechu, at the private number given us by the Ethiopian Chargé, he refused to see me. Moments later I was summoned urgently to the Foreign Ministry, to the office of Permanent Secretary[3] Tibebu Bekele, who lectured me sternly for having strayed from approved channels. Without mentioning Tesfaye or the advice he had given, I asked Tibebu to pass to Mengistu's office Washington's proposal to have Lyman come to Addis as US representative to the UNECA anniversary celebrations and meet Mengistu during that time. Tibebu took note of this non-commitally. Repeated requests for clarification as to whether Mengistu would see Lyman went unanswered. Lyman arrived in Addis on 22 April and left on 1 May without having seen Mengistu or anyone else who could speak for the Ethiopian government on the issue of US–Ethiopian relations.

What happened? Did Mengistu object to the timing of the visit or the level of the official chosen? If so, he said nothing about it. Did Tesfaye exceed his instructions when he told Crocker that Mengistu would be ready to receive an emissary? This hypothesis is impossible to verify but the Ethiopian Chargé was frequently out ahead of his government on the question of improving relations with the United States. Or did Mengistu simply have a temperamental change of heart? This last possibility cannot be dismissed. It recalls incidents that happened just a week after my meeting with Mengistu. On 22 February I was called to the Foreign Ministry, to meet the head of the Americas Department, Musa Yassin. Commander Musa, as he was called from his days in the navy, was a short, wiry man, a model of caution and of diligence in carrying out instructions received from higher up. He greeted me with the information that the Government of Ethiopia took strong exception to statements made by Assistant Secretary Crocker in an interview published several months earlier in an American scholarly journal. The next day I was summoned again to Musa's office and told in tones of even more stern reproof that President Reagan, in a speech the previous day to the American Legion, had made 'derogatory remarks about Ethiopia'. Knowing of no such statement, I asked Musa what the President had said that was objectionable to his government? Musa replied gravely that he did not have the text but it was 'a serious matter and Ethiopia will have to react publicly'. I replied that I expected to receive very soon the text of the speech in question; would the Government of Ethiopia not want to know precisely what was in it before issuing a public reply? Musa gave no answer. That afternoon I returned to Musa's office with the cabled text of the President's speech. Ethiopia was mentioned in only one brief sentence: Reagan said 'the Soviets sent their Cuban mercenaries to Ethiopia'. Could such a matter-of-fact remark be construed as a 'serious matter' requiring a formal and public Ethiopian reaction, I asked? Musa looked puzzled. He took the papers that I had brought and read through them carefully. Finding nothing, he asked if I were sure I had given him the correct text! I cautioned that he should not test my sense of humor too far and then said that, in view of the fact that there was nothing in the President's speech derogatory to Ethiopia, I hoped I could report that no Ethiopian statement would be issued. Musa replied that he could give no such assurance. The following day the *Ethiopian Herald* carried, under a banner headline, the text of a statement by the Foreign Ministry denouncing the United States for sending AWACs to Egypt and a carrier task force off the Libyan coast.

The cold shoulder given Lyman was discouraging but there occurred almost simultaneously another event that gave hope for brighter prospects. In late April a Cabinet reshuffle took place; Feleke was transferred to the Information Ministry and the Minister of Education, Goshu Wolde, became Foreign Minister. A handsome man in his early to mid-forties, Goshu enjoyed the reputation among the Western diplomatic community of a 'moderate'. He had no background in foreign affairs, but as education minister he had run one of the Ethiopian government's few successful programs, the literacy campaign. His new appointment was seen by Westerners in Addis Ababa as a sign that Mengistu wanted better relations with the West. Goshu's early actions abetted this impression. A new foreign minister traditionally receives the resident chiefs of diplomatic missions, but in groups rather than singly. In what order would he invite them? Rumor had it that Goshu had been advised to schedule the 'socialist' — that is, Soviet bloc — ambassadors first, but that he had rejected this counsel which was intended to underscore Ethiopia's ties with the East bloc. Whether or not the story was true, the new Foreign Minister received the African envoys first, followed by the other non-aligned, then the bloc, and lastly the Westerners. This was seen as indicating the order of precedence that he wanted to give to Ethiopia's foreign relations.

Such was the stuff on which the diplomatic corps in Addis Ababa — cut off by the authorities from all but the most limited official contact with Ethiopians and dependent on rumor for much of its information — thrived. It was an atmosphere that gave exaggerated importance to the smallest signs and in which judgment could easily go astray. On the afternoon that Western chiefs of mission were called to meet with Goshu I was not notified until they had assembled in his office. The Foreign Ministry telephoned to apologize for this 'oversight' and to ask that I come as speedily as possible. When I arrived, my Western colleagues were filing out of Goshu's office and I was escorted in for a private meeting. A clever ruse or nothing more than what it purported to be, an administrative mix-up? The meeting was very short. Goshu was extremely cordial, as was to be his manner in almost all of our dealings over the next two years. He said that while Ethiopia had adopted a socialist system domestically, in international affairs it was non-aligned, not subservient to any foreign power or bloc and desirous of better relations with all, including the United States. This could hardly be called an accurate description of Ethiopian policy at that moment but if it could be taken to reflect intent it was encouraging to hear.

Soon there were more encouraging signs. Early in July the Foreign Ministry notified us that Mengistu had approved a request by Congressman Howard Wolpe, Chairman of the House Africa Subcommittee, to visit Ethiopia during the first half of August. American legislators had not been in Ethiopia since 1978, when Senator Paul Tsongas and Congressman Don Bonker, stopped there briefly. The senator and the congressman found themselves stranded in Addis Ababa in transit for other destinations in Africa. Touring the city, they were shocked to see stacked on the curbsides the bodies of those executed during the night. They were even more shocked when, after mentioning this to Mengistu, they were told that the dead were counter-revolutionaries and had thus deserved their fate. Wolpe had asked to come in 1982 but had been turned down by the Ethiopians. He was a liberal Democrat, as were all but one of his delegation of eight congressmen and women, and a frequent critic of the administration's policies in Africa and elsewhere. After having passed up the opportunity to talk with the administration, the Ethiopian regime seemed to be saying that it preferred the opposition. Still, that Mengistu should have been ready to receive any American congressional group was seen in Washington as a favorable sign, and the administration gave full support to Wolpe's visit.

Wolpe and his delegation were accorded unusually broad and favorable attention by the Ethiopian media. Their arrival, their meetings in Addis Ababa and their travel to Assosa and Gondar got front-page headlines and top spot on the evening television news. Foreign Minister Goshu was even more cordial than usual. In his meeting with the delegation, he made with great enthusiasm all his standard points about Ethiopia's being non-aligned, independent and desiring better relations with the United States; he complained ever so politely about the United States' lack of understanding for the Ethiopian revolution. The delegation's meeting with Mengistu was less auspicious. Mengistu spoke harshly of the United States and of American policy, so much so that the sole Republican congressman, Gerald Solomon of New York, came close to walking out. Mengistu said it was up to the United States to come forward to seek better relations with Ethiopia — which of course, though he did not mention it, was what the United States had done earlier in the year. He added with some emphasis that, if it were to qualify for Ethiopia's friendship, the United States would have to mend its ways. When a Jewish congressman from New York asked for special procedures for emigration for Ethiopia's Falashas, the small peasant community in north-western Ethiopia that practices a unique form of Judaism, Mengistu abruptly refused.[4] Wolpe himself got just as brusque a turn-down when he suggested government-to-government negotiations between the United States and Ethiopia for settlement of American citizen claims. Wolpe, however, took encouragement from this meeting. Comparing notes afterwards, he and I could agree for the most part on what the Ethiopian leader had said but not on how he had said it or how it should be interpreted. Wolpe made it clear that he inclined to see Mengistu not as a Marxist–Leninist but as another African socialist, of the stripe of Mugabe or Nyerere. Publicly he summed up his view of the matter in the following words:

> There is great sensitivity in Ethiopia to the common American view and perception that they are simply the tools of the Soviet Union and do not have their own independent freedom of action, and they expressed very clearly to us, the Chairman himself and other officials of government, that that perception just really violated Ethiopia's sense of nationalism.[5]

It was obvious, however, that several of the other congressmen in the delegation did not share this view.

Wolpe and his delegation left Addis Ababa on 13 August, still to the accompaniment of much favorable publicity in the Ethiopian media. A few days later the Ethiopian press, radio and television began to attack the United States on every imaginable issue. This vitriolic campaign — for clearly it was a campaign — continued for several weeks. Finally, at the end of August, the State Department took the unusual step of instructing the Embassy to register a complaint. After that the crescendo diminished. One of the campaign's aims was obviously to reassure the Soviets. They were lauded in degree equal to that in which the Americans were vilified. But probably the more important purpose was to disabuse the Ethiopian public of any untoward notion that the visit of the American congressional delegation, and its reception by Mengistu, suggested some likelihood of change in Ethiopia's foreign or domestic policies. In fact, many Ethiopians did eagerly leap to the conclusion that change was in the wind. Early in August a flurry of invitations came to my wife and me to dine at Ethiopian homes.

Parallel to the congressional delegation's visit, another bizarre episode in US–Ethiopian relations was being enacted. The OAU had held its summit in Addis Ababa in June. Mengistu, as head of state of the host country, was elected Chairman of the organization. Tradition required that the Chairman of the organization attend the United Nations General Assembly to 'speak for Africa', and to meet with the President of the United States. Since the organization came into being in 1963, all OAU Chairmen had gone to New York to deliver the traditional address, and all but one — Idi Amin — had met with the American President. Would Mengistu go? Though he had made frequent trips to the Soviet Union and Eastern Europe, the Ethiopian leader had not visited any Western country since coming to power.[6] Even if made only in compliance with OAU tradition, a visit to the United States would be a significant new step for Mengistu.

During July and August the American Embassy in Addis Ababa was the object of a series of very strange approaches on this issue. All were by Ethiopian officials who claimed to speak in an entirely unofficial capacity. All wanted to know whether Mengistu would be received by President Reagan if he (Mengistu) were to go to New York in September or October for the General Assembly. None could say for sure whether Mengistu had in fact decided to go or whether he in fact desired a meeting with the American President, though most insisted that they thought he intended both. The most pointed and unusual of these approaches came from Kassa Kebede, until April 1983 Minister of Labor and Social Affairs in the Ethiopian government and after that Ambassador to the UN organizations in Geneva. Kassa received his university education in Israel. A friendly and personable man, he was known as favorably inclined toward the West and not fully in tune with the Ethiopian government's policy on relations with East and West. It appeared that Mengistu tolerated his deviations because the two had been childhood companions and were possibly blood relatives.[7] One evening in mid-August, Kassa burst into a dinner that I was attending at the Hilton Hotel, sat himself down next to me and, in order to conceal from others nearby the subject of our conversation, began addressing me in Hebrew, a language he knew I spoke. Kassa wanted a commitment from me that, if Mengistu went to New York, he would be received by the President. But like the others he could not assure me that he was speaking on Mengistu's behalf or that a decision to go to New York had been made. As soon as Kassa had delivered himself of his message, he rose from his seat and bolted from the room.

The ideal way to answer these feelers would have been to say that of course the President would be delighted to see the Chairman and that he should definitely plan to come. This would have put Mengistu squarely on the spot. Unfortunately, for reasons that will probably be fully appreciated only by those who have worked in foreign ministries, it was out of the question. The bureaucratic process for setting up meetings between heads of state is extraordinarily cumbersome, possibly more so in Washington than elsewhere. When those who propose the meeting cannot even offer the assurance that the visiting head of state wants such a meeting, or even that he is definitely going to be in the United States, it becomes practically impossible. The people charged with scheduling a president will simply not take the responsibility for committing him to a meeting that no one can say with certainty will ever take place. At the time of the General Assembly, in particular, there are many more foreign leaders in New York who want to see the American President than he can reasonably accommodate. Ethiopia's bad reputation in Washington made it a particularly poor candidate for consideration. If a meeting between the President and Mengistu could be looked upon as an opportunity, it could also be seen as a dangerous gamble. What if the President and Mengistu did not 'get on'? What if Mengistu were to lecture the President, as he did the United States in his speeches, about American policies in the Horn of Africa, Central America, southern Africa, and on arms control? So the best I could do was tell Kassa and others who came with similar messages that their approaches would be reported to Washington, and to urge them to return with more palpably official backing.

The most we were able to learn from the Foreign Ministry was that it was proceeding with planning as though Mengistu had decided to go to New York. The Ministry had also had talks with French, Belgian and EEC representatives and had made tentative arrangements for the Ethiopian head of state to stop in Brussels and Paris on his way back from New York. From contacts with officers of the Ministry, it was evident that they too did not know what their chief intended to do. But they had instructions from Goshu to make all arrangements so that visits to New York, Brussels and Paris could go forward if Mengistu were to decide in that sense.

Amid this uncertainty, I returned to Washington in September to attend a conference of American ambassadors in Africa and to prepare for the possibility of a visit by Mengistu to New York and a meeting with the President or the Vice-President. On the morning of 26 September I telephoned Ethiopian Chargé Tesfaye Demeke to ask if there were any late word from Addis Ababa on his head of state's visit. In hushed but agitated tones, Tesfaye replied that he had been called during the night from Addis Ababa and told that all plans for the trip to New York, Paris and Brussels had been canceled. Tesfaye invited me to his office and there, in whispers barely audible, confided that 'hostile people' had misled Mengistu. They had told him he would face a danger of assassination if he went to New York. The Ethiopian commercial counselor in New York, Tesfaye said, had sent many reports to this effect; he and others had also warned of plans by Ethiopian exile groups to demonstrate in New York and Washington if Mengistu came. Tesfaye himself had strongly advocated the visit and had hoped for a meeting between his head of state and President Reagan. The telephone call that he had received during the night troubled him deeply. He counted it a personal setback and feared that he might now be at risk not only of losing his job but his freedom. He reasoned that the 'pro-Soviet faction', having won out on the matter of a visit to New York, would not stop there; they would want to clear the decks of all those who had been in favor of the trip. Tesfaye's apprehensions may have been exaggerated but they were unquestionably genuine. He had worked long and hard for an improvement in relations between Ethiopia and the United States. His fears for his safety and that of his family, his disappointment over the meager results of his work, and his belief that his government had become irrevocably committed to the Soviet camp led him to resign his post and ask for political asylum in the United States in May of the following year. At the news conference he gave when he announced his decision, he said: 'I have found myself increasingly isolated within a Government established with Soviet power and perpetuated by Soviet arms.' He added that Mengistu 'is bent on pursuing Soviet policy instead of normalizing relations between Ethiopia and the United States'.[8]

I returned immediately to Ethiopia, disappointed but not surprised. The prospect of the Ethiopian leader's going to New York and meeting with the American President had seemed too discordant with all else we knew of him to be real. What did come as a surprise, in particular to African diplomats in the Ethiopian capital, was that a few days later, early in October, Mengistu left for a two-week trip to Aden and Pyongyang. He was also to have gone to Moscow, but the Soviet capital was stricken from his itinerary just before his departure, apparently because Andropov was too ill to receive him. Mengistu's decision not to go to New York to make the traditional OAU Chairman speech was a great disappointment to OAU officials and other Africans. His departure for the East struck most with dismay. It prompted bitter comments in these circles: the Ethiopian leader had shown contempt for the OAU and for Africa; he had shown where his true allegiances lay. It did in fact seem a turning-point, though perhaps more in appearance than reality. The

Ethiopian leader's passing-up a ready-made opportunity to visit the West and then flying off Eastward was deeply discouraging to those in Washington and other Western capitals who wanted to give him the benefit of doubt. Those who had argued all along that Mengistu was beyond redemption found in it confirmation of their view.

Of course, no explanation was ever offered for Mengistu's decisions in these matters. It seems unlikely that he could genuinely have feared assassination in New York. Other foreign leaders much better known and equally if not more controversial had been to New York regularly for UN meetings to no ill effect. The likelihood of demonstrations by Ethiopian opposition groups, while displeasing, could hardly have dissuaded Mengistu from going to New York if he had genuinely wanted to; demonstrations are commonplace and have never been allowed to become a personal inconvenience to visiting heads of state. To understand Mengistu's decision, one probably has to look to his Soviet tie. The Soviet Embassy in Addis Ababa was plainly nervous about the prospect of his going to the United States and meeting with high US officials. They asked pointed, agitated questions of their American counterparts and seemed little reassured when told that nothing definite had been arranged. It seems safe to assume that they found ways to make known their anxiety to Mengistu. The crisis over the Soviet downing of Korean Airlines Flight 007, on 1 September, must have made things even more difficult for Mengistu, particularly after Moscow announced later that month that Gromyko would not go to New York for the General Assembly. Could the Ethiopian head of state be seen to be breaking ranks with the Soviets? And would not a trip to New York be interpreted at home, by a public eager to see its government move closer to the West and take some distance from the East, as a harbinger of change? All these considerations must have entered into Mengistu's decision.

Whatever disappointment Africans and Westerners felt, the blow fell hardest on Foreign Minister Goshu Wolde and his staff. On Goshu's order, the staff had made detailed arrangements for Mengistu's travel to and sojourn in New York, Brussels and Paris, and even contingency plans for a visit to Washington. They were dismayed when told that he would not make the trip. For Goshu, the visit of the American congressional delegation had been only a lead-in; getting Mengistu to go to the West was his real project. It is not known whether the Foreign Minister had his chief's approval to go ahead with travel arrangements on a contingency basis, or whether he took this step on his own in the expectation that Mengistu would decide in favor of the trip. But that he wanted Mengistu to go and was pushing him to do so is beyond doubt.

In a way, Goshu's predicament was typical. He was one of a sizable group in the Ethiopian bureaucracy, perhaps more courageous than others, who all along hoped that Mengistu could be brought around to seeing the advantages of good relations with the United States and the unwisdom of relying so heavily on the Soviets. The Ethiopian leader kept these people around him, though never in positions of real authority, in the apparent expectation that some advantage could be got from them, through increased Western aid or trade or by keeping alive Western hopes for a shift in Ethiopian policies. But in the end he always disappointed them.

After the congressional delegation's visit, Goshu was harshly criticized in the top circles of the regime; he even received a mild rebuke from Mengistu. After the projected trip to the West fell through, he got an even more stinging dressing-down. This naturally caused him to become very cautious. He continued to put on the charm for visiting Western delegations, to assure all comers that Ethiopia was non-aligned and wanted good relations with all. But he took no more initiatives and wanted no more risks. When the United States later again proposed talks, Goshu turned his considerable talents not toward finding ways to get his government to agree but to the designing of clever strategems to avoid Ethiopia's having to bear the onus for the absence of talks.

Notes

1. Since 1977 the Carter administration had, on human rights grounds, abstained in votes on development loans in the IBRD and ADB, except when the loans met the criteria set for 'basic human needs'.

2. A settlement of American citizen claims was finally reached in December 1985, after the Ethiopian government accepted in June of that year the US offer, originally put forward in March 1979, for government-to-government negotiations. The settlement called for the Ethiopian government to pay the American citizen claimants $7m. in compensation.

3. The Permanent Secretary was the second ranking official of a Ministry and was usually a civil servant. After the tenth anniversary of the revolution, all Ethiopian government Permanent Secretaries were given the grander title of Vice-Minister, a return to the practice of imperial days.

4. The Ethiopian government took the position that the Falashas were just another of the country's countless minority ethnic and religious groups, much smaller in fact than most, and that they could not be granted the right to emigrate or

recognized any other special status; the revolution had liberated all minorities and given them equality, so there was no cause for anyone to talk about their wanting to leave. Emigration was permitted only in rare cases and illegal emigration was made a capital offense, though in fact the death sentence was only rarely applied. The Ethiopian Jewish community numbered no more than twenty to thirty thousand at the beginning of the 1980s and lived within a radius of a 150km from Gondar city. Israel's rabbinate did not recognize them as Jews until 1973. In 1975, the Israeli government extended to them the provisions of the law of return, which grants citizenship immediately to Jews immigrating into Israel. Drawn by the prospect of return to Zion and impelled by the upheavals and miseries of revolution and civil war, Falashas began to leave Ethiopia illegally in the late 1970s. In small numbers at first, they walked out, across mountains and deserts, to Sudan, a perilous and exhausting journey. Many died on the way or were caught before they reached the Ethiopian border and were taken back to Gondar. There they were treated with varying degrees of severity: some reported being beaten and tortured, and imprisoned for months or years, while others suffered little or no abuse and were released after brief detention. In 1984 the trickle of Falasha emigration turned into a flood; entire Falasha villages packed up and trekked to Sudan, and as many as eight thousand may have left during the year. There is no reason to believe that the government in Addis Ababa consented to the departure of the Falashas or even knew about it until the international press began reporting it from Sudan, though it is possible that certain officials in Gondar were bribed to turn a blind eye to what was happening. For an interesting account of Falasha emigration from Ethiopia, their travail in Sudan and their dramatic transfer to Israel in March of 1985, see Tudor Parfitt, *Operation Moses* (Weidenfeld and Nicolson, London, 1985).

5. Press conference in Harare, Zimbabwe, 16 August 1983.

6. As a young officer in Haile Selassie's army, Mengistu was in the United States twice for training, once in the early 1960s and again at the end of that decade.

7. See Chapter 6.

8. *The New York Times*, 8 May 1984.

4 THE UNITED STATES, ETHIOPIA, SOMALIA AND SUDAN

Definition of the United States' interests in the Horn of Africa has long preoccupied, and puzzled, the various categories of people who, for one reason or another, have given themselves to study of the issue. The protuberance at the eastern corner of the African continent, at the junction of the Red Sea and the Indian Ocean, is obviously of some strategic importance, but how much? And what weight should be given to the political element, as contrasted with the purely military one?

The answer, of course, is that geopolitical or strategic value, like beauty, is largely in the eye of the beholder. It is also a function of the times. In the 1950s and through most of the 1960s, the communications facilities grouped within the compound of the Kagnew station were, formally at least, deemed to be the greatest single element of American interest in Ethiopia. They were invoked repeatedly, almost in incantation, to wring money from a reluctant Congress and co-operation from an often recalcitrant Pentagon for military and economic aid programs for Ethiopia. By the early 1970s, Kagnew's importance was fast fading and the United States' commitments around the world were coming under harsh scrutiny. But the time of questioning did not last long and events soon returned the countries of the Horn to a position of prominence. Once oil from the Arabian peninsula, Iran and Iraq became of prime importance for the West — in the 1950s and much of the 1960s it was only auxiliary — the Horn acquired importance simply by virtue of its proximity to these regions. Nearby countries came to be seen as threatening to or supportive of stability in states that, after the 1973 Arab–Israeli war, were regarded as critical for the West. The quickening of the play of competition between the Soviet Union and the West added another element of interest. Somalia did not become greatly important in Western geopolitical and strategic thinking until its government allied itself with Moscow and gave the Soviets the use of naval and air facilities at Berbera and Mogadishu. Ethiopia gained considerable geopolitical and strategic importance for the West simply by going over to the Soviet side. Suddenly it began to look very ominous indeed, placed as it was bordering on Sudan, Somalia, Kenya and Djibouti and next door to Yemen and

Saudi Arabia, all countries in whose friendship and stability the United States had a substantial interest. At the end of the 1970s the Iranian revolution and the Soviet invasion of Afghanistan added yet another dimension: as the United States began to strengthen its military presence in the area to counter possible further Soviet moves southward, the friendly states — Somalia, Sudan and Kenya — became even more important and the unfriendly one — Ethiopia — came to seem even more threatening. The question of how to deal with Ethiopia became inextricably intertwined with that of how best to protect American interests in bordering and neighboring states.

As we have seen, it was Ethiopia's shift to alliance with the Soviet Union that first made Somalia attractive and important to the United States. Soon after President Carter dispatched David Aaron to Ethiopia to probe the possibilities of restoring some measure of American influence there, he sent Assistant Secretary Richard Moose to Somalia to lay the basis for a durable relationship with that country's government. Moose arrived in Mogadishu in mid-March 1978. His mandate was to get from President Siad Barre formal assurance that Somalia would keep its troops out of Ethiopia, would refrain from the employment of force against any of its neighbors, and would use American arms solely for defensive purposes and only within generally recognized Somali territory. The administration wanted no repeat of the embarrassing embroglio of the summer of 1977. It wanted to establish an American position in Somalia and recognized that this would inevitably entail the United States becoming a supplier of arms to Somalia, but it was not going to supply Somalia so that Somalia could resume the pursuit of its irredentist ambitions. Moose did not find it easy to extract from the Somali President the assurances that he required. He had to extend his stay in Mogadishu, but finally agreement was reached. On 23 April the Somali government gave the United States the requested assurances. Consultations began between Washington and Mogadishu over the amount and types of military equipment to be delivered. Barely two months later the United States learned that Somali troops and arms were being put at the service of guerrillas inside Ethiopia; accordingly, plans for the delivery of American weapons were suspended. Throughout the rest of 1978 and 1979 the Somalis continued to plead for American arms, but their record of deception caused Washington to be very suspicious of them. The United States continued to insist that

Somalia pull its forces out of the Ogaden and agree not to use American arms against any of its neighbors.

By late 1979 the interests of the two sides in reaching agreement began to converge. The Somalis became persuaded that the Americans meant what they said, and Siad evidently concluded that American arms and American encouragement to others to supply arms were vital if he were to be able to rebuild his army and stay in power. The events in Iran and Afghanistan persuaded the United States that it needed the use of naval and air facilities at Berbera and Mogadishu. A delegation of State and Defense Department officials arrived in Mogadishu in the second half of December 1979 to begin negotiations for an 'access agreement'. Talks first went well, but then the Somalis upped their asking price beyond what Washington was prepared to pay. By the early summer of 1980 the chances of reaching agreement seemed to be fading. Some in Washington argued that the Somali facilities were not needed by the United States. Learning of this American disenchantment, the Somalis reversed themselves and accepted the US offer. An agreement was signed in August. It specified that the United States would provide $65m. in credits and grants during US fiscal years 1980, 1981 and 1982 for the purchase of arms for Somalia and would undertake repairs and expansion of port facilities at Berbera; in return the United States would have use of naval and air facilities at Berbera and Mogadishu. Hardly was the ink of the signatures dry when the United States learned that Somali military units were again operating in the Ogaden. Notified of this, Congress balked at voting funds for the weapons to be provided to Somalia. Finally, at the end of 1980, in the last weeks of the Carter administration, Congress was informed that all Somali forces had been withdrawn from Ethiopian territory and was asked to go ahead with approval of money as provided in the access agreement.

The Reagan administration was eager to carry through the arms supply agreement with Somalia. The only question for it was whether to expand the amounts involved. After all, it was calculated, at the rate of $20m. per year, it would take something like a century for the United States to match in Somalia what the Soviets had done in the way of supplying arms to Ethiopia. On mature reflection, however, it was recognized that matching the Soviet arms build-up in Ethiopia was neither a desirable nor a feasible goal. Congress would not appropriate the money for very large programs of military assistance to Somalia, and the prospect of such programs caused alarm in Kenya, a chunk of whose territory was also coveted by Somalia. The Reagan administration, like its predecessor, did not want to arm Somalia to the point where it could plan another invasion of Ethiopia, though it was inclined not to consider that prospect a very likely one over any near term. For all these reasons, the new administration decided to stick initially with a program of $20m. yearly in military assistance for Somalia.

The issue of how to respond to Somalia's requests for arms was made more complicated, however, by Ethiopia's actions toward Somalia. In 1979 and 1980 the Ethiopian government began to encourage opponents of Siad Barre's regime to organize into military units. In 1981 Libya began to take an interest in this activity and to provide money and arms in support of it. By that time two organizations had emerged: the Somali Salvation Democratic Front and the Somali National Movement. The SSDF was the larger of the two but practically a creation of the Ethiopian and Libyan governments, by whom it was generously supplied with arms and money. The SNM took money and arms from Libya and Ethiopia but was more nationalistic and pro-Western and more jealous of its independence. Both, however, were based on Ethiopian territory and dependent on the goodwill of the Ethiopian authorities for their existence and their operations. They were cards for the Ethiopians to play against their enemy Siad Barre and a counterpart to the WSLF, the guerrilla organization sponsored by the Somali government.

Tension between Ethiopia and Somalia flared in the summer of 1982. In mid-June a Somali army force infiltrated into the Ogaden and, operating together with the local ethnic Somali guerrillas, attacked an Ethiopian army unit stationed outside Shilabo, a town some 100km inside Ethiopia. The Ethiopians lost some one hundred killed and wounded. Early in July, Ethiopian army forces, together with SSDF guerrilla units, attacked at several points along Ethiopia's southern border with Somalia. They captured the village of Balenbale and crushed the Somali army unit in garrison there; its survivors fled in panic. Throughout July and into the first half of August, the Ethiopians and their Somali dissident allies launched repeated forays across the Somali border. None seems to have gone very deep, but in August the Ethiopians and the SSDF took the village of Goldogob, north of Galcaio, and held it. These Ethiopian actions brought forth frantic appeals from the Somali government

for American help. Whether their alarm was genuine or calculated,
the Somalis greatly exaggerated the extent of the Ethiopian penet-
rations. They first claimed that the Ethiopian army was launched on
a march to Mogadishu, and they reported battles raging 40km inside
their territory. Washington was aware that the Somális were dealing
freely with the facts. Yet it was quite clear that the Ethiopian
actions, albeit limited, posed a political threat, if nothing else, to the
Somali government and to its policy of friendship with the United
States. If the United States did not help Siad in his hour of need, he
might be overthrown; or if not, he would almost certainly have
second thoughts about his association with the Americans and
about letting them use the installations at Berbera and Mogadishu.

More than this, however, the Ethiopian attack on Somalia was
just the kind of test that the Reagan administration welcomed. It
came to office persuaded that its predecessor had failed to stand up
for its friends and make itself respected by its adversaries. Here was
an opportunity to show Somalia that the United States could be
counted on and to demonstrate to Ethiopia that the United States'
restraint in arming Somalia was not to be construed as a sign of
weakness or as license for Ethiopia to work its will with its southern
neighbor. As a first step, it was decided on 15 July to airlift to
Somalia $5.5m. in recoilless rifles, small arms and ammunition that
was being prepared for sea shipment at the time the Ethiopian
attacks took place. Eight large US military air transport planes
would bring this consignment into Mogadishu airport in midday
hours for maximum publicity. I was instructed to inform the
Ethiopian government that its attacks on Somalia had made it
necessary for the United States to send weapons to Somalia to help
it defend itself, and to urge the Ethiopians to withdraw from Somali
territory. After I had done so, Foreign Minister Feleke called me in,
on 23 July, to lament the American 'ultimatum', to deny that
Ethiopia had attacked Somalia in any way and to complain of
aggression by Somalia against Ethiopia. Feleke warned of dire
repercussions for US–Ethiopian relations if Washington were to
send arms to Somalia. The next day, the Somali government, with
Washington's concurrence, announced the impending American air
lift. Two days later I was again convoked to the Foreign Ministry,
this time by Permanent Secretary Tibebu, to be given a harsh note
describing the American air lift to Somalia as 'massive' and stating
that, in the light of this 'hostile' American action, Ethiopia might
have to 're-examine its options'. This, of course, was a thinly veiled

threat to break diplomatic relations. It was the first of at least half a dozen such threats that the Ethiopian regime was to make during my three years in Addis Ababa. So indiscriminately did the Ethiopians use this weapon that its edge eventually became seriously blunted. In any event, it did not deter Washington soon thereafter from allocating an extra $10m. for purchase for Somalia of 24 late model armored personnel carriers mounted with TOW anti-tank missiles. The US also authorized, and encouraged, Italy to transfer to Somalia a large number of Korean war vintage American tanks that the Italians had just taken out of active service. Egypt sent Somalia some of its old Soviet-made tanks and artillery, and Saudi Arabia also transferred small amounts of equipment.

These deliveries were far too small to change the military balance, which remained heavily in Ethiopia's favor. Thanks to the in fact massive provision of arms by the Soviet Union, Ethiopia disposed altogether of over one thousand tanks, an equally large number of artillery pieces, and several dozen modern fighter-bomber aircraft. The Somali army was no match for it, but at least it would be able to make future Ethiopian attacks more costly. We hoped the Ethiopians would draw a lesson from what the United States and others had done to aid Somalia. To make sure that the point got across, I went to the Foreign Ministry to proffer a bit of friendly personal advice, after getting the Department's agreement to my doing so. Making clear that I was not threatening or giving an ultimatum, I said I was deeply concerned that, if fighting continued, the United States would move to arm Somalia beyond anything contemplated up to that time. Surely the Ethiopian government would not want that to happen.

All these several messages seem to have had their effect. Ethiopian attacks ceased in the second half of August and no more territory was taken. But Ethiopian forces did not evacuate Balenbale and Goldogob, and these two villages became another contentious issue between Ethiopia and Somalia. The Ethiopian regime at first did not want to acknowledge that anything had happened along its border with Somalia in July and August. Soon thereafter, however, it characterized the action as one of liberation of Somali territory by the SSDF. Later it claimed that Balenbale and Goldogob were within Ethiopian territory and therefore rightfully belonged to Ethiopia. Still later Foreign Minister Goshu declared that Ethiopia would be ready to return the two villages to Somalia if Somalia would agree to hold negotiations for demarcation of the border, and if these negotiations should show that they belonged to Somalia. It was an offer that the Ethiopian Foreign Minister knew he did not have to worry about the Somalis accepting, for acceptance would have meant abandonment of Somalia's claim to the Ogaden.

In the aftermath of the fighting, various efforts were made, or considered, to mediate between Ethiopia and Somalia. None got much beyond the stage of planning or early exploration. The United States wanted to make Balenbale and Goldogob a subject for discussion in the talks that it proposed to hold with the Ethiopian government but that never materialized. Italy had a project that called for Somalia to give assurances that it would make no territorial claims against Ethiopia, in counterpart for which the Ethiopians would withdraw from Balenbale and Goldogob. Before taking it to Addis Ababa they raised it with the Somalis and were turned down, so they shelved it. Early in 1983 the Egyptians presented a much more ambitious proposal. It was divided into three stages and spread over as many years: a first year in which armed actions and hostile propaganda would by mutual agreement be phased out; a second year in which there would be secret meetings between Ethiopia and Somalia under Egyptian auspices; and a third year in which Mengistu and Siad Barre would be brought together at the invitation of President Mubarak in a kind of Egyptian Camp David. This scheme was the product of the fertile mind of Egypt's clever and energetic ambassador in Addis Ababa, Samir Ahmad. It had the merit of recognizing that the substantial differences between Ethiopia and Somalia could not quickly be resolved and that the border issue needed to be deferred until a better understanding could be established between the two sides. But it was unrealistic in assuming that Ethiopia and Somalia actually wanted an accommodation or could be guided toward one by Egypt. The Egyptians had good relations with Somalia and some influence there, but not nearly enough to persuade the Somalis to abandon their territorial claims. The Ethiopian regime was deeply suspicious of Egypt, in the first place because of that country's close ties with the United States, and also because the Egyptians were believed to side with Somalia and were suspected — probably incorrectly — of helping the Eritrean insurgents. Even if they had been interested in Ambassador Ahmad's ideas, the Ethiopian regime was not about to award to Egypt the prize of settling Ethiopia's differences with Somalia. The project foundered on these difficulties.

The immediate issue between Somalia and Ethiopia is territorial. The borders between the two states were set in the colonial era, as were almost all African borders. An agreement between Ethiopia and Great Britain fixed the border of then British Somaliland in 1897; and in 1908 Italy and Ethiopia reached a similar agreement on the border of the then Italian colony of Somalia. The border with British Somaliland was actually demarcated on the ground, but no demarcation ever took place on the Italian side; the border remained simply a line drawn on a map. When Somalia became independent in 1960 it impetuously declared that it would not recognize any of its 'colonial' borders. Irredentist emotion ran too deep among the Somali population to permit any government to go back on that position, even though the Somalis found no support for it in Africa or elsewhere. This gave the Ethiopians a considerable moral advantage in the propaganda battle between the two sides. They proclaimed their acceptance of both agreements and took the position that all that needed be done was to demarcate the southern border, knowing full well that neither Siad Barre nor any likely successor would agree to accept that border.

Beneath the territorial dispute lie hatreds generated by centuries of warfare between the highland Christian kingdom of Ethiopia and its southern Muslim neighbors. A settlement between Ethiopia and Somalia based on some limited form of autonomy for the Ogaden under Ethiopian sovereignty is not hard to imagine, but it would require concessions that neither side currently is prepared to make. The quick American response to the Ethiopian attacks in the summer of 1982 laid down a marker and established a kind of crude balance: so long as the Somalis knew they had no reasonable hope of winning a military victory over Ethiopia and the Ethiopians knew that aggression against Somalia would bring a stepped-up flow of Western arms to that country, both sides would be deterred. Still the conflict is likely to fester until such time as deeply rooted attitudes begin to change on both sides.

By late 1982 it was Sudan's turn to become the object of Ethiopian pressures. Relations between Ethiopia and its northern and western neighbor have relatively little of the heavy emotional charge that dominates Ethiopian–Somali relations, despite the rich history of conflict between the Christian kingdom of Ethiopia and its northern Arab neighbors. Neither side any longer entertains territorial ambitions. Unlike the situation in the south, the Ethiopian–Sudanese border is undisputed. But the two countries share a lively distrust of one another and find themselves intertwined in a kind of perpetual mutual stranglehold. Each has insurgencies that can be fed effectively only from the territory of the other: for Ethiopia it is Eritrea and Tigray and for Sudan the Christian south. Ethiopia lays no claim to southern Sudan — the highland orthodox Christians of Ethiopia have no particular affinity for, or ethnic ties with, the lowland Catholics, Protestants and animists of southern Sudan — and Sudan does not covet Eritrea, though it has difficulty in resisting pressures from other Arab states to help the Eritrean rebellion. But Sudan and Ethiopia have not been able to regulate their dealings with one another on these issues in any consistent way. The two governments have oscillated between policies of accommodation and mutual restraint, in which each foreswore aid to the other's rebels, and of hostility and thinly disguised assistance to one another's rebels. In the late 1960s, with a government friendly to Moscow, Sudan afforded the radical Arab states and the Soviet bloc an unrestricted channel for aid to the Eritrean rebels, and it allowed the Eritreans the free use of the sanctuary of its territory. After Nimeiri's close brush with assassination at the hands of the Sudanese communists, he began to rethink his ties with the East and to see the potential benefits of an understanding with Ethiopia. In 1972 he and Haile Selassie met and composed differences: the Emperor lent a hand to understanding between southern Christian Sudanese and the Arab government in Khartoum, while the Sudanese President agreed to cut back on assistance to the Eritreans. With Haile Selassie's fall from power in 1974, the Derg's decision to try for a military solution in Eritrea and its move toward alliance with the Soviet Union, the agreement fell apart. The Sudanese were troubled by the killing of General Aman, whom Nimeiri considered a personal friend. They were even more disturbed by the new government's policy of repression in Eritrea and by its opening to the Soviet Union. Clearly, Sudan and Ethiopia were moving in opposite directions. Early in 1975, Sudan lifted restraints on aid to the Eritreans, a move that contributed substantially to Eritrean successes in the mid-1970s. The Derg, caught in the throes of the revolution it had launched and pressed from all sides by ethnic and regional rebellion, was not able to bring pressure to bear on Khartoum through southern Sudan. But by 1979, after the Ethiopians had pushed out the Somalis and pushed back the rebels in Eritrea, and with rebellion again stirring in southern Sudan, Mengistu and Nimeiri were ready to talk. They reached a new set of agreements.

The alliance that Mengistu concluded with Libya and South Yemen in August 1981 inevitably undermined relations between Addis Ababa and Khartoum. For some time one of Qadhafi's main aims had been to overthrow Nimeiri. Now Ethiopia seemed to be joining the Libyan effort; with Libyan money, supplies and instructors, camps for the training of Sudanese dissidents, at this stage for the most part northerners, sprang up inside Ethiopia. Mengistu's immediate motive for linking up formally with Qadhafi appears to have been monetary; the Ethiopian treasury was strapped for funds and the Libyan leader promised large amounts.[1] But mainly Mengistu seems to have wanted to put pressure on Nimeiri, either to bring about his overthrow or to make him more co-operative with Ethiopia on Eritrea. After the 1979 agreements, Mengistu had pressed his search for a military solution in Eritrea ever more vigorously. But his yearly offensives made little progress. The 1982 offensive ended embarrassingly, with Ethiopian forces not only failing to take their objective, the town of Nacfa, but pushed back behind their earlier lines. The Ethiopian leader began to chafe and to blame the Sudanese for his failures.

At Ethiopia's request, Sudanese Vice-President Omar Tayeb came to Addis Ababa in late July of 1982. Mengistu wanted to enlist the Sudanese in much more active arrangements for the suppression of the Eritrean rebellion. He pressed Tayeb for agreement that Sudan would hold joint military operations with Ethiopia aimed at sealing the Ethiopian–Sudanese border against penetration by Eritrean and Tigrean rebels. This went much further than anything the Sudanese had contemplated or would be able to undertake without risking serious complications in their relations with Arab states that continued to support the Eritreans. Tayeb refused Mengistu's demand, upon which the Ethiopian leader is said to have threatened Sudan with a choice between 'peace or war' in its relations with Ethiopia. After the unsuccessful meeting between Mengistu and Tayeb, the Ethiopians stepped up their support for terrorism and sabotage against Sudan. Relations between the two countries cooled markedly, and when the Sudanese ambassador left Addis Ababa in June 1983 at the end of a long tour of duty he was not replaced.

Libyan and Ethiopian activities did not at first meet with much success, until Nimeiri took steps that rendered his government vulnerable. At some particular moment in 1983 the aging Sudanese leader was struck by a vision of his country as a pure Islamic state. Perhaps he thought that by embracing Islamic fundamentalism he could overpower the opposition that had long been building to his rule. In August 1983 the laws of Islam were decreed to be those of modern day Sudan and the Christian south, since the 1979 agreements united in a single governate, was divided into three districts. These measures threw the south into turmoil and alienated moderate Arab opinion in the north. It was one thing to apply Islamic law to Muslims, to hold public floggings, sever limbs and prohibit the sale or use of alcholic beverages; it was quite another to inflict these practices upon Christians already chafing under the domination of the Muslim north. Armed dissidence immediately reawakened in the south. By the end of 1983 Sudanese troops were being regularly ambushed by guerrillas and their reprisals were sending thousands of southerners across the border into Ethiopia as refugees. Ethiopia began to step up assistance to southern Sudanese dissidents. From among the factions and leaders that competed for their support, the Ethiopians chose former Sudanese army colonel John Garang to be their preferred instrument. Garang's professions of socialism, among other things, presumably marked him for Ethiopian favor. The Ethiopians began to supply Garang money and arms and to open training camps in Gambela, near the Sudanese border, for his recruits.

The deteriorating situation in Sudan caused alarm in Washington. It had long been thought that Nimeiri's days in power were approaching their end; he had ruled since 1969, was in poor health, and the accumulated burden of his mistakes had begun to weigh heavily upon his regime. But if Sudan were to come under an unfriendly government, particularly one of the stripe of Ethiopia's, the consequences for the United States' position in the Near East and the Horn of Africa would be serious, perhaps catastrophic. A possibly uncontrollable threat to Egypt and Saudi Arabia, the United States' two very important friends in the area, could develop. The new American ambassador to Khartoum was dispatched repeatedly to see Nimeiri and try to persuade him to step back from the dangerous course on which he had embarked. The Egyptians pleaded with the Sudanese leader in the same sense, and even the Saudis discreetly made known their concerns. All to no immediate avail.

While it sought ways to bolster Nimeiri domestically, and in particular economically, Washington began to look with renewed hope toward an accommodation with Ethiopia that might ease the pressure on Khartoum. There was a flare-up of tension at the end of January 1984 when the Ethiopian government expelled four members of the staff of the American Embassy in Addis Ababa and the United States sent home two officers of the Ethiopian Embassy in Washington. But at the end of March the United States proposed to send Ambassador-at-Large Vernon Walters to Addis Ababa for talks with Mengistu and Goshu aimed at clarifying and improving relations. I was instructed to convey this proposal to the Foreign Minister. He received it very non-committally; he said only that he would 'consult' within the Ethiopian government and let us know. When by late April no reply had been received, I was instructed to see the Foreign Minister once more to reiterate our interest in having Walters come to Addis Ababa or meet with Goshu in Europe or anywhere else the Ethiopian government might find convenient. This interview also produced no answer; Goshu sent me away with the very doubtful assurance that 'the matter is under consideration'. This should have been enough to make clear that the Ethiopians were not interested, but Washington was in no mood to settle for hints, however heavy. In May I was instructed to press Goshu once more. Summoning all the eloquence that I could, I urged the Foreign Minister not to pass up the opportunity for high level meetings that could put relations on a more sound basis. He replied, with an air of resignation and deep regret, that he could see no possibility that the talks proposed by the United States could lead to any positive result. Goshu added that it would be 'an embarrassment' to the government of Ethiopia for Walters to come to Addis Ababa, and a meeting elsewhere would be out of the question for it would give the impression that Ethiopia 'had something to hide'. Goshu said Walters was, in any case, suspect in the eyes of the Ethiopian government because he had once been Deputy Director of the CIA; there were people in the Ethiopian government who objected to dealing with him for that reason. As might be imagined, Goshu's reply was not well received in Washington. A few weeks later, I was instructed to convey to him that the United States deeply regretted that Ethiopia should have no interest in talking with it or in improving relations. Goshu heatedly denied this and proposed talks between himself and me, with Washington providing me with instructions, but this was clearly only a maneuver to avoid being put in the disadvantageous position of seeming not to want to talk.

By the summer of 1984 the Ethiopian regime was, in any case, of no mind to seek an accommodation with the government of Sudan. It had committed itself to the support of John Garang and sensed that Nimeiri was on the defensive. Its aim was to use the rebellion in southern Sudan as leverage against the government in Khartoum to force it to close down operations of the Eritrean and Tigrean insurgents. Mengistu and Goshu were explicit about this in their conversations with visiting Western officials. Mengistu went even further on one occasion, declaring that, if Eritrea should break away from Ethiopia, Sudan could not expect to retain its territorial integrity. During the remainder of 1984 and in 1985 the Ethiopian government stepped up its support for Garang and his Sudanese People's Liberation Army. The numbers of southern Sudanese crossing into Ethiopia for refuge continued to grow; by the end of 1984 the Addis Ababa office of the United Nations High Commission for Refugees estimated that there were eighty thousand of them in camps in south-western Ethiopia. Fighting spread in southern Sudan, and SPLA camps in Gambela, near the Sudanese border, grew in size. The Ethiopian government speeded up work on the road connecting Gambela with Jimma and Addis Ababa and construction was begun on a paved airstrip near Gambela town capable of accommodating jet fighter and transport aircraft. These projects were given top priority. When completed at the end of 1985, the road and the airstrip would give Ethiopia much improved means for supporting the southern Sudanese insurgency.

As Mengistu stepped up his assistance to Garang, he also consolidated his control over the Sudanese dissident leader, who became very nearly a captive of his Ethiopian sponsor. Garang was given a house in Addis Ababa and evidently spent a good part of his time there. His movements were closely controlled. The Sudanese government that succeeded Nimeiri, after the latter's ouster in April 1985, tried repeatedly to make contact with Garang. Each time it was rebuffed. The United States was much interested in these efforts and supported them as best it could, seeing in them a hope for bringing peace to southern Sudan and stability to the government in Khartoum. But quite clearly, the Ethiopian government did not want to promote either of these aims. In May of 1985 an African intermediary proposed to the State Department to arrange to bring Garang from Addis Ababa to Kenya to meet with US officials. When the intermediary's representative arrived in Addis Ababa to collect Garang for the meeting, Ethiopian authorities placed both him and Garang under house arrest.

In its preoccupation to shield Somalia and Sudan, the United States was quick to condemn Ethiopian actions against its friends but inclined to pay less attention to the problems Somalia and Sudan caused for Ethiopia. The Ethiopians frequently complained of American bias against them. It evidently did not occur to them that they might have got more impartiality, and possibly some help, had they been ready to talk with the United States. The difficulties between Ethiopia on the one hand and Somalia and Sudan on the other topped the list of American concerns. The Ethiopian regime seemed to regard this US interest in the stability of Somalia and Sudan as a meddlesome intrusion into Ethiopia's sovereign affairs. Perhaps it did not understand that it was passing up an opportunity to make the United States a more impartial player in the affairs of the area. Or, as many on the American side came to believe, perhaps it did not care, because it did not want to see the United States play any role at all in the area.

Note

1. The Libyans actually paid the Ethiopians only a few hundred million dollars, a fact that contributed to Ethiopia's later disenchantment with the Tripartite Pact.

ETHIOPIA AND THE SOVIET UNION

'The most remarkable feature of relations between our two countries is perhaps the fact that they have never been troubled by anything in all their history.'
Anatoly A. Gromyko, speech before the eighth International Conference of Ethiopian Studies, November 1984, Addis Ababa.

When the Italians entered Addis Ababa in May 1936, one of the first things they did was haul down the equestrian statue of Emperor Menelik II. They did not wish to be reminded of the victor of Adowa and did not want their new Ethiopian subjects to be. One of the first things Haile Selassie did after re-entering his capital five years later was restore the bronze likeness of the great emperor and his steed to a pedestal at the center of the round point in front of Saint George's cathedral.[1] Later two statues of Haile Selassie were put up, only to be dragged down in 1974. From then until 10 September 1983 Menelik's statue was the only graven image of man to adorn the public roads and gardens of Ethiopia's capital, though from 1977 on a large billboard poster of Marx, Lenin and Engels dominated Revolution Square.

The statue unveiled in September 1983, on the eve of the ninth anniversary of the Ethiopian revolution, was a gigantic Vladimir Illich Lenin, standing 7 meters tall. With gaze fixed sternly ahead and right leg arched forward, the great revolutionary is obviously marching toward an irresistible goal, in this case the building of socialism in Ethiopia. It is the standard, mass-produced statue of Lenin found in the central square of every provincial Soviet city, and of course it was the gift of the Soviet Union. The symbolism of its emplacement in Addis Ababa, in the heart of the city's international district at the apex of a small park separating the UNECA from Haile Selassie's former palace, could not be heavier or more pointed. The statue was said to be the only one of the father of Soviet socialism on public display anywhere in Africa. The message it proclaimed was that, a little less than six years after their massive air and sea lift of arms and five after their treaty of friendship and cooperation, the Soviets were solidly entrenched in Ethiopia. The Ethiopian public was all too familiar with the message. It was nonetheless outraged by the statue. An armed guard was placed around the statue and photography of it was prohibited. Since it faced in the direction of Addis Ababa's airport, Ethiopians invented the whimsically wishful story that Lenin was headed home.[2]

Soviet scholars and propagandists go to considerable lengths to show that their country's interest in Ethiopia has deep roots. Anatoly Gromyko, Director of the Institute for African Studies of the USSR Academy of Sciences, dates Imperial Russia's first attempt at establishing political relations with Ethiopia as far back as the seventeenth century. Ethiopia unquestionably did exercise a fascination for Russian scholars and adventurers, as it did for those of other European nations. Ethiopians were aware of and curious about Russia. In mid-nineteenth century, Emperor Tewodoros sought to enlist the Czar in a bizarre scheme to liberate Jerusalem from the Turks. Facing Italian invasion in the mid-1890s, Emperor Menelik sought Russian arms, and a Russian officer adventurer was with his forces at Adowa and may have advised during the battle. After the Russian revolution, the Soviet government sent an official of the People's Commissariat for Foreign Affairs, one I.A. Zalkind, to Ethiopia in 1921 to try to re-establish the diplomatic relations that Imperial Russia and Ethiopia had entertained since 1897. Zalkind made his way on horseback to Addis Ababa. He was given the kind of reception that Ethiopians traditionally reserve for importunate foreigners. He was assured that his proposal was of great interest but was made to understand that there were nonetheless certain problems, in this case over the likely reaction of the *entente* powers which at the time were making every effort to isolate the new Soviet state. Zalkind returned to Moscow empty handed and disappointed. He published a bitter article warning that Ethiopia was at a crossroads and faced a choice between taking 'the road passing through the white-hot crucible of capitalism' or entering 'the era of productive forces under the aegis of the power of the working people'.[3] In its early phase, the Soviet state had high hopes of spreading the fires of revolution to Asia and Africa. As Africa's only independent state at the time, other than Liberia, Ethiopia was obviously of much interest. But the Soviets had no more immediate success there than elsewhere.

From 1936 until its pact with Nazi Germany in 1939, the Soviet Union sided with Ethiopia at the League of Nations, and in public pronouncements in other fora, against the Italian invasion and occupation. The Soviets and the current Ethiopian regime attempt to give the impression through their joint propaganda that the Soviet Union played some role in Ethiopia's liberation from the Italians. In fact, this was entirely the work of the British and of Ethiopians who rallied to Haile Selassie. The Soviets played no role whatsoever; they were still allied with Nazi Germany and Fascist Italy when Haile Selassie re-entered Addis Ababa in May 1941.[4] Having switched sides soon thereafter, the Soviets took advantage of their wartime alliance with the United Kingdom and the United States to open a legation in Addis Ababa in 1943 while Ethiopia was still under British occupation. They evidently sought to play on Ethiopian fears that the British would try to substitute their colonial domination for that of the Italians. The Soviets diligently set about building for the future. The Russian hospital was reopened in 1947, scholarly and cultural delegations were sent to Ethiopia, and efforts were made to establish ties between the Russian and the Ethiopian Orthodox Churches. In 1959 Haile Selassie accepted a Soviet invitation to Moscow and was promised $102m. in economic aid.[5] The main component of the Soviet grant was an out-of-date oil refinery disassembled and moved from Baku to Assab. The full amount of the grant had not yet been disbursed when the imperial regime was overthrown in 1974.

But it must have been clear to the Soviets that they had no chance of gaining a position of influence in Ethiopia so long as the imperial regime continued in power. After the Eritrean rebellion broke out in earnest in the mid-1960s, they began to support it with clandestine shipments of arms. Encouragement of the Eritrean insurgency could serve several purposes: it could weaken and hasten the day of demise of the monarchy; it could establish Soviet credentials with the Eritreans in case they should succeed and form an independent state; it could put pressure on the United States; and it could gain the Soviet Union popularity with radical Arab states that were supporting the separation of Eritrea from Ethiopia. When Siad Barre put an end to the parliamentary regime in Somalia and established his own dictatorship, the Soviets eagerly responded to his appeal for arms. This brought more pressure to bear on the Ethiopian government and caused friction between it and the United States when the Americans failed to increase their supply of arms to Ethiopia in answer to what the Soviets were doing in Somalia. But it was not until late 1974, after Haile Selassie had been overthrown, that the Soviets began to channel arms to Somalia in truly large quantities. Was this coincidental or deliberate? In retrospect one may be tempted to think that the Soviet move was a calculated one, intended to drive Ethiopia into their arms. But to suppose the Soviets capable of forecasting in 1974 everything that was to happen over the next three years is to credit them with far more clairvoyance than they or anyone else could possibly have had, or to make them out to be absolutely reckless gamblers. More Soviet arms for Somalia would probably only have caused Ethiopia to move closer to the United States had power not been seized there by a group that was intent on aligning itself with the Soviet Union. And as we have seen,[6] the United States did in fact substantially increase shipments of weaponry to Ethiopia in 1974 in an effort to shore up its position there and to offset Soviet deliveries to Somalia.

Ethiopia presented a very favorable terrain for the Soviets in the years just before the revolution. The stagnation of the imperial regime produced much disaffection and discontent. A substantial part of this rubbed off on the United States, which as Haile Selassie's main foreign friend could not escape identification with both the real and the imagined shortcomings of his regime. The American presence in Ethiopia was very large; in Addis Ababa alone it numbered about one thousand, and in Asmara three thousand until 1971. As always the Americans were highly visible and very active. Though Americans formed many ties of friendship with Ethiopians, the numbers in which they swarmed across Ethiopia inevitably produced a reaction among a proud and independent people who had always resisted foreign encroachment. Some Americans, in particular academics and many of the young men and women of the Peace Corps, encouraged discontent by criticizing the regime for its authoritarian practices and by extolling the virtues of democracy, free speech and a more equal distribution of wealth. Marxism did not have a large or serious following but it did enjoy a kind of vogue, particularly among students. The Soviet Embassy in Addis Ababa diligently cultivated relations with student activists and middle-grade military officers.

The revolution did not immediately present the Soviets with clear-cut choices. They must have realized very early on that in Mengistu and others they had good friends in the Derg, but there were also many who inclined toward the United States or toward a virulently nationalistic neutrality. On the civilian side, a bevy of leftist political groups and intellectuals returned from abroad competed for Soviet favor. The Soviets had links with the major ones, the EPRP and MEISON. They seem to have given their support both to these two semi-clandestine groups and to their friends in the Derg. This encouragement to opposing factions unquestionably contributed to the bloody confrontations first between the regime and the EPRP in late 1976 and in 1977, and then between the regime and MEISON beginning in September 1977.

In 1975 the Soviets sent a first group of officers from the Derg to the Soviet Union for ideological training. This group included Lt-Colonel Fikre-Selassie Wogderess, later to become Mengistu's number two, and Legesse Asfaw, now a member of the Politburo ranked seventh from the top and reputed to be very closely associated with the Soviets. Indoctrination and money were useful adjuncts for the Soviets, but only through the supply of arms could they establish their primacy in Ethiopia. As we have seen, they were long reluctant to take this step, because they feared its consequences for their position in Somalia. But once their decision was taken and they had been expelled by the Somalis, all restraints were off. Western estimates of Ethiopia's debt to the Soviet Union for the supply of arms since 1977 range between $2b. and $4b. Even the figure of $4b. probably does not cover everything supplied by the Soviet Union, for it appears that substantial amounts have been delivered gratis. One has only to look at the size of the Ethiopian military establishment to realize what an enormous amount of weaponry and other equipment the Soviets must have had to supply. Ethiopia's armed forces stood at 45,000 in 1974 at the time Haile Selassie was deposed. Ten years later, reliable Western estimates put the army at 306,000 with another 5,000 for the airforce and navy, and para–military forces of 169,000.[7] For a country that ranks among the world's poorest, or for almost any country other than a major power, this is a very large military machine. The Ethiopian army is reported to have over 1,000 tanks, almost all Soviet and most T–54 and T–55, and 160 combat aircraft, many of advanced model, all Soviet supplied except a few American F–5Es no longer in use owing to a US embargo on spare parts.[8] Almost all other equipment is supplied by the Soviet Union. The cost to the Soviets may be reduced by their disposing to Ethiopia of items no longer in use by Soviet and other Warsaw Pact forces — a practice of which the Ethiopians complain — but the burden of equipping such a large force must still be very great.

The Soviet Union's readiness to assume that burden reflects its deep concern not to lose its position in Ethiopia. The Soviets did not easily reach their decision to link up with Ethiopia. They were not clear about what course to take in 1975 and 1976, and even into 1977 some elements of the Soviet government must not have been enthusiastic about embracing Mengistu. But having been thrown out of Somalia in 1977, after having been shown the door in Egypt and Sudan only a few years before, the Soviets became quite determined that the same should not happen to them in Ethiopia. As elsewhere, however, they have judged the economic sector to be less important to the protection of their position than the military. The economic assistance given by the Soviet Union, though not so small as some Western writers make it out to be, is nowhere near the scale of its military assistance. A recent Soviet compilation lists the following major projects in which the Soviets are involved in Ethiopia: a project to irrigate 10,000 hectares along the Baro river in Gambela province, recently expanded to 40,000–50,000 hectares; construction of six refrigeration plants; building of silos for grain storage (50 commissioned, 18 completed by November 1984); six large repair shops for agricultural machinery; a tractor assembly plant, and a cement plant at Dire Dawa.[9] If this list sounds impressive, Soviet performance has been disappointing to the Ethiopians. The tractor assembly plant was declared operational in August 1984 along with the cement factory. Both were touted in the Ethiopian media, in the build-up to the celebration of the tenth anniversary of the revolution, as shining examples of the generous help given to Ethiopia by its socialist friends. Yet by wholly reliable report, both factories were incomplete at the time of their opening and unable to produce anything.

The Soviets seem to recognize, and the Ethiopians to accept, that they cannot play a role in Ethiopia's economic development similar to the one they play on the military side. There is agreement, tacit or explicit, that Ethiopia can look to the West for help on the development side without damage to its ties with the East. The Soviets do, however, supply all of Ethiopia's petroleum requirements, except for small amounts of specialized oils, at a discount of 10 per cent below the world market price. The Soviets have also refrained from pressing the Ethiopian government to begin payment on the arms debt, evidently in recognition that the amounts involved are far too large for Ethiopia to afford. In a visit to Moscow in May 1984, Ethiopian Finance Minister Tesfaye Dinka reached agreement with his Soviet counterparts for the postponement of the first payment, scheduled for earlier that year, until 1986. Clearly, both the Soviets and the Ethiopians regard the arms debt as political. So long as political relations between the two sides remain good, further postponements seem assured.

The number of Soviet advisors and technicians in Ethiopia has been put at as many as five thousand but the correct figure at the end of 1985 was probably lower, around three thousand, divided more or less equally between military and civilians. General Vasily Petrov, commander of Soviet ground forces, has visited Ethiopia frequently since the end of 1977 when he took charge of the offensive to clear Somali forces from the Ogaden. Petrov's visits to Ethiopia have for the most part been unannounced, though he did make a well-publicized trip in August 1984. They have usually coincided with preparations for Ethiopian army offensives in Eritrea and Tigray. Soviet civilian advisors and technicians hold posts in several government departments, in particular in the planning commission. Soviet instructors teach in all the institutions of higher learning and at the Yekatit political school, the party's institute for the training of cadres in Marxist–Leninist doctrine. The East Germans and the Cubans also have substantial numbers of technical and advisory personnel; the former specialize in electronic intelligence and the media and the latter in medicine, where their doctors have earned themselves a fearsome reputation. In 1984 and 1985 the Bulgarians became active in economic and technical assistance and established a program of several hundred scholarships yearly for Ethiopian students. The East Germans also have a large program of university scholarships. The Soviets acknowledge giving out five hundred scholarships a year for undergraduate and graduate study, but the actual number is much greater if Ethiopians sent for shorter-term training are included. The Soviet Union, East Germany and Cuba also have substantial numbers of instructors in Ethiopian institutions of higher learning, where they play an influential political role. Other bloc states have embassies in Addis Ababa but their economic and technical assistance programs are very small.

The Cuban troop contingent was until 1984, and probably remains, the largest single element in the Soviet bloc presence in Ethiopia. While the Soviets have a large contingent of military advisors and technicians, and a few specialized teams, only the Cubans have had actual combat units in Ethiopia. In the spring of 1978, at the conclusion of the offensive against Somalia, Cuban forces probably numbered about sixteen thousand. Their number subsequently settled to between twelve and fifteen thousand, depending on rotation schedules, and stayed at that level until the end of 1983. But after the close of the campaign against the Somalis, the Cubans had little to do. They may have taken some part in the Ethiopian army's offensive in Eritrea late in 1978, and they have certainly provided some technical and advisory services in Eritrea and Tigray, but they did not otherwise participate in combat operations there.[10] After the 1978 fighting they trained and sat in their barracks, and had serious morale problems. Ethiopia was a long way from home and living conditions were usually difficult. In May 1980 two Cuban enlisted men climbed over the wall into the compound of the American Embassy in Addis Ababa and asked for asylum. The United States refused the Ethiopian government's demand that they be handed over. They were given residence on the compound. One was arrested by the Ethiopians after voluntarily leaving the compound in December of that year. The second stayed on the Embassy grounds until February 1982, when he fled after getting into a fight with one of the Embassy's marine guards. When the then US Chargé d'Affaires, Owen Roberts, told the Foreign Ministry of the Cubans' departure, Permanent Secretary Tibebu Bekele, in apparent seriousness, accused the Embassy of having killed the two men and buried them on the compound.

The Cubans stayed in Ethiopia as a kind of praetorian guard for the regime and also probably as a show of defiance to Western pressures for their removal. But over time all concerned came to tire of these roles. The cost of maintaining this large expeditionary force weighed heavily on Ethiopia and Cuba, and at least indirectly on the Soviet Union as well. The Ethiopian army cast jealous glances at the heavy equipment with which the Cubans were outfitted and which sat unused in their casernes in Dire Dawa, Harar and Jigjiga when it could have been put into action in the north. And with the bulk of their forces in these south-eastern towns, a day's drive at the very least from the capital, the Cubans were poorly placed to rescue the regime from a surprise takeover. At some point in 1982, Mengistu, Castro and Brezhnev came to agreement on reducing the Cuban force in Ethiopia. No announcement was made but word leaked to the Western diplomatic corps in October 1983. A process of gradual reduction was begun at the end of that year and by the end of 1984 the Cubans were believed to have only two combat brigades, of about 1,500 men each, left in Ethiopia, one near Addis Ababa and the other in the Dire Dawa–Harar area. The operation seems to have been poorly co-ordinated, for some Cuban units with specialized equipment that Mengistu wanted kept in Ethiopia were transferred out.

The Soviets, Cubans and Ethiopians also had trouble keeping together on how to answer Western inquiries about what was happening. In Havana, a Cuban deputy foreign minister spoke publicly about withdrawal of Cuban troops from Ethiopia. The Ethiopian government, however, consistently denied that there had been or was to be any change in the numbers or status of Cuban troops. The Soviet and Cuban ambassadors in Addis Ababa made poker-faced denials when asked by their Western colleagues. But initially Soviet Embassy officers confirmed that the number of Cuban troops was to be reduced; evidently they did not know what their ambassador was saying on this subject. Why the denials? One can only suppose that all three parties wanted to avoid or minimize speculation that the withdrawals were the result of a cooling in relations between Ethiopia and Cuba, or that they meant that Ethiopia was loosening its ties with the Soviet Union. Fear of being seen to be bowing to Western pressure — though by 1983 no great pressure was being brought to bear — may also have been a consideration for the Ethiopian government. In one of those surrealistic scenes commonplace in my official dealings with the Ethiopian government, Vice-Minister of Foreign Affairs Tibebu referred, in December 1984, to the stories about reduction in the number of Cuban troops. Tibebu suggested that, 'if the stories are true', the United States should be pleased, because it had long called for the removal of Cuban forces from Ethiopia; the United States should accordingly give the Ethiopian government due credit. When I reminded Tibebu that his government had always denied the stories but said I was glad now to hear that he was confirming them, Tibebu disavowed any such intent and promptly dropped the subject.

What has the Soviet Union wanted, and what has it got, from its massive investment in Ethiopia? Some writers have argued that it has got very little.[11] The best that can be said of such evaluations is that they tend to obscure the extent to which the Ethiopian regime is aligned with and beholden to the Soviet Union. The case that the Soviet Union has got little or nothing from Ethiopia is based mainly on the assumption that its objective in Ethiopia was principally to get military bases for itself, and upon a deliberate effort to make little of what the Soviets did get in the way of military facilities.[12] The Soviet naval installation at Dahlak houses repair and resupply facilities for Soviet ships in the Red Sea and Indian Ocean; two battalions of Soviet marines, and more recently surface-to-air missiles, are believed to be emplaced there. The Soviets also have the use of the military side of the Asmara airport for the basing of their long range Indian Ocean reconnaissance aircraft; two of these airplanes were in fact destroyed in an Eritrean guerrilla raid on the airport in May 1984.

Even these relatively small favors done to the Soviets are a source of embarrassment to the Ethiopian regime, whose leader has repeatedly denounced his predecessor Haile Selassie and his neighbor Siad Barre for giving 'bases' to the United States. The Ethiopian regime has consistently denied that there exists a Soviet installation on Dahlak. These denials prompted American officials, in the fall of 1981, to show satellite photographs of the Dahlak installations to a very surprised and discomfited Ethiopian Foreign Minister during a meeting on the margins of the UN General Assembly. It has been reported, though not on particularly good authority, that the Soviets have sought facilities at the Ethiopian mainland port of Massawa.[13] It does seem entirely plausible that the Soviets would want to set up an operation at Massawa and that they may have asked the Ethiopian government for permission to do so. Had they considered it essential, they certainly had the means to force it upon the Ethiopian regime. Evidently, they have taken into account Mengistu's vulnerability on the issue of foreign bases or installations and decided not to press the issue.

Clearly, the Soviet Union has neither wanted nor felt it needed important military installations in Ethiopia. Its central and overriding aim has been political. The whole point of Marxist–Leninist doctrine is that the 'socialist' order should spread throughout the world. It was the prospect of establishing a Marxist–Leninist state in one of Africa's most populous, important and strategically located countries that brought the Soviet Union into Ethiopia, and it is that prospect that has kept it there and made it ready to add to its already considerable investment. Whether it sought a satellite or only a faithful friend — and it would be hard to reach any widely agreed definition of the former or of the line to be drawn between the two — it obviously feels quite satisfied with the return that it has got on that investment. For each of the two contending blocs, the name of the game is to win friends and emulation, at the other's expense. Those inclined to belittle what Mengistu's regime has given to the Soviet Union should imagine what joy there would be in Washington and other Western capitals if suddenly a large and important country under Soviet sway were to adopt a democratic system of government, align itself with the West and cast its vote with the West in the UN and elsewhere, all the while retaining membership in the non-aligned movement enabling it to plead Western causes there.

The Soviets very quickly came to know Mengistu as someone they could work with. There were others in the Derg who might have been more pliant — Legesse Asfaw easily and probably Fikre-Selassie Wogderess as well — but none that showed so much promise. As we have seen,[14] Soviet congratulations arrived so promptly after Mengistu's seizure of power that they aroused suspicion of complicity in it. Nonetheless, as in any relationship between patron and client, there have been difficult moments between them. At first, neither side seems fully to have trusted or to have understood the other. The Soviets had to learn the hard way that Mengistu Haile Mariam was not someone they could order around. Two Soviet ambassadors had to be sent home before this lesson was well understood. In May 1978, while Mengistu was in Havana thanking Fidel Castro for his help against Somalia, the Cuban Embassy in Addis Ababa smuggled Negede Gobeze, a Marxist–Leninist ideologue and former leader of MEISON, into the country. Evidently it was the intention of the Cubans and the Soviets that Negede should take on the job of setting up the party that had so long been talked about, that Mengistu agreed to in principle, but that was slow in coming. This was not at all the way Mengistu saw things. The Cuban ambassador and all his staff were expelled, along with Negede, and the Soviet ambassador departed soon thereafter. Early in 1982 a second Soviet ambassador left Addis Ababa prematurely after having admonished Mengistu that he should consult with his socialist friends before inviting Western European officials to Ethiopia. This incident followed Ethiopian invitations to the Italian and French Foreign Ministers.

It was over the party that the first and most serious clash between Mengistu and the Soviets took place. The idea of setting up a party had been in the air virtually since the beginning of the revolution, but beyond the notion that it should be the sole expression of the new order there was no agreement on how it should be formed or what guidelines it should follow. Teferi Bante and his group, and many others, wanted a party that would encompass all factions favorable to the revolution. The clash between Teferi and Mengistu that led to Teferi's death was ostensibly over this issue. What Mengistu essentially wanted was to build a party of his own, staffed by people he could trust not to conspire against him. He did not want to assemble a party from a hodgepodge of individuals who might have good credentials as revolutionaries and even as Marxist–Leninists but whose loyalty could be in doubt. The Soviets seem not fully to have understood, or not to have taken to heart, their friend's concern on this point. They considered the establishment of a vanguard Marxist–Leninist party to be a prime means for assuring that Ethiopia would not stray down wayward paths. They saw a lot of good party material around. If some were not exactly loyal followers of Mengistu's, perhaps they welcomed that as giving them more leverage. In his speech in Moscow in May 1977, Mengistu promised that a party would be set up very soon. When he stalled, the Soviets pressed him. The Soviet view was put very plainly in a paper presented by two Soviet academics, A. Kokiev and V. Vigand, at the fifth International Congress of Ethiopian Studies in December 1977:

> Our conception of the question is that a vanguard party is indis-
> pensible, a party which is equipped with the revolutionary theory
> of scientific socialism and guided by the Leninist idea of the
> union between the working class and peasantry and embraces
> within its ranks all progressive members of the working class, the
> peasantry and the intelligensia.[15]

Mengistu's tardiness in moving as the Soviets desired did not deter them from consolidating their ties with him through the signing of a treaty of friendship and co-operation in November 1978. A little over a year later, on 17 December 1979, Mengistu announced, in a radio and television address, plans for the creation of a commission to organize a national party. Twenty-four hours afterwards a proclamation was issued detailing the structure of the organization that came to be known as COPWE. This was to be Mengistu's party, built from the top down of his own materials and in good time, not of a scattering of whatever might be immediately at hand. Even then, many Westerners remained skeptical that the Ethiopian leader truly intended to establish a party. This skepticism deepened as years passed and COPWE languished, still only a Commission, and it nourished Western hopes — perhaps for a while not entirely without foundation — that the Ethiopian leader was not yet committed to Moscow. The three years that COPWE passed in relative somnulence — from December 1979 to January 1983 when Mengistu announced that the party would be formed no later than September 1984 — obviously were a sign that Mengistu was in no great hurry and they suggested that he might have doubts about the undertaking. If doubts there were, his resolving them in favor of moving ahead with the party was almost certainly not wholly the product of Soviet urgings. With the passage of years, as many of the members of the Derg were purged or moved to government jobs and set aside their military titles and connections, his government took on a more heavily civilian flavor. In any case it was never a classic military regime. The army was kept in its place. It was not called upon to produce senior officers to replace those in the Derg who fell by the wayside, or to fill ministerial jobs. It remained the mainstay of the regime but it understood that its mission was to make war on the insurgents, not to staff the government or make policy. Since his regime was not the ordinary kind of military junta at the beginning and became less so as time passed, the Ethiopian leader must have come to feel that he needed an organization to underpin his rule, to mobilize and control the public in ways that the army did not, and to assure political and ideological conformity in a society with a long tradition of anarchy and stubborn independence. As Mengistu said in his address to the founding congress of the Workers Party of Ethiopia in September 1984:

> It is only under the correct leadership of the Party that the relationships and interactions that exist among the various bodies of the political system, that is, the Party, the State and Mass Organizations, can be unified and made more productive.[16]

And a bit further on:

> As the Workers Party of Ethiopia is the core of the new political system, its main task is to make its relationships and working procedures with the state and with mass organizations harmonious and unified in a manner that will enable it to realize its objectives.[17]

There can be no doubt, however, that Mengistu turned to the Soviets for help in setting up the party and that they played a major role in its establishment. Several Soviet and Eastern European

Communist party delegations visited Ethiopia in the first half of 1984 and COPWE delegations flew off to Moscow and to Eastern European capitals. From early 1982 on, Soviet ambassadors to Ethiopia were no longer career diplomats but senior party officials, members or candidate members of the Communist Party of the Soviet Union. Konstantin Fomichenko, who was appointed early in 1982, had previously been Moscow's party boss in one of the Soviet Eastern republics, where his job was to keep the natives in line. A short, heavy-set and boisterous man in his early sixties, he carried forward this task quite ably in Ethiopia. He was frequently seen entering and leaving the former parliament building where COPWE had its headquarters. Fomichenko's successor, Gennadi Andreev, who arrived in Addis Ababa in May 1985, was of similar background, having come directly from being the Soviet party's chief representative in the Armenian SSR. The East German ambassador, Hans Jagenow, sent out to Addis Ababa in the summer of 1983, was also a senior party functionary. Mengistu's speech to the founding congress of the WPE was cast in Marxist–Leninist jargon and bore the mark of ample East bloc counsel. It proclaimed the WPE a 'Marxist–Leninist vanguard party' whose immediate objective was to be the establishment of the 'People's Republic of Ethiopia'. Of the latter, Mengistu had this to say:

> The social basis, the organizational structures and the working procedures of the People's Democratic Republic of Ethiopia are based on the fundamentals of Marxist–Leninist state formation and working procedures. Accordingly, democratic centralism, socialist legality, internationalism, and the conscious participation of the people are its defining characteristics.[18]

The Soviets had every reason to be pleased with what they heard in September 1984. They could also count themselves satisifed with their Ethiopian ally in other respects. Under Mengistu, Ethiopia's voting record in the UN came into perfect conformity with that of the Soviet Union. In the time when it was the Soviet fashion to do so, Mengistu duly excoriated China. With hardly a moment's hesitation, the Ethiopian media followed the Soviet line on Afghanistan and the Ethiopian Foreign Ministry issued a statement supporting Soviet intervention there. When Conor Cruise O'Brien interviewed Mengistu early in 1980, the Ethiopian leader told him that 'the Soviet Union entered Afghanistan in conformity with the treaty of friendship and co-operation that was signed between the two countries'.[19] Of his talk with Mengistu, Dr O'Brien remarked:

> As a whole, Colonel Mengistu's answers seem clearly designed towards one end: to make clear, directly to the west and indirectly to the Kremlin, that the stability of his alliance with the Soviet Union is very much more important to him than any idea of 'building bridges' to the west or improving his image there.

In 1983, as we have seen, Mengistu passed up the opportunity to go to New York for the UN General Assembly, at least in part out of solidarity with Gromyko's boycott of that particular session. In June 1984, in a decision heavy with symbolism, Ethiopia joined the Soviet boycott of the Los Angeles Olympics.[20] More generally, in every one of his speeches, regardless of forum or subject matter, Mengistu has denounced 'imperialism' and reaffirmed his government's dedication to 'socialism' and to solidarity with the Soviet bloc.

The one thing Mengistu could not give the Soviets in Ethiopia is popularity. Unlike Americans in the heyday of their influence in Ethiopia, the Soviets generally keep out of sight. Very little is seen of them on the streets of Addis Ababa. They keep themselves to themselves — in Addis Ababa on a residential compound built on land that before the revolution was a golf course — and do not mix with the Ethiopian population; and they do not spend much on the local economy. This has the advantage of making their numbers seem smaller than they actually are but it has the very distinct disadvantage of preventing them from getting to know and making friendships with Ethiopians, to whom they seem aloof and arrogant. Westerners have almost always been well liked because they mixed in Ethiopian society. At the eighth International Congress of Ethiopian Studies held at Addis Ababa University in November 1984, Western academics lunched, dined and traveled with their Ethiopian colleagues daily; Soviet academics were whisked away by a Soviet Embassy bus at noon and in the evening and had no contact with Ethiopians outside the formal sessions. Some Ethiopians who studied in the Soviet Union in the 1970s and early 1980s returned persuaded that racism is by no means exclusively a practice associated with capitalistic society and might in fact be more widespread in Soviet socialist society.[21] The heavy-handedness of many Soviet officials has also frequently alienated Ethiopians.

Among Ethiopian officials, stories of Soviet Embassy officials calling on them at home or arriving unannounced at their offices with a set of demands are common currency.

In fairness to the Soviets, it must be said that the Soviet Union's position as the foreign power most closely associated with the Ethiopian government virtually assures that they would be unpopular in any event. Ethiopians tend to blame their government's shortcomings, and the country's ills in general, on the Soviet Union. Before the drought and famine of 1984, food shortages were commonly laid at the Soviet doorstep; it was, for example, said — and believed by many Ethiopians — that teff, the grain from which traditional Ethiopian bread is made, was unavailable or very expensive because large amounts were being shipped to the Soviet Union where it was being used, according to one version, to feed pigs, or, according to another, to make vodka.[22] In this atmosphere, the usual fare of anti-Soviet jokes abounds. In a fairly typical one, an Ethiopian teacher instructing his elementary school class in Marxism–Leninism enthusiastically tells them that their mother is Russia and their father Lenin. The teacher then asks what the children want to be. They answer, in chorus, 'orphans'.

The Soviets are well aware of their unpopularity among the common run of people in Ethiopia. They are to some extent concerned about it, but they incline to write it off to unreconstructed reactionary attitudes that will disappear once the population achieves the proper level of education in socialist principles. They are popular with the top level of the government, which is what matters for the time being. And they know that their role as supplier of weapons for the Ethiopian army makes them practically indispensable to the regime. The Soviets have something very close to a monopoly here, for they know, and the Ethiopians know, that the West would not be ready to supply weapons in the massive quantities that the Ethiopian army has become accustomed to receiving from the Soviet Union. The arms supply relationship locks Ethiopia into virtual dependency on the Soviet Union, a dependency that could be broken only if the insurgencies in Eritrea and Tigray could be brought under control and the size of the army reduced. Knowing this, many Ethiopians suspect that the Soviets are secretly supporting the rebels with arms and money. The suspicion is probably without foundation, but it shows how widely distrusted the Soviets are.

One might conclude that Ethiopia has no choice but to remain the faithful friend of Moscow while it awaits the far-off and uncertain prospect of an end to its northern insurgencies. This seems overly simplistic. If the Ethiopian government is beholden to the Soviets for arms, the Soviets have too big a stake in Ethiopia to cut its government off short of an outright break. A strong Ethiopian leader who wanted to be his own man could play East and West off against one another and get a lot more from the West without losing what is essential in Soviet support; and win the admiration and applause of his people. It is a game that has never seemed to interest Mengistu. At least he has never tried it. To understand why, we need to take a closer look now at the extraordinary figure of the Ethiopian leader, the man who has shaped his country so decisively into the mold of his own personal vision.

Notes

1. The Italians had not bothered to destroy or carry off the Menelik statue; they simply discarded it on a trash heap in Addis Ababa. Haile Selassie had it dug out and set back in its place.
2. Ethiopians were not the only ones to be unhappy about the Lenin statue. There was also considerable, albeit muffled, discontent at the OAU. The plot of land on which the statue was put up was covered with trees planted by African governments to mark the founding of the OAU. The Ethiopian government cut down a large number of these trees without bothering to consult the OAU Secretariat or the African governments concerned.
3. Anatoly Gromyko, speech before the eighth International Conference of Ethiopian Studies, November 1984, Addis Ababa.
4. Soviet and Ethiopian propagandists deal with this painfully inconvenient fact by suppressing it in so far as they can.
5. Gromyko, in his speech before the eighth International Conference of Ethiopian Studies, mentions the aid but conveniently omits mention of the Emperor or the connection of the grant to his visit to Moscow.
6. In Chapter 1.
7. International Institute of Strategic Studies, *The Military Balance, 1984–85* (London, 1985).
8. Ibid.
9. Anatoly Gromyko, speech before the eighth International Conference of Ethiopian studies.
10. Until the mid-1970s, Cuba strongly and openly supported the Eritrean cause. Castro was apparently reluctant to be seen to be turning against his former friends. After the end of the campaign against Somalia, Cuban combat units stayed in southeastern Ethiopia, well away from the combat zone in the north.
11. In particular, see Marina Ottaway, *Soviet and American Influence in the Horn of Africa* (Praeger, New York, 1982), p. 151, for this statement: 'Even politically the Soviet Union had not derived any tangible benefits from its relation with Ethiopia.'
12. Again see Marina Ottaway, *Soviet and American Influence*, p. 149 'The initial Ethiopian concession to the Soviet Union was to allow it to anchor in the Dahlak Islands off the port of Massawa in Eritrea, the dry dock originally stationed in

Berbera. The Islands . . . were an inconvenient location, consisting for the most part of waterless sandbars.' Dahlak in fact has an excellent harbour. During their time in Eritrea, the Italians kept a naval base there.

13. Marina Ottaway footnotes this information to the publication *Emirates News*, hardly a source that would inspire confidence. Ibid., p. 149.

14. In Chapter 2.

15. Paper presented at Conference of Ethiopian Studies at Nice, December 1977 and published in Joseph Tubiana (ed.), *Modern Ethiopia from Menelik to the Present* (Rotterdam, Balkema, 1980).

16. *Central Report Delivered by Mengistu Haile Mariam* (Addis Ababa, September 1984), p. 28.

17. Ibid., p. 30.

18. Ibid., p. 30.

19. *Observer*, 9 March 1980.

20. The Soviet boycott got support only from Ethiopia, Angola and Burkina Faso, and the position of the last was ambiguous. The Los Angeles Olympics offered the government of Ethiopia an easy opportunity to show some small degree of independence from the USSR. Even the Department of State, not usually inclined to optimism about Ethiopia's choices on East–West issues, would not believe — until it happened — that the Ethiopian regime would join the Soviets in their boycott.

21. The Soviet Embassy in Addis Ababa treated Soviet women living in Ethiopia married to Ethiopians as outcasts. It wanted nothing to do with them, and would not accept their children at the Russian school. The American Embassy in Addis Ababa befriended several of these women, and their children attended the American school there.

22. There was never any evidence to corroborate this and other such stories.

6 MENGISTU HAILE MARIAM

'Insofar as Ethiopia has freed itself from the imperialist sphere of influence and opted for socialism, it is well on the road of achieving its goal of justice and progress. . .'

Mengistu Haile Mariam, address in Revolution Square,
12 September 1985.

Looking back over the course of the Ethiopian revolution, one is struck by how little of what happened was inevitable. Under slightly different circumstances, the mutinies that broke out in the army, and the discontent that swept — but was confined to — Addis Ababa early in 1974, might have caused no more than a large ripple. As one astute observer of the Ethiopian scene has put it, 'The imperial regime in Ethiopia fell victim to a combination of problems in 1974 none or all of which in themselves would have constituted an unmanageable challenge just a few years before'.[1] At several points, events might easily have been turned in a different direction: in June 1974, had Haile Selassie not forbidden the chief of his guard to attack the mutineers; in November, had General Aman played his cards differently in his confrontation with Mengistu and the hardline faction in the Derg; even in February 1977, had Teferi Bante and his group been more on guard — or taken the initiative — against Mengistu.

Soviet bloc and Western Marxist writers make the Ethiopian revolution out to be the product of mass uprisings by workers, peasants and intelligentsia that moved ineluctably along a well-charted path. Their version is a theoretical construct designed to meet the need for an ideologically acceptable explanation of how a particular result was achieved. It ignores a great many facts that it finds inconvenient, in particular this central one: that the Ethiopian revolution was not made by the masses but by a small group of middle-grade officers who set out to destroy the existing order and create a new one. Like so many others, the Ethiopian revolution, after being put through many violent contortions, fell into the hands of the most ruthless contender on the scene. This, of course, is what happened on 3 February 1977, when Mengistu Haile Mariam executed Teferi Bante and his followers and seized absolute power for himself.

To understand what happened after that time, we must dispense once and for all with the notion that Ethiopia is governed by a military junta or that Mengistu sits only as *primus inter pares*.[2] Even today Western writers on Ethiopia continue to use the term 'the Derg' to describe the body supposedly responsible for the governance of Ethiopia. This fosters a wholly inaccurate impression of collective decision-making when in fact the direction of affairs is concentrated in the hands of a single individual. Regimes of collective governance are a rarity everywhere, but there is no precedent for them in Ethiopian history and no place for them in Ethiopian culture.

Though Mengistu is a very different kind of person from Haile Selassie, and the institutions he has set up are a world removed from those of the old regime, the practices of the two are in many respects similar. Decision-making in the imperial regime ultimately reached a point of strangulation because all matters of any importance, and many of none, had to be referred to the Emperor, and as the Emperor aged he lost his ability to deal with such a heavy burden. Haile Selassie fought against this practice fostered by Ethiopian culture but to no avail.[3] Mengistu has deliberately sought to exercise tight and very comprehensive control over all the major branches of government and policy. He is relatively young, in good health and very intelligent and hard-working, but there are not enough hours in the day for him to deal with all the matters that, under this system, require his attention. As a result, the Ethiopian government frequently finds itself paralyzed for long periods of time while important matters wait to be decided. Ministers refuse to make decisions, for the penalty for the wrong move can be quite severe. They are sometimes reluctant even to ask Mengistu's guidance on a controversial matter; months may go by as they seek the 'right moment' to raise an issue with their Head of State or try to divine his wishes in some obscure way. There is a story, probably apocryphal, that once during a meeting with his cabinet Mengistu calmly drew his revolver and shot a minister whose attitude caused him irritation.

Like Haile Selassie, Mengistu inclines to keep the same people around him. The Emperor kept the same prime minister for 16 years. The top hierarchy of the PMAC has stayed the same since Mengistu reshuffled it in February 1977, with one exception: Atnafu Abate, a competitor from the first days of the revolution, was removed from the position of Vice-Chairman and executed in

November 1977 for challenging Mengistu's policies. Ministerial changes have been infrequent and when they have occurred, as in April 1983, have been mainly reshuffles. But they have been the work of Mengistu alone. Mengistu's deputy, Fikre-Selassie Wogderess had no prior knowledge of the April 1983 shift; he is said to have gone briefly into hiding upon learning about it, out of fear that it signalled a coup or a purge. Mengistu's ministers stand at attention in his presence and do not venture dissenting opinions. In his rare public appearances in Addis Ababa, the Ethiopian leader sits on a kind of throne, a red velvet upholstered gold-lacquered chair emplaced above and in front of the less ornate seats provided for the other senior figures of the regime. In these and in other ways, Mengistu Haile Mariam is a figure in the mainstream of Ethiopian tradition, one who can be looked upon as a monarch, an emperor, a successor to Haile Selassie and to Menelik.

Very little is known of Mengistu's early life. No official biography has been issued and the Ethiopian leader has yet to become the subject of an unofficial biographer. Even the circumstances of his birth are shrouded in ambiguity. On the face of it, his origins were at the bottom of the then heavily structured Ethiopian social scale. His father, a low-caste Amhara, was a night-watchman at the Addis Ababa residence of a nobleman, Dejazmatch Kebede Tessema. His mother, a Konso, worked as a servant in the Dejazmatch's household. But there is another version, with two subplots, that awards the Ethiopian leader noble lineage. The first, which gives the larger degree of nobility, has Mengistu descendant from a woman who was a mistress of a chamberlain of Emperor Menelik's court. Her illegitimate daughter in turn had an illegitimate daughter by Dejazmatch Kebede whom Kebede married off to his night-watchman, Mengistu's father Haile Mariam. The second version has the Dejazmatch as Mengistu's real father, obliging the night-watchman, Haile Mariam, in this version only the putative father, to take Mengistu's mother as his wife for the sake of legitimation. Some Ethiopians credit these stories; many consider them nothing more than an attempt by Mengistu, or his sycophants, to build a geneology. Mengistu is not known to have pronounced himself on the matter. But rumors of a blood relationship with Kebede were given a not very subtle endorsement when the Dejazmatch died in May 1985 and was accorded something very like a state funeral, with Mengistu in attendance.

For whatever reason, as a child Mengistu did catch the Dejazmatch's sympathetic attention, a fortunate development for Kebede who, unlike most of his class, not only lived through the revolution but did so without ever seeing the inside of a jail. Evidently with Kebede's help, Mengistu's real or putative father Haile Mariam was able to gain entry into the army as a non-commissioned officer. He was posted in Jimma, the administrative capital of Kefa province, and served there and in neighboring Sidamo. Mengistu received an elementary school education and then, possibly with assistance from Kebede or possibly only because Haile Mariam served in the army, gained entry into the Holeta military academy. Holeta, located just outside Addis Ababa, was the far less prestigious of two such institutions in Ethiopia. An academy at Harar, Haile Selassie's birthplace, trained the sons of the aristocracy and the wealthy bourgeoisie for service in Ethiopia's armed forces in a four-year course of study closely resembling that of West Point. Holeta was for promising and ambitious youngsters from the lower reaches of society and offered only a one-year course of instruction. As might be imagined, students at Harar looked down on those at Holeta, and those at Holeta hated their counterparts at Harar. All but a few of the members of the Derg were from Holeta. The revolution was Holeta's triumph over Harar. After the revolution, the Harar academy was closed.

Mengistu is believed to have been born in 1940 or 1941. If so, he would have been 20 or thereabout when General Mengistu Neway, head of the imperial guard, took advantage of Haile Selassie's absence from Addis Ababa in December 1960 to try to depose the Emperor. The defect of this particular Mengistu was that he was hesitant, and he wanted to reform the system rather than do away with it altogether. Mengistu Haile Mariam may have been a student at Holeta at the time. In any event, he and others of his generation seem to have given Mengistu Neway's attempted coup a lot of thought and to have spent many hours analyzing the reasons for its failure.

Upon graduation from Holeta Mengistu was commissioned a second lieutenant and went on to posting in the army. He quickly gained a reputation as a trouble-maker, a brawler who won his fights because he did not hesitate to hit first and very hard, and a womanizer. One of Mengistu's commanding officers is said to have put a notation in his personnel file warning that the young man was to be regarded as dangerous. Among other unverifiable stories is one that, after having made his way up the ladder to captain, he was demoted to first lieutenant for some breach of discipline. Yet Mengistu's superiors must have seen promise in him as well, for he was twice sent to the United States for training, in 1963 to a base in Alabama and again in the late 1960s to the Aberdeen Proving Grounds, outside Washington DC, for training in his speciality of ordinance. Sensitive over his very dark skin (official portraits of Mengistu issued in the early years after he seized power show him as light-skinned, as though to suggest that he came from an upper-caste background; in later years his complex over color eased and he was portrayed more accurately) and not a little arrogant, Mengistu is said to have suffered racial discrimination in Alabama, and during his time at Fort Meade to have got into a bar-room brawl over a racial slur. In any event, his two sojourns in the United States seem to have left him with an aversion to it as a society and a government. In the rare dealings that Mengistu had with members of the American military mission in Addis Ababa after he became prominent in the Derg, he left the pronounced impression that he was no friend of the United States. Some thought the coldness Mengistu and others in the Derg showed toward the United States might be nothing more than shyness or defensiveness. Perhaps, it was postulated, Mengistu and others in the Derg thought the United States would seek reprisal against them for having overthrown the regime of Haile Selassie, the United States' friend. Was this not the reason the Derg repeatedly alleged itself to be the object of CIA-hatched conspiracies or that Mengistu persisted in asking, even years later, whether the United States was hostile to Ethiopia because it disliked him? Such contorted feelings of guilt suppose a sensitivity that Mengistu did not show in any other of his dealings, and it is hard to take them seriously. Eventually, Mengistu became known to the American Embassy in Addis Ababa as chief among those in the Derg who wanted the Americans out of Ethiopia and the Soviets in.

The senior ranks of Haile Selassie's army were not closed to commoners, but Mengistu, with his low-class origin, his very dark skin, his inelegant Amharic, and his record of obstreperousness, was an unlikely candidate to move to the top. He seemed destined for a military career of obscurity and stagnation. For the eight years that preceded the revolution he was an ordinance officer for the third division stationed in Harar, a job that must have been infinitely boring for a young man of intelligence and ambition; it must, in fact, have seemed a total dead end. Mengistu much later made the following oblique observation on the state of mind of officers of low-class background in the imperial army:

> members of the downtrodden and oppressed classes managed to enter the ranks of officers, thereby strengthening the participation of the supporters of the broad masses. In particular, as the life and duty assignments of the majority of the men-in-uniform did not make them beneficiaries of the existing system, their attitude was not dissimilar to that of the broad masses.[4]

One writer has described Mengistu before the revolution as 'consumed with class hatred, visceral and elementary'.[5] The disturbances in the army and in the capital in the early months of 1974 opened up prospects that he certainly must have welcomed. There is no public record of his activities during that time, but he is said to have taken part very early on in organizing committees of junior officers and NCOs, urging them to take power into their own hands and calling for the arrest of senior figures in government and members of the aristocracy. But he did not attain prominence until the founding meeting of the Derg, at the end of June. There his decisiveness and determination are said to have deeply impressed the group and to have established him as a leading figure. By some accounts, he was elected Chairman of the Derg. If so, he soon pulled back and took the post of Vice-Chairman. The reason for this has never been explained. It is commonly assumed that Mengistu hesitated to push himself out front too fast. Most probably he sensed that the time was not yet ripe for him to claim first place and feared that the future was still too uncertain to make it safe for him to do so.

It would be fanciful to suggest that Mengistu came on the scene in mid-1974 with the outline of all he wanted to do over the next several years full blown in his head. A great deal of what later happened must have been the result of circumstance or spur-of-the-moment decision. Yet by all testimony the main reason he made such a forceful impression on his colleagues in the Derg was that he was one of the few who genuinely seemed to know what they wanted. Where others were uncertain or timorous over the role that the group should seek for itself, Mengistu had no hesitation in proclaiming that it should seize power. Beyond this, it seems clear that he knew from the outset that he wanted to destroy not only the monarchy but the entire structure of government and society. He was not out to make modest changes in course. In a limited way, the basic institutions of liberal democracy were already in place in Ethiopia in 1974; there was a constitution and a parliament. The restricted scope of the latter grew considerably through *de facto* usage during the spring and summer months. Yet the Derg seems not to have given a moment's thought to the possibility of strengthening or preserving the parliament, even as a façade. The parliament was dismissed and the constitution revoked by the decree that on 12 September dissolved the monarchy and established the PMAC. Mengistu wanted, and got, a clean sweep of all institutions.

There are many questions that can be asked about Mengistu at this early stage. Was he a Marxist–Leninist at that time or did he arrive at a coherent ideological formulation only later as a result of buffeting by competing forces? There seems to be no way to answer this question. It is as plausible to suppose that he was simply a young man with deep grievances impelled by an overriding ambition to seize power as it is to hold that he was a Communist from the beginning, one who had a reasonably well-defined program in mind even if he had not yet worked out the details. What is reasonably well established is that he did not come to prominence with a profound knowledge of Marxist–Leninist doctrine. He thought of himself as a revolutionary and knew that socialism and alliance with the Soviet Union were grounds on which revolutionaries position themselves. But he seems to have understood that he was not well versed in matters of doctrine. He did not hesitate to turn to advisors who could play the role of guide or tutor in ideological matters, notably Senay Likke and Haile Fida. He did prove a quick learner. Mengistu's name is usually identified with the December 1974 'ten-point program' that first proclaimed socialism to be Ethiopia's chosen path and that foreshadowed the expropriation decrees of early 1975. He himself delivered the speech, on 20 April 1976, announcing the program of National Democratic Revolution, although Haile Fida is said to have drafted it.

Two things stand out in Mengistu's actions after he became Vice-Chairman of the Derg: his consistent espousal of extreme positions and his extraordinary ruthlessness. Both came to the fore in his showdown with General Aman in November 1974. Aman advocated conciliation in Eritrea and opposed execution of the chief notables of the former regime. He had favored deposing Haile Selassie but did not want change to go a great deal further. What

Aman proposed, Mengistu opposed. He wanted a military solution in Eritrea and the notables put to death. These were real and well-defined issues, but one can only wonder how much of the struggle between Mengistu and Aman had to do with them and how much with competition for power. Would Mengistu have advocated compromise in Eritrea if Aman had opposed it? Whether Aman saw Mengistu as a competitor to be eliminated is not known. It has been remarked that one of the reasons for Mengistu's success in the bloody disputes that wracked the Derg was that his opponents always underestimated him.[6] Clearly, however, Mengistu saw Aman's ambitions as a threat to himself as much as to the programs that he advocated. He did not hesitate. He confronted the general with the demand for the dispatch of more troops to Eritrea and for executions. When Aman made the mistake of resigning, Mengistu cut him down. Both his readiness to act quickly, to seize the moment, and his lack of scruple at shedding blood became characteristic. While opponents hesitated, he struck: against Aman in November 1974, against Lieutenant-Colonel Negussie Haile in March 1975, against Sisay Habte in July 1976, against Teferi Bante in February 1977, and against Atnafu Abote in November 1977, to cite only the best-known instances. What is surprising is that his enemies did not learn to take their precautions. After Sisay Habte's execution, there was a reaction against Mengistu in the Derg and an effort was made to shunt him aside. That anyone would have thought this would make him less dangerous seems unimaginable, unless one supposes a very substantial degree of guile and cunning on Mengistu's part in misleading adversaries about his intentions. Perhaps luck played a more important role than can be appreciated. Repeatedly attempts were made to assassinate him. Their number altogether has been put at nine,[7] but it may be greater. He was wounded at least once, but his escapes must reflect good fortune as much as quickness of mind or any other quality.

More than anything else, Mengistu has defined himself through his consistencies: consistently extreme, consistently ruthless, consistently anti-American, and consistently pro-Soviet. Over the years, none has changed. His attachment to the Soviets evidently derives from his vision of himself as a revolutionary. But he also seems genuinely and deeply grateful to Moscow for having saved him in 1977 when the Somali invasion and the Eritrean insurgency brought him very close to the abyss; in his speeches he has made frequent appreciative references to Soviet help in that difficult moment. And when Mengistu thanks the Soviets for what they did for him in 1977, he no doubt also means that he counts on them to be his ultimate support in future times of need.

Mengistu's admiration for the Soviet system is another important element in the ties that bind him to the Soviet Union. The Soviet system offered a readymade formula for imposing tight controls over Ethiopian society, unlike the Western model. Under Mengistu's leadership, Ethiopia has transplanted from Eastern Europe every dreary institution that could be made to take root: neighborhood committees (Kebeles), mass organizations for youth and women, government trade unions and controlled media, a plenitude of informers, a secret police and since September 1984 a Marxist–Leninist party. Until the establishment of the party Mengistu went by the title of Chairman of the PMAC. Since that time, in emulation of Soviet leaders, he uses that of General Secretary.

This man who played such a critical role in directing the Ethiopian revolution in its formative phase and who eventually seized it for his own is short, of medium build and, in his mid-forties, beginning to thicken slightly at the middle. He admires Castro but is himself a plodding, uninspiring public speaker. He sports a swagger stick on the parade ground but is not one to bedeck himself with medals or don fancy uniforms; for military dress he sticks to the plain khaki uniform of his days in the army. Western visitors find his intelligence and his mastery of detail impressive and they are often charmed by his cordiality.

Haile Selassie was renowned for his statesmanship and his diplomatic successes, thanks to which both the OAU and the UNECA have their headquarters in Addis Ababa. Mengistu has made only one foray into this arena and it turned out badly. In August 1982 and again in December the OAU called summit meetings in Tripoli that failed to reach the necessary quorum for convening. At issue was the question of seating the Polisario, or Saharan Democratic Arab Republic, as a member state. On both occasions Morocco was able to muster a blocking third. In an effort to break the deadlock and save the African organization from paralysis, it was decided to try again at Addis Ababa. Mengistu seems to have sought this opportunity in the hope of proving himself the equal of his predecessor and certainly in the expectation of gaining for himself and his regime the stamp of legitimacy that the Chairmanship of the OAU confers upon the host head of state.

African leaders converged on Addis Ababa in June 1983. There were three days and nights of tense negotiations before the compromise formula that permitted convening was agreed upon: the Polisario would 'voluntarily' abstain from taking 'its' seat in the assembly. Others, in particular Tanzania's elder statesman Julius Nyerere, played a role, but the success was basically Mengistu's. It required that he bend his radical principles more than a little, and it cast a pall over his relations with Qadhafi. The Libyan strongman struck a more than usually colorful figure in Addis Ababa that month; he came surrounded by a dozen or so female bodyguards clad in white and sporting machine pistols. He left in a fit of jealousy, spurning the Ethiopian honor guard at the airport, after it became clear that Mengistu and not he would be elected Chairman of the organization.

Momentarily, Mengistu basked in the glow of diplomatic success. Western and African hopes for pragmatism in Ethiopia's foreign policy briefly revived. But the effort expended on the successful OAU summit seemed to exhaust the Ethiopian leader's slender fund of diplomacy. He was too dogmatic, too rigid and too committed to radical causes to take on the role of arbitor in the disputes that continued to encumber the OAU: the Western Sahara and Chad conflicts. Under a very thin pretext of impartiality, Mengistu consistently took the side of the Polisario against Morocco and, on Chad, in support of Libya's man Goukouni Oueddi against the recognized government of Habre. Mengistu's failure on Chad was spectacular. After long and exhaustive preparations, in January 1984 Mengistu called Habre and Goukouni to a meeting in Addis Ababa. Versions of what was agreed in advance were contradictory. The Ethiopians claimed that Habre agreed to come to Addis Ababa. Habre, however, clearly did not consider Mengistu an impartial arbitor. Fearing a trap, he insisted that he be received as Chief of State and that Goukouni be given no official reception. The assurances the Ethiopians gave Habre on this score apparently fell short of what he felt was required, for at the last moment he announced that he would send a subordinate. Rather than accept this and try to salvage something, Mengistu reacted vengefully. He sent his deputy Fikre-Selassie Wogderess to give Goukouni a full dress reception, with honor guard and flags flying, on his arrival at Addis Ababa airport. It was just short of what a recognized head of state might expect. Habre's representative, a minister in the government of Chad, was welcomed by the Ethiopian Foreign

Minister with no fanfare whatsoever, not even a news photo-grapher. This display of pique cost Mengistu whatever chance there still may have been to convene a meeting between the contending Chadians. To complicate matters still further, Goukouni's side demanded that its flag should mark its place at the negotiating table. Habre's representative stoutly refused to sit at any table bearing the Libyan protégé's banner. He demanded that the only flag at the table be that of his government. After a day or two of wrangling over this, he issued a bitter statement complaining of Ethiopian high-handedness and left Addis Ababa. The Ethiopian Foreign Ministry replied with a statement casting all blame on Habre's government. This shambles ended Mengistu's first and last serious effort to negotiate a solution to an African dispute, though he remained Chairman of the OAU until the following November.

Some Ethiopians and an even greater number of Westerners continue to hope that Mengistu's embrace of Communism domesti-cally and the Soviets internationally is nothing more than a sly act aimed at assuring a steady flow of arms from Moscow. Western visitors to Addis Ababa are invariably surprised to find themselves so warmly greeted there. Indeed, living in Ethiopia one quickly develops a very disconcerting sense that nothing is quite what it seems. The people are very friendly, the government is hostile; or is it hostile? It proclaims non-alignment, and the literal-minded visitor might come away from the Ethiopian Foreign Minister's briefings wondering what it is that impedes better relations between the West and Ethiopia. Certainly, it cannot be ruled out that Mengistu might one day begin to reassess both his domestic policies and his alliance with the Soviet Union. Other Third World leaders have done as much, and he may yet follow in their footsteps. He has in fact played quite effectively on the hopes of Western governments and the Ethiopian public that he might eventually take some distance from the Soviets. But on every occasion on which an opportunity to do this has arisen, Mengistu has instead reaffirmed and even moved to strengthen his ties with the Soviet Union. If he has actually secretly contemplated changing course, he has not dared do it. As we examine next the crisis brought on by the great Ethiopian drought and famine of 1984, we shall see to what extent this same pattern prevailed.

Notes

1. Paul Henze, 'Marxism–Leninism in Ethiopia: Political Impasse and Economic Degradation', paper prepared for symposium on African revolutions in the Marxist–Leninist mode, June 1985 p. 1.

2. The term is used by Rene Lefort, *Ethiopia, an Heretical Revolution?* (Zed Press London, 1983), p. 282, to describe Mengistu's position as Chairman of the PMAC.

3. Though how strenuously he opposed it has been questioned. Harold Marcus, *Ethiopia, Great Britain and the United States, 1941–74* (University of California Press, 1983) gives the impression that the Emperor's efforts to put more authority in the hands of his ministers were largely a sham.

4. *Central Report Delivered by Mengistu Haile Mariam* (Addis Ababa, September 1984), pp. 18–19.

5. Lefort, *Ethiopia, An Heretical Revolution?*, p. 227.

6. Ibid., p. 197.

7. Ibid., p. 192.

7 THE GREAT DROUGHT AND FAMINE OF 1984 AND 1985

After being in the spotlight of world affairs in the mid-1970s, Ethiopia faded into obscurity at the end of the decade and in the early 1980s. The revolution had expended its furies; calm followed the storm. Western journalists rarely visited, in part because the government rarely let them in. All this changed abruptly at the end of September 1984 after films of emaciated Ethiopia children, taken by British and Kenyan newsmen, were broadcast over BBC television.

Famine has been Ethiopia's companion throughout its history. In Ethiopia, as in most societies in which subsistence farming predominates and which lack a good road transport network, there is no way to cope when the rains fail or pests invade. People may starve in one province while in another, only a few tens of kilometres removed, there is plenty. When food runs out, the population has the choice of fleeing or dying on the spot. A distinguished British scholar of Ethiopia has found record of 23 major famines in just over two and a half centuries from 1540 to 1800.[1] The great famine of 1888–92 was caused not by drought but by an epidemic of rinderpest that killed about 90 per cent of Ethiopia's livestock; unable to farm, a third of the human population in the north-central regions of the country may have perished. In the mid-twentieth century, three famines struck Ethiopia's north-central highlands: in Tigray in 1958, in Wag-Lasta in 1966 and in Welo in 1972 and 1973.

In traditional Ethiopian culture, famine was not the outgrowth of natural calamity or the failure of a political and socio-economic system, but an act of god. It was punishment for sin. As such, no human being or institution was to be held responsible. Governments did not mobilize to fight it, for, even if they had viewed it otherwise, there would have been little that they could have done. This changed in the twentieth century as Ethiopia's road network expanded and the world's food stockpiles grew. But traditional attitudes lingered. The famines in Tigray and Wag-Lasta drew practically no response from Haile Selassie's government in Addis Ababa. Neither did the Welo famine, until it was projected on to Western television screens and from there captured world attention and brought universal condemnation on to the Emperor and his regime. Western television, more than anything else, mobilized world opinion and made it dangerous for governments to ignore famine.

Tardy and ineffectual response to the famine of 1972 and 1973 did not, contrary to widespread impression, bring down the imperial regime but it unquestionably contributed to its fall. The young Ethiopian radicals who seized on the Welo famine and used it to bludgeon the regime propounded the doctrine that famine was not really at all a consequence of natural phenomena, such as drought or locust invasion, but the manifestation of the stark failure of a political and socio–economic system: 'neither the work of God nor that of nature, but of man and his institutions.'[2] Recurrent famine, they argued, exposed 'the utter failure of the state and its machinery . . .'[3] From this reasoning they drew a rationale for the abolition of the old order and the creation of a radically different political system.

The Welo famine of the early 1970s subsided but never really disappeared. Drought continued to afflict northern Welo and Tigray, as well as much of Eritrea, through the late 1970s and into the early 1980s. Its effects were compounded by civil war as the population of these areas rose in revolt against the new government that proclaimed itself in Addis Ababa. The new government's policy of requiring peasants to sell their crops at artificially low prices discouraged peasant farmers from producing more than they minimally needed. In most parts of north-central Ethiopia, overpopulation, deforestation and excessive cultivation had in any event seriously depleted the soil. Although 1982 was, for Ethiopia as a whole, a relatively good crop year, hungry, emanciated peasants began to show up in Makelle, the province's administrative capital, in the late summer and early fall. Catholic Relief Service, one of the few private Western relief agencies operating in Ethiopia at the time, appealed to the United States government, in November 1982, for food and money to open a feeding center in Makelle; money for this was not approved until May 1983. The situation worsened somewhat in 1983. Destitute, starving peasants began to arrive in towns and relief camps along the main road running through Tigray and northern Welo, and in eastern Gondar, at Ibnet, in the summer and fall of 1983, but still only in relatively small numbers. The 1983 harvest was not so good as that of the preceding year, but it was only marginally under the average.

Though much has been written about the Ethiopian famine of

1984, it remains widely misunderstood. Some, in particular the Ethiopian government and its apologists, attribute it almost exclusively to drought, deforestation and soil depletion; others, almost entirely to bad agricultural policies. In fact, it was the product of an explosive mix of these elements. Poor rainfall in the north-central areas of Ethiopia, in Eritrea, Tigray, northern Welo and eastern Gondar, induced the beginnings of a crisis during 1982 and 1983. But in 1984 a searing drought hit these areas and most of the rest of highland Ethiopia. Highland Ethiopia has two rainy seasons: the summer or *mehr* rains that ordinarily begin about mid-June and last until early or mid-October; and the early year or *belg* rains that begin toward the end of January or in February and last until April or early May. The former produces the main grain crop, which is harvested at the year's end. The latter makes possible a harvest that may account for between 5 and 15 per cent of the year's crop, but just as important it produces fodder for animals and softens the soil for planting before the summer rains. There was no rain in highland Ethiopia, except for a few scattered showers of no utility to agriculture, between mid-October 1983 and mid-May 1984. The spring crop was wiped out and early summer planting was made unusually difficult. This seven-month drought devastated Tigray, northern Welo, eastern Gondar and widespread sectors of southern Ethiopia, all areas where agricultural production was already in trouble. It did considerable damage even in normally prosperous areas, in Shoa, particularly in eastern Shoa, in Gojjam and in Arusi. Few starved there but the surplus that these regions usually produced, and that the regime counted on to feed the population of the capital and other cities, did not materialize. The summer rains were lighter than usual in these areas and failed altogether in Welo, Tigray and eastern Gondar, and in much of Eritrea. Visitors to northern Welo later in 1984 found it so dry that even the cactus was wilting.

Even had Ethiopia had a strong and resilient system of agriculture, seven months with no rainfall would have left its mark. For its system based on subsistence farming, undermined by agricultural policies aimed at discouraging private farming and encouraging collectives and state farms, and by civil war, the blow was terrible. By May 1984 it was clear to foreign experts and embassies in Addis Ababa that a crisis was in the making. By mid-summer frightening reports began to come in from the field staff of Western private voluntary organizations. The trickle of destitutes was turning into a flood into Makelle, Korem, Alemata, Kobo and Kambolcha and other towns along the main roads. A few alarmed Ethiopians began to whisper to Western embassies their fears that widespread famine was imminent and that hundreds of thousands might die, and to speak of their shock that their government was doing nothing about it.

For the Ethiopian government was following hallowed tradition. The RRC did launch an appeal to Western governments at the beginning of May. Commissioner Dawit warned that the early year drought had depleted food stocks and had put as many as 5.2 million people at risk of starvation. But inside Ethiopia nothing was said or reported about major drought and famine. No senior official raised the alarm. The government took no measures to grapple with the crisis that its RRC Commissioner had proclaimed, and Dawit made no further public appeals to foreign donors until August. From early June through the rest of the summer, the attention of the government of Ethiopia was directed exclusively toward preparations for the founding congress of the WPE and the celebration of the tenth anniversary of the revolution. Famine was obviously a painful embarrassment to a regime that claimed to have the solution to all problems, particularly at a moment when the glories of the regime were to be celebrated. Months later, the Ethiopian press and the RRC began to rewrite history in an obvious attempt to shift from the regime the burden of responsibility for failure to recognize and act on the crisis in good time. Typically, contradictory versions were put about: in one, it was claimed that the regime was in fact the first to realize that a crisis was in the making and to appeal for help; in another it was said that the regime had not ignored the drought and famine but acknowledged that it had underestimated its extent. In both versions, it was the Western governments alone who failed to act in time: the West was put in the docket while no mention at all was made of Ethiopia's 'socialist' friends, who evidently were considered excused of any responsibility in this particular matter. The Ethiopian government's after-the-fact versions were a cynical distortion of the record. Throughout the summer of 1984, day after day with dreary regularity, the Ethiopian press filled its pages with stories of meetings, usually addressed by the regime's top figures, held in preparation for the party founding congress. Not a word was said about famine before mid-October. Even then the Ethiopian media approached the subject very cautiously. Not until late November and December did the media bring the country's massive drought and famine fully into the open. The first close-up pictures of famine victims were published in newspapers and broadcast on Ethiopian television only in late December, and even then the people shown were not the emaciated semi-skeletons that the Western public had beheld on its television screens since the end of September, three months earlier. It was by word of mouth or from foreign radio broadcasts that most Ethiopians in Addis Ababa first learned of the magnitude of the crisis that had engulfed their nation.

In the five-hour speech that he delivered in the Workers Party's new convention hall on 6 September, Mengistu made no mention that Ethiopia was facing a crisis. He spoke of recurrent drought and famine, of deforestation and the danger of desertification. But these few remarks were buried deep in his long text and were fundamentally no different from what he had been saying on these same subjects for years. Elsewhere in his speech he even spoke in glowing terms of 'the success of the measures taken to raise production in the agricultural sector [that] has helped especially to alleviate the shortages of food crops',[4] as though to say that prospects were promising. Nowhere in a document that runs to 150 printed pages did he convey a sense of immediacy or urgency. One wonders whether he in fact knew what was happening. As in Haile Selassie's time, bad news did not easily make its way to the top of the Ethiopian government, and when it did it was not gladly received. The September speech was a major policy document, one that offered the Ethiopian leader the opportunity to proclaim to the public and to the world that a crisis existed and to appeal for national and international mobilization to combat it. The fact that Mengistu did not use it to do so suggests two hypotheses: that he had not been informed of the scale of the disaster or that he was indifferent to it. Both were charges made against Haile Selassie in the aftermath of the famine in Welo in 1972 and 1973.

While thousands, perhaps tens of thousands, starved to death, the Ethiopian regime busied itself during the critical weeks of July, August and early September with the beautification of Addis Ababa for the thousands of guests to come from the Soviet bloc and Western Communist parties for the September ceremonies. It was a time of frantic activity. Triumphal arches were erected and adorned with revolutionary slogans, enormous posers of Mengistu were put up, sidewalks were repaired and streets patched and painted with traffic lines, stars with hammer and sickle hoisted atop buildings and archways, and fencing put up to hide slums. Paint was applied to shops and buildings along all the main avenues. Huge neon signs displaying revolutionary insignia and mottos were installed on the highest buildings. A bust of Karl Marx — a gift, appropriately, of the German Democratic Republic — was unveiled in the park opposite the University. In the field in front of the Black Lion hospital, stairs and fountains were built leading to a soaring stele crowned by a red star, bronze statuary representing three Ethiopian soldiers of the revolution and the 1977–8 war, and bronze bas-reliefs of Mengistu in military and civilian roles, all with features slightly orientalized. They were the gift of the North Koreans, Ethiopia's special friend since Mengistu's visit to Pyongyang in October of the previous year; meanwhile, North Korean instructors trained the population of Addis Ababa in mass marching and dancing for the 12 September parade. Higher up in the city, in the field between the Menelik palace, now Mengistu's compound, and the former parliament building where COPWE was headquartered, the finishing touches were being put on the Great Hall of the People, the three-thousand-five-hundred-seat convention center built for the WPE. Only the tape on the upper windows remained to be removed. Equipped with the latest gear to carry simultaneous translation to each seat, and with conference rooms and a large cafeteria, it was built to specification and completed on schedule by a Finnish contractor, with all materials except rock siding imported from Finland and cash paid by the Ethiopian government on the barrelhead. Less than a kilometre down the street the Addis Ababa Hilton Hotel now sported a huge sign proclaiming 'Peace Solidarity Friendship'. But since July work on its annex, meant to lodge guests for the ceremonies, had slowed as it became apparent that the September deadline would not be met. Contrary to popular rumor, neither the work-force nor the Tourism Commissioner, under whose responsibility the project operated, was taken out to be shot for the failure to make schedule (though a few months later the Tourism Commissioner, Fisseha Geda, was sent off to be Ambassador to Pyongyang).

By the beginning of September all energies were concentrated on the drilling of the population for the mass marches to be held on revolution day. The city's main streets resounded to the megaphoned cries of drill instructors. Revolution Square and the avenues leading to it were closed each day until 1 p.m. while the 'broad masses' were marched down from the slums on the surrounding hills to be exercised there. They spent all day at it on the Sunday just before the big event, got drenched by a late afternoon downpour and trudged miserably back to their homes in the early evening. If there was any popular enthusiasm in these preparations, it escaped detection. People dutifully showed up, formed and marched, and returned home when dismissed. They had little alternative; those who shirked this 'voluntary duty' were punished by imprisonment or beating, or by withdrawal of their ration cards or loss of their jobs. Addis Ababa, always a heavily policed city, now bristled with police; they were at every intersection, patroling in pairs, carrying side arms and looking very alert. The September festivities were to pass without any known incident, but the regime took no chances. The old airport, long a military compound, was now packed with combat helicopters, armored personnel carriers, tanks and artillery pieces, ready to do heavy battle. Bole International Airport was so heavily guarded that it was practically inaccessible except to diplomatic officers and personnel of the regime with special passes. More than usually, the city was awash in rumors. A few days before the arrival of the East bloc dignitaries, one more curious change occurred: the lines stretching out from the government ration stores on the main avenues disappeared. Since the beginning of the summer they had grown longer and thicker as severe shortages forced up the price of flour, beans and cooking oil on the free market. Now, miraculously, the crowds were gone.

Just how much the adornment of Addis Ababa cost became a matter for intense and often bitter speculation in the West. *Time* magazine put the total at $150m.; others said $250m. The Ethiopian government protested that these were ridiculous figures and assured that the amount was paltry because the work was done by 'volunteer' labor and the materials were furnished by 'friendly governments'. But it never itself gave a figure. Even if its claims of no-cost labor and donated materials were more or less true, the bill still had to be substantial. The convention hall alone cost, according to reliable report, $17m. Another $12m. was spent on the most up-to-date television equipment, including vans loaded with cameras and transmitters, purchased from the United Kingdom and flown to Ethiopia to be on hand in time for the September celebrations. Another $8m. to $10m. must have been expended on decorations. Over and above these sums, the government of Ethiopia spent large amounts of money to import food and drink to host the thousands of delegates from East bloc and Western Communist parties who came to celebrate the founding of the Party and the tenth anniversary of the revolution. The total expense could not have been less than $50m. and may have run as high as $100m. or more. In a normal quarter, Ethiopia spends foreign exchange at a rate of $300m. to $350m. In the third quarter of 1984, Ethiopia's outlay soared to approximately $600m.

Despite serious political differences with the government of Ethiopia, and the cut-off of development assistance in 1979, the United States continued thereafter to provide $5m.–$6m. a year to CRS for humanitarian relief programs. These grants came under attack within the administration in 1982, and in the spring of 1983 they were deleted from the Agency for International Development's budget for the following fiscal year. But as the administration became aware of the incipient famine in Tigray and Welo, the money was restored and more was added. American humanitarian assistance to Ethiopia amounted to $11m. in fiscal year 1983. In fiscal year 1984 it jumped to $23m. Most of the increase came in the summer months of 1984 as the United States moved, before the Western media ran the story of the famine or the Ethiopian government acknowledged that there was one, to help feed the growing number of starving.

The Western media did not immediately take to this story. Those few Western journalists allowed into Ethiopia to cover the September ceremonies for the most part stuck to their assigned beat. *Washington Post* reporter David Ottaway and his wife Marina, both well versed on Ethiopia from their assignment in Addis Ababa during the mid-1970s and from subsequent writing on it, and *New York Times* reporter Judith Miller, were the only American press representatives accredited. Ottaway and Miller came to the American Embassy in the first days of September for a briefing. In a session that lasted over an hour they were told, in as much detail as the Embassy knew at the time, of the terrible famine developing in Tigray and Welo and of the indifference of the Ethiopian government. As this information was conveyed to Ottaway, a look of deep skepticism came across his face. Miller sent in a short report on drought and famine but it gave little idea of the scope of the disaster. Ottaway consigned the story of the drought and famine to a brief paragraph buried midway through an article that led off with a report on a prosperous collective farm to which he was taken by Ethiopian officials and that described Ethiopia as crippled by an 'East–West squeeze'. The real story of Ethiopia's famine did not break until late September when films taken by Kenyan television journalist Mohammed Amin were shown on British television.

In the second half of September, after receiving alarming reports forwarded by the Embassy, Washington decided to launch a much expanded program of humanitarian relief for Ethiopia. An AID team was sent to Addis Ababa at the end of the month to make a survey. The Embassy asked and quickly received from the RRC permission for the team to travel to Welo. Foreigners could not travel outside the Ethiopian capital without special permits, which were often refused or came too late to be used. In this instance, however, the RRC gave speedy co-operation. The AID team returned from their trip with harrowing tales. The summer crop had failed or was about to fail throughout Welo and in most of northern Shoa. Neither the RRC nor Western private relief agencies had enough food or shelter to cope with the vast numbers seeking refuge in the roadside towns. These towns had suddenly become overrun by the destitute, who huddled in the streets or in nearby barren fields. Western relief workers reported dozens of deaths daily in each of these places. On the drive back to Addis Ababa from Dessie[5] the AID team's vehicle was repeatedly stopped by gangs of starving children who sat in the middle of the road and refused to move until food or money was thrown to them. One of the members of the AID team estimated that ten thousand people might die in Welo in the month of October. On 5 October, as the AID team was cabling its report to Washington, Ambassador Vernon Walters and Assistant Secretary Chester Crocker met Foreign Minister Goshu Wolde in New York on the margins of the UN General Assembly. They told the Ethiopian that the United States intended to step up substantially its deliveries of food and other items for emergency relief. They asked for assurance that American aid personnel would be allowed the freedom of movement needed to carry out the program, and that the Ethiopian government would co-operate in the delivery of food to all parts of the country; that is, that no one would be precluded for political reasons from getting food. Goshu gave both assurances unhesitatingly.

On 13 October I was instructed to advise RRC Commissioner Dawit that the United States was prepared to provide food directly to his organization for emergency relief feeding. This was an important new step. Up to that time, the American government had given food and money for feeding the hungry in Ethiopia only to private Western relief organizations. It had refused to donate to the Ethiopian government, because of concern that donations might be misappropriated. The Ethiopian government took this as a snub; it refused to give publicity to American donations made through private organizations and said it would only acknowledge aid that was given directly to it. Washington had no intention of changing its policy to suit the complaints of the Ethiopian government, but it recognized that the magnitude of the crisis made it desirable to use all possible channels. The visiting AID team had made a study of RRC procedures and had concluded that adequate accountability could be expected. The one condition that I was to put to Dawit was that food should be delivered to 'all needy parts of the country'. Dawit readily gave his oral agreement to this. On 17 October I sent Dawit a letter spelling out this and other terms for the United States' stepped-up humanitarian assistance program and on 18 October he replied in writing formally assenting. At the end of October Dawit went to New York to talk with UN officials and on 1 November he took the shuttle to Washington to meet with AID Director Peter McPherson. The two men had already clashed publicly; Dawit had accused the United States of tardiness in coming to Ethiopia's assistance, and McPherson had criticized the Ethiopian regime for being slow in responding to the crisis and for making no effort to get food to people in rebel-held areas. But in person they hit it off well together. On 2 November they announced agreement on a memorandum of understanding that called for the United States to provide immediately to the RRC 50,000 tons of grain for humanitarian relief. The memorandum held out the prospect of a second 50,000 tons if distribution of the first were deemed to have been carried out satisfactorily. The memorandum also specified that the Ethiopian government undertook to make food available to all parts of the country, on the basis of need alone.

After this, American government grants for relief assistance in Ethiopia shot up. By the end of November, only two months into the fiscal year (the American government's fiscal year runs from 1 October to 30 September) the United States had committed just over $112m. for food, medicines and other supplies for famine relief in Ethiopia. By the end of June 1985 the United States had obligated $250m. for humanitarian assistance to Ethiopia, a sum that included provision of 440,000 tons of grain; by the time the 1985 fiscal year closed, on 30 September, the program had reached $280m.[6] In launching this massive program, the United States made it clear to the Ethiopians that it neither expected nor required any political counterpart. Walters and Crocker again offered Goshu the possibility of high level talks but emphasized that this would be entirely separate from the matter of famine relief assistance. When Goshu said he would like to see such talks take place, Washington was much encouraged. It was natural to hope, if not to expect, that the West's Herculean effort to save the lives of millions of starving Ethiopians would be appreciated and would cause the Ethiopian government to take a second look at its international position. Surely, some in Washington reasoned, the Ethiopian regime would see that, when it came to basic matters of survival, the West had a lot more to offer than the East. Moscow could give arms to prosecute endless civil wars, but it could provide neither food in time of emergency nor an economic model that would assure Ethiopia the ability to produce enough food to feed its burgeoning population even in normal times. Would the 1984 drought and famine not make Mengistu and his government understand, after seven years of striving to imitate the Soviet model, that the time for at least modest changes had come?

It soon became clear, however, that the Ethiopian government and the West had quite different views on how to deal with the crisis. The United States and other Western governments considered the delivery of food to starving people to be the first priority; before all else, lives had to be saved. The Ethiopian government's priorities lay elsewhere. On 22 October, Mengistu convoked the ambassadors of the Warsaw Pact states, together with the Cuban and Vietnamese envoys, to appeal for their governments' help in a massive new program. The Ethiopian leader said six million people would be transferred from drought-afflicted areas in north-central Ethiopia to fertile, well-watered and unused lands in the south-west and west. The aim, he declared, would be to assure that 'this catastrophe will never happen again'. Mengistu told the East bloc envoys that those transferred would be set up on collective farms. The next day he called in the French and West German ambassadors to tell them of his resettlement plan and to ask for their governments' help with it. He did not mention the figure six million or say that they would be collectivized, but he did let drop a remark that shocked the two Western diplomats: only the able-bodied would be resettled; the old and young would be left in the drought-stricken areas. RRC Commissioner Dawit later told the French and German ambassadors that Mengistu had not said this. Both men had heard it quite distinctly and were taken aback by Dawit's straightfaced denial. Mengistu had apparently not understood what effect such a callous remark would have on Western listeners; Dawit had.

A few days after his meeting with the ambassadors, Mengistu left the capital to survey resettlement sites in Wellega, Kaffa and Illubabor. He had not yet been to famine relief camps to visit the starving and was not to get around to doing so until a month later, at the end of November.

The Ethiopian government's argument that the land in the drought-stricken areas was depleted, and that people had to be given the chance to become self-sufficient, was plausible and aroused sympathy. Yet Western reaction to the plan was almost uniformly one of reserve. Western development agencies had ample experience with resettlement. It could be very useful, but they knew that careful preparation and substantial investment were needed to assure success. But what the Ethiopian government was proposing was a hastily thrown-together scheme in which enormous numbers of people would be sent to new and unfamiliar lands with little or no preparation. Early announcements spoke of moving between 1.5 million and 2.5 million people in the first year of a program launched in November 1984, though in fact the numbers sent in the first year turned out to be well under a million. Other aspects of the program also troubled Western governments. No thought seemed to have been given to helping people stay and farm in the stricken areas; it was as though these vast regions were to be abandoned. Western embassies and governments feared that people would be forced to go, and the West had deep misgivings about collectivization of those resettled. Several Western envoys in Addis Ababa had visited collective resettlement farms set up in the late 1970s and early 1980s and had come away deeply disturbed by what they saw. I visited the large resettlement farm in Assosa, in western Wollega, twice in 1983, and the British Ambassador had seen resettlement farms in the south. None of these farms was successful. All were still dependent on Western-donated food years after their creation. At Assosa, the largest single element of the work-force were the guards, who numbered over 600 and whose task was as much to keep the reluctant resettlers in as to keep marauding locals — who regarded the resettlers as foreign intruders — out.

All in all, the program's hidden political agenda seemed more substantial than its avowed developmental one. It was aimed at carrying out the regime's plans for the collectivization of agriculture and at emptying as much as possible the north-central highlands, not by coincidence areas of insurgency, of able-bodied population.

No sooner was the program launched than stories confirming the worst of Western fears began to filter back to Addis Ababa and from there to the outside world. Western relief workers in the field witnessed people being rounded up at gunpoint and forced on to trucks taking them to the south-west and west. They saw families being separated, the able-bodied singled out for resettlement while the young and old and the ill and crippled were left behind; Catholic workers began a project to care for children left behind when separated from their parents in the round-ups. At first, many of those taken for resettlement were packed into open trucks and driven off with no shelter from the fierce African sun for a journey of a week or more. Many died along the way or fled when the trucks stopped to refuel. In many cases no arrangement had been made to feed people in transit or even to supply safe drinking water; food was often requisitioned from local populations, both *en route* and on arrival at destination. Western governments protested at these practices. The Ethiopian government stoutly denied them, but they continued. On 10 February 1985 the BBC international service reported eye-witness testimony of approximately two hundred people taken away at gunpoint from a camp at Makelle. On 10 March, field-workers of Save the Children UK watched while a battalion of Ethiopian troops surrounded their camp in Korem and forceably extracted several hundred persons for dispatch to resettlement areas. One of the foreign relief workers photographed the event and succeeded in smuggling his film out of Ethiopia. In late October, Western papers reported hundreds forceably taken away from Korem for resettlement while thousands of others fled the camp to escape the same fate. A British journalist reported this description of the event, given by a representative of a Western relief agency who was there: 'There is no doubt that they were forced to leave . . . They were herded like cattle. Some of the people taken were still receiving medical treatment. Two of them were TB patients.'[7]

These were only a few instances, the visible part of a common and routine practice. The Ethiopian government, while protesting that resettlement was entirely voluntary, assigned quotas for each district. The army, acting at the direction of the local branch of the WPE, proceeded to fill them. People were rounded up indiscriminately, both from famine relief camps and from villages along the roads controlled by the army. No effort was made to distinguish between those who had crops and those who were destitute. A Western relief worker who made a survey at the camp at Damazin where people rounded up for resettlement were held in transit, while awaiting transportation to resettlement areas, found that only 14 per cent of those questioned had had no harvest the previous year. Approximately 38 per cent had had some crop and 34.5 said they had had a normal harvest. Another 14 per cent had had an above average harvest.[8] The Ethiopian government proceeded as though the entirety of Welo and Tigray, regions with a population estimated variously at four to six million, had become permanently unfit for cultivation and habitation when in fact some peasant families were still able to bring in a satisfactory harvest despite the drought.

As word of forced resettlement spread through the dry hills of Welo and Tigray, many starving peasants turned away from the relief camps in government-controlled territory and began a long trek to Sudan. By early 1985 it was estimated that four to six hundred thousand Tigreans had crossed into Sudan seeking food. To fill their quotas, the authorities often had to resort to subterfuge. In one district in Tigray, the local administration announced a compulsory vaccination program for livestock. The population complied by bringing in their flocks, only to be rounded up for resettlement and forced to abandon their animals.[9] Promises of food distribution were frequently used to lure peasants to a town where they would be seized by troops.

These practices assured that no Western government would associate itself with the resettlement scheme, though a few were tempted to do so and late in 1985 the Canadian government made a small grant for resettlement. Food and Agriculture Organization Director Saouma impulsively espoused the program at its outset but drew back when warned that the FAO's endorsement could undermine Western support for the organization.

The scruples that constrained Western governments were not shared by the Soviets and Ethiopia's other 'socialist bloc' friends. After receiving Mengistu's appeal, they directed all their assistance to resettlement. The Soviets sent military transport aircraft, helicopters, and three hundred trucks, all with military crews to operate and maintain them; and later the Soviet Union provided a fully equipped military field hospital. The Antonov military transport aircraft were immediately put to the task of flying resettlers from Makelle to Addis Ababa (from the capital they were sent on by truck to resettlement areas in the south-west). Conditions during these flights have been described as atrocious.[10]

To its assistance, the Soviet Union attached a value of $173m., which UN personnel skeptically but dutifully recorded in their official reports. The Soviet Union made its annual donation of 10,000 tons of rice[11] in June, months before the Ethiopian government acknowledged the famine, but it provided no further food after that time. Some of the Eastern Europeans gave small amounts of food. The Bulgarians sent a ton of good quality feta cheese which the RRC sold on the market in Addis Ababa and which was snapped up by the Western diplomatic community.

Every Soviet and East bloc contribution, no matter how small, was given lavish publicity in the Ethiopian media. Often East bloc donations were counted three times: when announced, when delivered to port, and when actually in the field. If the Western European and Canadian ambassadors pressed hard enough, they could usually get a clip on television or a story in the newspaper about their most recent donation. But American food donations were a great embarrassment to the regime. The Ministry of Information steadfastly refused to publish the overall figure for American government donations after they grew to the tens of millions of dollars in late summer 1984, and then to one hundred million dollars and beyond at year's end. It was a certainty that no very large American donation would be reported, but small ones were readily featured in the newspapers and on television and radio. This of course gave the impression that American assistance was minuscule. Many Ethiopians knew better, but anyone who believed the regime's propaganda had to think that most help came from the Soviet bloc. Needless to say, the Ethiopian government's distorted reporting of Eastern and Western assistance caused much irritation in Washington.

Out of the fundamental disagreement between Western governments and Ethiopia over goals and methods grew a crude unspoken division of labor. The West did famine relief while the Ethiopian government, with what help it got from the Soviet bloc, did resettlement. If this sounds logical in theory, it proved highly unsatisfactory in practice so far as famine relief was concerned. (Because the Ethiopian regime devoted almost all of its resources to resettlement, it had very little to offer for famine relief. It paid the salaries of those RRC employees — many of them able and dedicated individuals — assigned to the famine relief program, and it provided some equipment. But it gave little if any other support, and first priority for allocation of trucks, always in short supply in Ethiopia, was accorded to resettlement. There were never enough to clear the ports of the hundred thousand or so tons of grain that began arriving monthly from January on, or to assure a steady supply of food to the emergency relief camps.

This was the case from the very beginning of the crisis. At a meeting of Western ambassadors at the ornate residence of the Italian ambassador in Addis Ababa on 8 October, alarmed officials of CRS announced that food stocks for relief feeding were close to exhaustion in Makelle, where some forty to fifty thousand destitute peasants had by that time sought shelter. The reason was that the Ethiopian army had not run a food convoy into Makelle since August; evidently it felt it had more urgent tasks than to get food to the starving in the administrative capital of Tigray. (Because of the insurgency, all road transport had to be in convoy with military escort, even in daylight hours.) The CRS officials appealed for Western help. They warned that, if nothing were done, within a short time their operation and others there would have bare larders, and thousands would die. They pointed out that there were at that very moment more than 30,000 tons of grain sitting in the port of Assab. Could the Western governments do something to get enough to Makelle to prevent mass starvation? The assembled Western envoys, moved by this plea, decided to make a representation to the Ethiopian head of state. They elected the Italian ambassador to be their spokesman and he proceeded to file an urgent request for an audience with Mengistu. Eight days later just before noon the Italian envoy was convoked to the palace. There RRC Commissioner Dawit met him and warned him sternly against specifically mentioning the situation in Makelle. The Italian was in a quandary; he had a mission to carry out but had been enjoined from doing it by the senior Ethiopian government official in charge of relief programs. He maneuvered with characteristic skill. He told Mengistu of the Western ambassadors' concern about shortages in the emergency feeding camps. On their collective behalf he asked that the government of Ethiopia make available air and land transport to assure distribution of food to 'hard-to-reach places', and he referred eliptically to 'cases discussed with Commissioner Dawit'. The next day's *Ethiopian Herald* turned this *démarche* on its head: it reported that the Italian ambassador had expressed concern to Chairman Mengistu over transport of food to remote areas and had promised to 'take steps to correct such problems'.

Meanwhile, after urgent exchanges of cables with Washington, on 15 October I was authorized to offer Dawit $100,000 to pay fuel costs for the Ethiopian airforce to fly grain to Makelle from Asmara. To my consternation, when I presented the offer to Dawit in his office that some morning, he turned it down. Unbelieving, I asked how it could be possible that the Ethiopian airforce could not fly food to starving Ethiopians even if the United States paid the transportation costs? Dawit merely shook his head, but three days later he telephoned me to advise that the Ministry of Defense had agreed to put 'one or two Antonovs' at our disposal to carry food into Makelle. The Ministry's agreement must have been less than enthusiastic, for the planes were not made available until ten days later and the flights ran only intermittently. Over a period of several weeks only 19 or 20 took place, and it was impossible to verify if we got full return on our $100,000. But the air lift caught the imagination of the Western press and made headlines. It sounded, quite falsely, as though everybody were pulling together to rescue the starving: American grain flown in Soviet-made planes by Ethiopian airforce pilots, with fuel purchased by the United States.

Since the Ethiopian government could not be got to move food to Makelle in any reliable and regular way, the Western nations set about doing this job themselves. This was to become a regular pattern; as the Ethiopian government defaulted on its responsibilities, Western governments stepped in to fill the resulting void. AID contracted with TransAmerica corporation for two L–100 aircraft[12] to fly shuttle daily between Asmara, where American grain was delivered from the port of Massawa, and Makelle. Britain assigned an RAF C–130 to the same mission and West German and Italian military aircraft occasionally joined in. This Western air shuttle carried the bulk of the food that reached Makelle from November 1984, when it began, until June of the following year when it was phased down.

The camps at Makelle were a pitiful, heart-rending sight that November. Though starving people had been arriving there in great numbers for several months, little had been done to provide shelter and only a fraction received enough food. CRS, the only private Western relief agency operating in Makelle at the time, had stretched its resources to the breaking point; it set up a hospital and provided some tents and clothing. But the need far exceeded its resources, and the Ethiopian government had done virtually nothing. Most of the people in the several camps on the outskirts of Makelle huddled miserably in the open, day and night, with only a few stones, a goatskin or a piece of cloth to break the wind and protect occasionally from the fierce sun. At 2,500m altitude, Makelle was bone chilling at night and broiling hot during midday hours. People in the camps run by CRS received a more or less adequate supply of food, depending on what CRS was able to provide at a given moment, but those in the RRC-run camp were given rations below the starvation level. In the makeshift hospitals in Makelle, Korem, Alemata and other camps, the chorus of pitiful rasping coughs mingled with the putrid smell of the dying and the sharp odor of disinfectant. In December, AID brought into Makelle a large quantity of heavy plastic sheeting from US military stocks in Europe. Tents were fashioned from this material, and by early 1985 Makelle looked like a model for the administration of humanitarian relief. Private Western relief agencies sent in clothing. The people in Makelle became the more fortunate of Ethiopia's drought victims.

The matter of getting food to all in need in Ethiopia became an issue between the United States and Ethiopia almost from the start of the crisis. The assurances that the US side had sought — and got — from Dawit and Goshu were important for several reasons. One was simply humanitarian: there were between 2.5 and 3.5 million people in areas that escaped the control of the Ethiopian government; they could not be left to starve while people in governmentally controlled areas were provided for. The American program was supposed to be non-political, but the administration was concerned that it would become politically controversial in the United States if it were seen to be neglecting people who happened to live in areas held by the rebels. Moreover, people in these areas who could not find food, and who feared to go to camps in government controlled territory, were beginning to flood into Sudan. There they put an enormous burden on the already hard-pressed government of Sudan, in whose stability the United States had a great interest.

In Tigray, a region roughly the size of the state of New Hampshire, only the towns along the main roads were in government hands. Everything else, including after dark the roads, were guerrilla territory, loosely held and administered by the

Tigrean People's Liberation Front. The same was true of the northern part of Welo and northern and eastern Gondar. The government's writ was somewhat broader in Eritrea but a substantial part of that region also escaped its control. People in these areas were particularly hard hit, for they suffered the distress not only of drought but also of civil war. The Ethiopian army, in its offensives in Tigray and Eritrea, practiced a policy of scorched earth; it burned crops, killed livestock and destroyed houses. In both Tigray and Welo, the greater part of the population was thought to be at risk of starvation.

What Washington and senior UN officials hoped for was a 'food truce', an arrangement between the Ethiopian government and the rebels that would permit passage of trucks with food through government-held territory into rebel areas. I was not enthusiastic about raising this with the Ethiopians because I knew it would be rejected; the Ethiopian government, in its usual paranoia, would see it not as a practical expedient for feeding the starving but as a ploy to get it to accord recognition to the rebels. I also seriously doubted whether the Ethiopian regime wanted to get food to people in the rebel-held areas. But in December I was instructed to raise the food truce idea at the highest available level of the Ethiopian government. Setting aside my doubts, I called on the Acting Foreign Minister, Tibebu Bekele, and presented Washington's arguments. Tibebu rejected the proposal flatly and scathingly. With characteristic unconcern for logic, Tibebu first accused the United States of asking the government of Ethiopia to 'make an arrangement with criminals'; he then proceeded to deny that any area within the border of Ethiopia escaped the control of the government. Tibebu claimed the Ethiopian government could get food to people in need anywhere inside its borders; American concern was therefore misplaced and all the United States needed to do was to give food to the Ethiopian government.

There the matter stood until Senator Edward Kennedy visited Ethiopia just before Christmas and raised it with Berhanu Bayih, the Politburo's co-ordinator for foreign assistance, and Fikre-Selassie Wogderess, the regime's number two figure.[13] They rejected it every bit as starkly and bluntly as had Tibebu and denied, as had Tibebu, that the rebels controlled any territory in Ethiopia. So incredible was this denial that even their Ethiopian interpreter stumbled over it.[14] Rendering into English Fikre-Selassie's reply to Kennedy, the unfortunate Foreign Ministry official who had been called in to interpret said the Ethiopian government could deliver food 'anywhere except in some places where there are bandits'. He was halted by a chorus of reproof from Fikre-Selassie, Berhanu Bayih, Dawit and Tibebu, after which he meekly corrected himself: 'any place except that in some places bandits hinder'. Fikre-Selassie told Kennedy, as Tibebu had earlier told me, that the United States should stop worrying about the problem and rely on the Ethiopian government to get food to 'people in remote areas'.

This would have been perfectly agreeable to Washington. The problem was that the Ethiopian government was making no effort to get food to these areas, and could not have done so even if it had genuinely wanted. Other avenues had to be found. Private relief agencies had for some time been getting food into northern Ethiopia via Sudan. In April 1984 AID contributed 5,000 tons of grain to a private organization working with the Relief Society of Tigray and the Eritrean Relief Association. These two agencies were the relief arms, respectively, of the TPLF and the EPLP. The United States took care to have no dealings with REST and ERA. Despite profound political differences with the government in Addis Ababa, Washington avoided involvement with the insurgent organizations and held to its long-standing policy of support for the territorial integrity of Ethiopia. AID dealt only with the Western private voluntary agencies, who in turn handled all necessary arrangements with REST and ERA. This mechanism did not offer absolute assurance against American relief food falling into the hands of rebel soldiers, just as the United States could not be absolutely certain that food it gave to the RRC would not be diverted to improper use. Bringing food across from Sudan was only a partial solution to the problem of famine in northern Ethiopia. There were no roads, only tracks, and trucks had to travel exclusively at night to avoid detection and attack by Ethiopian aircraft. Still, unless the Ethiopian government agreed to the food truce proposal or some similar arrangement, it was the only way to get help to people in the large rebel-controlled enclaves.

In mid-November AID made a grant of 23,000 tons of grain for delivery via Sudan, and at the beginning of December a further substantial amount was allocated for this purpose. This raised the question of how to address this activity in our dealings with the Ethiopian government. The 5,000 tons donated in April was a relatively small amount, not enough to be noticed or, if it were, to be taken very seriously by the Ethiopians. But 30,000 or 40,000 tons was quite another matter. The Ethiopian government was bound to object strenuously to this food being brought across its border without its consent, and it was certain to accuse the United States of helping the insurgents. Nonetheless, the initial view in Washington was that we should say nothing to the Ethiopian government about these donations. To tell the Ethiopians what we were doing, it was argued, would be to set a deliberate challenge to them; if not formally notified, they might prefer to ignore the shipments. This was valid for small amounts, but I did not think the Ethiopians could or would turn a blind eye to the much larger program that we embarked on in November. They would learn of what we were doing and exaggerate and distort it to accuse us of all manner of nefarious activities. Our humanitarian assistance to people in northern Ethiopia was not some sort of guilty enterprise, and I felt that we should not be seen to be going about it in stealth. We should be forthright. This might irritate the Ethiopians but it would also surely command their respect and, more important, permit us to keep our own self-respect.

Washington fell in with these views, and the Ethiopian government was notified of the shipments via Sudan and our reasons for making them. It protested loudly and petulantly. On 24 December, Tibebu, still Acting Foreign Minister, called me in to complain about press reports of US food aid 'for the secessionists'. In the course of our exchange on this subject, Tibebu blurted out with more candor than he probably intended that 'food is a major element in our strategy against the secessionists'. The Ethiopian army, Tibebu added, tries to cut the rebels off from food supplies. He threatened that it would destroy any food it found being brought into Ethiopia from Sudan. He warned that the United States supplying food 'to the secessionists across Ethiopia's border and without its permission' was 'a very serious matter'. When Goshu returned to Ethiopia at the beginning of January he called me in to deliver a protest, evidently on Mengistu's instruction, on this same subject, albeit in milder terms than Tibebu. Ethiopian officials continued to raise this issue from time to time and to make vague threats, but these were never translated into action. They claimed that the food shipments were only a cover for the delivery of arms to the rebels; weapons, they said, were hidden under the bags of grain carried by the REST and ERA trucks crossing from Sudan. Had they actually thought this was true, they might have broken relations with the United States. They knew it was not, and they realized that they would find no public support in Ethiopia or elsewhere for a break in relations with the United States over the fact of American food shipments to starving Ethiopians in Tigray and Eritrea. In any event, by that time American assistance for relief in government-controlled areas had grown so large that a break with the United States was hardly affordable.

Another issue that caused friction and public recrimination between the United States and Ethiopia was the pile-up of Western-donated grain on the docks at Assab and Massawa, Ethiopia's two ports. This was not a new problem. Even before the large Western relief effort was launched in the fall of 1984, the ports were chronically congested and food almost always had the lowest priority; it sat on the docks, or in ships at anchor in the harbor, while weapons and cement were unloaded and sped away. In December 1984, while the RRC was complaining that food promised by the West was not arriving fast enough, large amounts accumulated at Assab. They were cleared from the port by special order from Mengistu. But by January more very large shipments were arriving and grain again began to pile up at Assab. From then on between 100,000 and 150,000 tons came in each month. Even with a concerted effort, movement of such large amounts would have strained Ethiopia's meager transport resources. But only rarely was such an effort made. Trucks were assigned to the area that had first priority for the regime, resettlement. From time to time Mengistu would order more trucks allocated for the movement of emergency relief grain, after urgent appeals by the Western ambassadors and the UN. But for long periods nothing was done. Great mounds of bagged grain spread across the dock and port areas at Assab, Ethiopia's main port. Warehouses could only accommodate a small portion of what was arriving; most sat in the hot sun. The temperature of the Red Sea port was over 100° and plastic bagging burst and grain began to rot. (Burlap would have stood up under the heat but plastic was preferred because, unlike burlap, it did not allow penetration by insects.) Western embassies and the UN repeatedly urged the government to allocate trucks to move it to inland warehouses. They warned that, if nothing were done, there could be great loss through spoilage. The RRC repeatedly assured that measures were being taken, yet the grain continued to pile up in the open, unprotected. On 5 May the inevitable happened: it rained heavily at Assab and over 10,000 tons of Western-donated grain was ruined. Thereafter the Ethiopian government made another fitful try at reducing the accumulation. But only a protracted effort, through diversion of trucks from the resettlement program and from the military, could solve the problem. The regime was not prepared to take these steps. To keep the count of tonnage sitting on the docks as low as possible, Ethiopian port authorities deliberately kept ships waiting in the harbor and delayed unloading, a step that resulted in heavy additional charges to the accounts of the Western donor governments. Much more grain could have been brought in through the port of Djibouti but the Ethiopian government did its best to discourage donors from using Djibouti, even though Massawa and Assab were overburdened. Relief organizations that used Djibouti complained that the Ethiopian railway authority deliberately allocated too few rail cars to move their food promptly into Ethiopia.

At the end of June 1985, Western and UN relief experts estimated that there were over 210,000 tons of grain donated for famine relief sitting on the docks in the three ports of Assab, Massawa and Djibouti or in vessels at anchor in their harbors. According to RRC figures, the rate of distribution of food to the needy was at that time between 65,000 and 75,000 tons a month, so the 210,000 tons in the ports was enough to keep the program going for over three months. The Embassy's estimate was far lower, approximately 30,000 tons a month. At the end of 1984, the number of people 'at risk' of starvation was estimated by the Ethiopian government, and by the UN which by then had set up an office in Addis Ababa under the very able direction of Assistant Secretary general Kurt Jansson to co-ordinate the relief effort, at seven to nine million. The figure was of course only an educated guess; no one knew with any precision how many people were starving in Ethiopia. What all the Western and international agencies did know was that far too little food was reaching the famine areas. Almost every emergency feeding center was, at one time or another and often chronically, short of the food needed to feed the thousands upon thousands of destitute that waited miserably outside their fences. Adequate rations were reaching only between 2.5 million and three million people. The efforts of the relief agencies to reach greater numbers were stymied by lack of road transport and by bureaucratic obstacles raised by the Ethiopian government.

Many Western relief workers wanted to complain publicly of the Ethiopian government's failure to support famine relief and of its many other abuses, in particular those connected to the resettlement program, but they were constrained from doing so by order from their headquarters and by fear of being expelled from Ethiopia. The threat of expulsion of individual workers, or the closure of entire programs, was constantly held over the heads of the foreign relief organization by the RRC. It added considerably to the emotional strain under which those who worked so selflessly, indeed heroically, to save lives themselves lived. It effectively silenced many but by no means all. In the fall of 1985, as resettlement resumed after a brief summer hiatus, the distinguished French relief organization Médecins Sans Frontières raised with the RRC its deeply felt concern over the program. In a series of meetings with senior RRC officials, MSF pointed out that the absolute priority given to resettlement was causing serious disruptions in the effort to save lives, that many of those sent for resettlement were taken against their will, and that because of haste and poor preparation tens of thousands of those sent for resettlement — perhaps as many as one hundred thousand altogether — had died. MSF asked the Ethiopian government to suspend the resettlement program for three months to allow time for clarification of three issues: the viability of the northern territories (that is, Tigray and Welo, from which people were being taken for resettlement) and the scope for local rehabilitation; the accommodation facilities in all the resettlement lands; and freedom of choice as regards relocation and the possibility for separated families to be reunited. For its temerity in criticizing resettlement and in making this proposal, MSF was summarily expelled from Ethiopia at the beginning of December 1985. The British relief organization Oxfam also issued a statement critical of Ethiopian government practices in resettlement, albeit reluctantly and only after one of its workers in Ethiopia had spoken out. Carol Ashwood, described as a twenty-eight-year-old nurse and midwife who worked for Oxfam in a remote district of Welo, told the British press that coercion had been used systematically to enforce mass migrations from the area in which she was stationed.

> Half of the 250,000 people in the district were earmarked for removal . . . Grain was deliberately denied by the Ethiopian authorities to force people to agree to leaving their homes. We found that hungry children to whom Oxfam was distributing food were losing weight, not gaining it. This, we discovered, was because the children were taking the food from our centre and

sharing it with their entire families, who were getting nothing else.[15]

Although MSF's figure of as many as one hundred thousand deaths as a result of the resettlement program after one year of its operation has been challenged, there can be no doubt that the toll has been high. The Ethiopian government has opened a few resettlement sites for inspection by Western journalists and relief officials, but most have remained closed. Despite this effort to preserve secrecy, a good deal has become known about conditions overall, from Ethiopians who have returned from the sites, from resettlers who fled into Sudan, and from the occasional Westerner who inexplicably managed to get into the forbidden areas. Numerous accounts, both private and published,[16] attest to widespread deaths as a result of lack of food, overexertion owing to intensive forced labor, lack of sanitary facilities and rampant disease for which no prophylaxis was provided, notably malaria, typhus, typhoid, yellow fever and sleeping sickness. Some of the land chosen for resettlement has turned out to be far less fertile than expected. Ethiopians returning from Gambela province, in the south-west near the southern Sudanese border, have told of settlements established on land cultivable only with great difficulty owing to the poverty of the soil and the alternation between wet seasons of intense rain and flooding and dry seasons that leave the ground parched and arid. Those resettled have not been the only ones to suffer. In some instances local peoples have been driven off land that they had long used for cultivation or for the grazing of livestock. Just how many have been affected is impossible to know. The Ethiopian government denies that anyone has been evicted to make way for resettlement. But according to Survival International, a private voluntary organization specializing in the defense of the rights of indigenous groups, some fifteen thousand people of various tribes from the Gambela area of Ethiopia have taken refuge in southern Sudan as a result of the 1984/5 and earlier resettlement programs.[17]

Notes

1. Richard Pankhurst, 'The Great Ethiopian Famine of 1888–1892, A New Assessment', *Journal of History of Medicine and Allied Sciences* (April 1966), p. 96.
2. Mesfin Wolde Mariam, *Rural Vulnerability to Famine in Ethiopia: 1958–1977*

(Vikas Publishing House, New Delhi, 1984), pp. 15–16.

   3. Ibid., p. 103. Professor Mesfin's excellent study is replete with statements of this sort and others that, unintentionally no doubt, ring true of the 1984–5 Ethiopian famine; for example: 'The response of the ruling class to an impending famine appears to be remarkably similar everywhere. Officialdom has a characteristic propensity to receive any information on famine with scornful disbelief' (p. 10). He was, of course, writing about Haile Selassie's regime. His book was published in the spring of 1984, on the eve of the massive famine that struck Ethiopia that year. At the end of the year it could no longer be found on the shelves of the bookstore of Addis Ababa university or elsewhere in the city.

   4. *Central Report Delivered by Mengistu Haile Mariam* (Addis Ababa, September 1984), p. 52.

   5. Administrative capital of Welo region.

   6. For a detailed breakdown of American humanitarian assistance to Ethiopia in US fiscal years 1984 and 1985, see Appendix II.

   7. David Blundy, *The Sunday Times* (London) 27 October, 1985. See also 'Ethiopians Took Over Aid Trucks for Resettlement', *International Herald Tribune*, 30 October, 1985.

   8. Report by Peter Niggli, representative of the West German organization Berliner Missionwerk, cited in Médecins Sans Frontières, 'Les Déportations de masse en Ethiopie', December 1985, pp. 9 and 10. Niggli's observations include the following: 'Among the "victims of famine" were such absurd cases as that of Tewolde Gebreegziabher who owned irrigated farmland and who was a rich peasant by Ethiopian standards.'

   9. Médecins Sans Frontières, 'Les Déportations de masse en Ethiopie', p. 11.

   10. Survival International, *Ethiopia's Bitter Medicine* (Calvert's Press, London, 1986), p. 22, offers this vivid description of the nightmarish conditions in which the flights took place:

> From Makelle, refugees were then taken in unheated and unpressurized Antonov jets to Addis Ababa; Peter Niggli's investigations reveal how they were able to get between 300 and 350 people into each flight. People were lined up against the back of the cockpit and those on the edges of the plane had to suspend themselves from bars running along the sides, their feet dangling helplessly. In this manner, more and more people were packed into the planes; they were belabored with a stick if they resisted. When the doors were closed by force, the people were crushed up into the plane. Children had to be held above the adults heads to avoid being crushed by the force of take-off and landing. During the one hour flight, the refugees reported that many people died, some from being trampled and crushed; on one flight several women miscarried. Upon arrival, the dead were removed on stretchers while the others were marched out between rows of soldiers and loaded onto buses.

   11. Rice was unknown to the people of highland Ethiopia and they would generally not eat it. The RRC complained loudly when Italy and Austria offered it for famine relief but gave grateful thanks when it came from the Soviet Union.

   12. The civilian version of the C–130. These were what is known as the stretch version of the aircraft and could carry a load of 20 tons.

   13. Mengistu was in Moscow at the time.

   14. Fikre-Selassie spoke excellent English but, like Mengistu, used Amharic when receiving foreign visitors.

   15. *Sunday Observer*, 8 December, 1985.

   16. See, notably, Médecins Sans Frontières, 'Les Déportations de masse en Ethiopie', and Survival International, *Ethiopia's Bitter Medicine*.

   17. Cited in 'Les Déportations de masse en Ethiopie', p. 37.

From the early 1980s, destitute peasants sought refuge in the relief camp at Ibnet in the hilly plateau country of south-eastern Gondar region, some 90 km east of lake Tana and of Gondar city. Many came from Tigray and Welo regions, hundreds of kilometres distant, in the word-of-mouth knowledge that at Ibnet food and medical treatment were to be found. Members of the American congressional delegation that visited Ethiopia in August 1983 made a brief stop at Ibnet. It was then a relatively small camp of only a few thousand, but the delegation was struck by the misery it witnessed there. The terrible drought of 1984 caused the numbers to soar, and an extraordinary turn of events made Ibnet briefly famous.

At the end of March 1985, the camp at Ibnet presented a picture of extreme dereliction on the part of the RRC, which was responsible for its administration. An employee of the Embassy's AID mission who visited Ibnet at that time found some thirty to forty thousand destitute peasants huddled there on the hillside with only what little shelter they could manage to construct themselves of sticks and stones. Foreign relief workers told our employee that there was so little food in the camp that rations could only be provided to a few thousand, so dozens were dying daily. The AID employee was shown a warehouse where several thousand blankets donated by the US government were stored, neatly folded in piles, while outside at night the temperatures dipped into the forties and people suffered terribly. The RRC officer in charge of the camp had done nothing to attend to the needs of the people there. He had been ill for the previous two weeks and had kept to his room. It seemed an incredible situation. Thousands stood to die because of the indifference of this one official.

Our employee returned to Addis Ababa and made his report. The Embassy immediately appealed to RRC Commissioner Dawit and UN Assistant Secretary General Kurt Jansson for the dispatch of food and tents to Ibnet and the replacement of the camp's administrator. Dawit responded promptly. A new administrator was appointed and a convoy was dispatched with emergency supplies. In the meantime we learned that there was a substantial amount of grain in Ibnet but that it too had been kept under lock by the former administrator of the camp. We learned also that the RRC had been trucking very large amounts of food to Gondar but sending it westward, in the opposite direction, to the resettlement camps. AID let a contract to Israeli philanthropist Abie Nathan to put up several hundred large tents at Ibnet to shelter the refugees.[1]

Unfortunately, however, this was not to be the end of Ibnet's travail. On 29 April, alarmed members of the field staffs of Western relief agencies operating at Ibnet got word to friends in Addis Ababa that the Ethiopian army had moved in the previous evening and begun clearing the camp. Within 24 hours half the sixty thousand or so estimated then to be in the camp had been forced out, at gunpoint when verbal order did not suffice. The thousands of makeshift straw and stone huts built by the refugees had been burned or torn down. By happenstance, an officer of the Embassy's AID mission had a travel permit that enabled him to fly to Ibnet the next day. What he saw and was told there by foreign relief workers was even more alarming. By then the Ethiopian army had expelled all but about two thousand very ill people housed in the compounds of Irish Concern and World Vision. The others, well over fifty thousand by the estimate of foreign relief workers, had been sent away without foot or water. Many were quite ill. Since there was no food or medical treatment available to them anywhere else around, it was certain that large numbers would die. The camp lay in ruins, in silent testimony to what had been done. Foreign relief workers did not see everything, for the expulsions took place in the main at night, during which time the foreign workers were confined to their quarters several hundred meters from the RRC camp. But they heard the shrieks and sobs of people being forced out with no hope of survival, and the sound of rifle fire. Ethiopian officials on the spot were obviously surprised and annoyed to see our AID employee, and they gave him a very cold reception. The local Workers Party chief told him that the camp was being closed because the people there were from Welo and Tigray; they should go back to their homes, he said, and they would be taken care of there. This of course was nonsense. Relief camps in Welo and Tigray were at least two weeks' hard march, over difficult terrain, from Ibnet. There was no possibility that people without food and already severely weakened and ill could make it there. Under the eyes of our AID employee, the local Ethiopian authorities added a cruel twist. They opened the RRC warehouse and distributed the grain there, much of it American-donated, to members of the district peasants' association, farmers who were working their land and had crops.

Western relief workers at Ibnet said the order for closure of the camp was given by Major Melaku Teferra, the head of the WPE for Gondar Administrative Region. This individual was surely one of the more strange and ominous figures to emerge to a position of authority as a result of the Ethiopian revolution. A founding member of the Deg, Melaku was one of Mengistu's faction. He was a native of Gondar, and there were rumors that there was Falasha blood in his family background. After Mengistu seized power, Melaku returned to Gondar to run that province, first as Chief Administrator and later as head of the party apparatus. There he ruled with an iron fist, terrorizing the population and Ethiopian officials visiting from Addis Ababa. Rightly or not, Melaku was said to have murdered and tortured hundreds of people, with his own hands. He was of medium build and unremarkable except for his eyes, which all who met him described as those of a fanatic, or, less charitably, of a madman. He had got himself a particularly bad name among American Jewish groups concerned over the well-being of the small Falasha community in the Gondar area, though it does not seem that he treated the Falasha more harshly than other elements of the population. On occasion, Melaku enjoyed harassing American tourists who came to Gondar to see the crumbling castle of Emperor Fasiladas and the biblical scenes painted in a primitive style of great charm on the walls and ceilings of the local churches. American Senators Denis Deconcini and Paul Trible got a taste of this, though not directly, when they visited Gondar in February 1985. Two of the Ethiopians in the party accompanying them, one a senior Ethiopian employee of the Embassy and the other purportedly an officer of the Ethiopian Government's Tourism Commission, were taken from the delegation's hotel by Melaku and a gang of thugs and brutally beaten during a dinner at which the two Senators and the Governor of Gondar were exchanging friendly toasts. This incident, about which the two senators protested vigorously, had a small twist of irony. The Tourism Commission man was in all likelihood an officer of the security service in Addis Ababa. He was beaten before he could identify himself.[2]

Our AID employee flew back to Addis Ababa late in the afternoon of 30 April. As his plane took off from the airstrip at Ibnet and turned to head toward Addis Ababa, he saw thousands of people scattered over the barren, rocky hills within a radius of a few kilometres around Ibnet. Back at the Embassy, he gave us a detailed account of what he had seen and heard in Ibnet. This was quickly put into a cable and dispatched to Washington, but I knew that whatever Washington decided to do could not come quickly enough to help the thousands of people threatened with certain death as a result of the brutal and unexpected closure of the camp. Jansson and Dawit had to be informed and appeals had to be made to the government of Ethiopia to reverse the closure order. But we all knew that in the absence of some force that would impel action days or even weeks could pass before something would be done. So as we filed our cable to Washington I sent the AID employee and the head of the AID office to the Hilton Hotel to look for *Washington Post*-reporter Blaine Harden, the only American journalist still, temporarily, in Addis Ababa. They found Harden in the hotel lobby and gave him the full story. He telephoned it to Washington that evening and it made the front page of the *Post* the next day.

Because of the time difference between Washington and Addis Ababa;[3] the *Post* story did not reverberate back to Ethiopia until late in the day of 1 May. The next morning Dawit told Harden that he was to be expelled within 24 hours (though through the Embassy's intervention with Information Minister Feleke, Harden was enabled to stay another week) and in a meeting with the foreign press denied everything: 'only' about thirty thousand people had left, all of their own free will; they had not been forced out by the army; their shelters had not been destroyed, and they had been given food, seed and tools so that they could return to their homes and farm. The rationale that Dawit gave for closure of the camp, which he admitted was the regime's intent, was that people must not become dependent, they must return and farm their land. It might have sounded entirely reasonable had one ignored the fact that most of the people were too weakened by famine or disease to farm, that their oxen were dead or sold, and that they were not given food to tide them over until a harvest or seed and tools with which to plant a crop. And of course it flew in the face of the Ethiopian government's main argument in justification of resettlement, namely that the land was too exhausted to be farmed. On 3 May, the Ethiopian Foreign Ministry issued a vitriolic statement denying that anyone had been forced out of Ibnet and denouncing the *Washington Post* story as a malicious lie, a product of American propaganda.[4]

After Dawit's denial, the burden of turning the Ethiopian regime around on this matter fell upon Jansson. It was a situation that required tact, firmness and courage, qualities for which the Finnish UN civil servant had a reputation and that he displayed in ample measure in this instance and at all other times during his ten months in Ethiopia. On 2 May he went to see Berhanu Bayih, the Politburo's co-ordinator for foreign assistance and the regime's fifth-ranked official. Berhanu, a short, thin and coldly reserved man, replied to Jansson's representation with the observation that what had been done at Ibnet was 'an ordinary thing'. That same day, despite bad weather, Jansson flew to Ibnet accompanied by two British journalists. On his return to Addis Ababa he met with Western ambassadors and told them that what he had seen and heard in Ibnet essentially confirmed what had been reported in the Western press. Jansson did however accept the RRC's figure of thirty-five thousand as the number in the camp before the expulsions. He may have seen this as a sop to the Ethiopian government, or he may have got conflicting testimony about the numbers in the camp. On 30 April, foreign workers at Ibnet had placed the number at sixty thousand but by 2 May they had been threatened with expulsion if they spoke candidly.

Jansson immediately sought a meeting with Mengistu. Four days passed before the audience was granted, on 6 May. Jansson told the Ethiopian leader that he had been to Ibnet and seen with his own eyes what had been done there. He called it 'unacceptable' and urged that steps to reverse the closure be taken immediately. To his surprise, Mengistu agreed, saying that he considered the action taken at Ibnet to be 'stupid'. It was done, Mengistu said, without the knowledge of officials in Addis Ababa. Jansson urged Mengistu to issue a press statement to this effect. The Ethiopian leader begged off with the excuse that it was late now for him to do so but said he would have no objection if Jansson wished to convey his 'clarification'. That same afternoon Jansson issued to the press and to Western donor embassies a written statement, headlined 'this is not a press release', in which he announced that Mengistu had told him that what had occurred at Ibnet was a mistake and had not been authorized by the government of Ethiopia. Jansson said Mengistu had promised that measures would be taken to punish those responsible and that the people expelled from Ibnet would be allowed to return and be given food and shelter there. Mengistu visited Ibnet a few days later. He is said to have spoken harshly to Melaku but no disciplinary measure was reported and Melaku kept his job.

Ibnet was reopened and destitute peasants began to return there in large numbers. Within a few weeks the camp's population surpassed its former level and by early June more than ninety thousand were there by official RRC estimate. This great number reflected the considerable distress of the population of eastern Gondar and western Welo and Tigray, caused as much by civil war as by drought. The Ethiopian army carried out an offensive in western Tigray and north-western Welo in March and April 1985, and there was heavy fighting in eastern Gondar too. Some of those who sought refuge in Ibnet both before and after its closure at the end of April were probably insurgents who had thrown away their arms. A substantial number of the women and children in the camps in Tigray and Welo were probably the families of insurgents. This, very likely, is why the camp was closed at the end of April, and it may explain why the Ethiopian government decided, soon after the camp's reopening, to close it a second and final time, at the end of June. This second closing was handled much more carefully than the first; the Ethiopian government did after all learn a lesson in public relations. They informed Western embassies and relief agencies well in advance; they assured that the camp would be closed gradually, over a period of weeks, and that no one would be forced out; and they said that all who left would be given adequate food, seed and tools to carry them through to the fall harvest. It was hard to believe any of this. But a gradual, orderly closing was much more difficult to contest than the sudden, brutal action that took place at the end of April. In July, the camp at Ibnet was closed for the second and last time.

*   *   *

The Ethiopian government's failure to face forthrightly the problem of cholera in the camps was another frustration for Western embassies and relief organizations. Sanitation in the camps was, unavoidably, very poor. This probably made cholera inevitable. It first broke out in a small camp in eastern Welo, in January. From there it quickly spread westward to the larger camps, at Bati, Korem, Alemata and Kobo, and southward where nomads carried it across the border into Somalia. As soon as the epidemic struck there, the Somali government made it known and appealed for international help to combat it. The Ethiopian government, however, refused to acknowledge that there was cholera in Ethiopia, though thousands died of it in the first half of 1985. The issue went to Mengistu and it was on his order that the Ethiopian government adopted its ostrich-like position. The reason he did so is obscure; perhaps the Ethiopian leader considered it inappropriate for a country that had chosen the path of socialism to have something so nasty as a cholera epidemic. But it could not be denied that there was a disease, and a name had to be found for it. So the RRC and the Ministry of Health called it 'acute diarrheal disease'. This worthy euphemism was understood by all, but the regime's wish to keep the whole thing quiet ruled out large-scale foreign assistance to combat cholera. At a meeting with Western embassies and relief organizations in mid-April, Dawit was taken severely to task about this by one relief worker who asked why cholera could not be called cholera? The questioner pointed out that the requirement to use the euphemism 'acute diarrheal disease' (even Western private relief agencies were forbidden by the government of Ethiopia from employing the word cholera) impeded the ordering of proper medicines and the taking of proper measures to prevent the disease's spread. The Ethiopian Vice-Minister of Health, himself a physician, replied with a half-hour lecture on the etiology of diarrheal diseases, never once mentioning the word cholera. Dawit, more candidly but flippantly, commented that 'on the Somali side of the border we call it cholera, here we call it acute diarrheal disease'. Predictably, by mid-summer, 'acute diarrheal disease' had reached Addis Ababa.

*   *   *

Though the Ethiopian government provided no food for distribution in the relief camps, it took care to assure that stocks should not run out in Addis Ababa. Peasants starving in remote areas could safely be ignored, for a time at least, but even a police state could not afford the risk of food riots in the capital. The September celebrations left the treasury depleted, so the regime first tried to get donations. I was called in by the Minister of Foreign Trade and was asked for a grant of 100,000 tons of grain to help feed Addis Ababa. Since this did not fall into the category of emergency humanitarian relief, Washington refused, but offered to sell grain to Ethiopia on concessional terms. The Minister was not interested. He asked the British, who also turned him down. In the end, the Ethiopian government bought 100,000 tons of wheat from France at below market price with provision for long-term, low-interest payment; and a second purchase was made from France, in the same amount and on the same terms, in the spring of 1985. Food supplies never ran out in the capital though there were often shortages. Western television correspondents arriving to cover the drought and famine found the long lines in front of the government's food stores — reopened after the September ceremonies — a graphic back-drop for the filming of their daily reports. To their disappointment, and even more to that of the local population, early in 1985 the stores on the main avenues were closed once and for all.

Even before the 1984 famine and the big foreign shipments that began to reach Ethiopia in the fall of that year, there were frequent rumors that the government was secretly siphoning off for its own use grain donated by Western governments for famine relief. These stories often came from exile groups or insurgent organizations and were, by their origin, automatically suspect. No large unauthorized diversion was ever proven. Even reports of donated grain being found in army camps or seen being unloaded from military vehicles could not be taken as proof of diversion, since in remote areas military transport and storage in military installations was the only reasonable way to protect food stocks intended for famine relief. But after the large relief shipments began to come in, cans of oil and bags of grain marked with US or EEC labels did begin to show up in market places in cities throughout Ethiopia. To a certain degree this was unavoidable. What was much more troubling were persistent reports from credible sources of the existence of a system under which the RRC, upon Mengistu's personal order, secretly transferred to the army or to the civilian administration stocks from warehouses where donated food was kept. It was, of course, never possible to verify or even to investigate these stories.

In the last months of 1984, under the impact of the drought and famine, Ethiopia opened its doors to Western visitors to an extent unknown since the mid-1970s. Western parliamentary delegations, government officials and journalists swarmed through Addis Ababa airport, along with representatives of charitable organizations come to find a project on which to spend their freshly raised monies. Platoons of new relief workers arrived. Any Westerner with cash to donate to the RRC — the winner of a New Jersey lottery showed up to pledge half of his windfall — was welcome. A typical Sunday morning at the VIP lounge at Addis Ababa airport found a British ministerial delegation in one corner, a French parliamentary group in another, a Finnish woman parliamentarian being interviewed here, an American mayor there, and scattered around the room a

UN mission, Abie Nathan and his Israelis, and half a dozen Western reporters on the prowl for a story.

One might have judged that the West was making a big comeback in Ethiopia, thanks to the massive aid it was sending. In this particular instance, however, appearance and reality in Ethiopia were even further apart than usual. The high level talks that Walters and Crocker had proposed to Foreign Minister Goshu when they met him in New York at the beginning of October 1984, and that Goshu said he welcomed, never materialized. The Americans had agreed with Goshu that the US side should draw up an agenda for talks and give it to the Ethiopians, who would make whatever changes and counterproposals they wished; once there was mutual agreement on the agenda, talks would be held. In the proposal that it put to the Ethiopian government, that I gave to the Ethiopian Foreign Ministry in mid-November, the United States took the significant new step of suggesting that it would be ready to help achieve a peaceful settlement in Eritrea. Months passed without any reply from the Ethiopians. When I left Addis Ababa the following July, eight months after the US agenda was given to the Foreign Ministry, there was still no answer, and when Goshu came to New York for the General Assembly again in October of 1985 he was still unable to reply. We were repeatedly assured that the US proposal was 'under consideration'. In fact we learned that in December 1984 the Foreign Ministry drafted a reply and sent it to Mengistu's office for approval, but there it was rejected. The Ministry was told that it should not raise the matter again, and it did not.

The Ethiopian regime, in fact, was greatly concerned to reassure its East bloc friends that its attitude toward them was not in the least affected by the food and money sent by the West. In the second half of December 1984 Mengistu made a ten-day trip to Havana, Moscow and several capitals in Eastern Europe. Mengistu seemed to regard the famine as a test of the steadfastness of his alliance with Moscow, one that he was determined to pass — and in fact did pass — with high marks. Early in 1985 civilian Marxist–Leninist ideologues for the first time emerged in top place among his advisors. Shimelis Mazengia, Alemu Abebe, Fassika Sidelel and Shewandagan Belete were credited with having gained Mengistu's ear and having urged radical measures upon him. The Ethiopian public promptly dubbed them 'the gang of four'. Mengistu's experience with the West and the Soviets during the fall of 1984 and early 1985 must have confirmed him in his preference for the latter. The West pestered him about feeding starving people in rebel-held areas, complained about lack of Ethiopian government support for emergency relief programs, and criticized resettlement. The Soviets and their Eastern European and Cuban followers did not importune him on any of these issues; they expressed no humanitarian concern about people on the rebel side, ran no programs for the hungry on the government side and did not protest about the use of coercion in resettlement or raise doubts about that program. In fact, Soviet aircraft carried thousands of peasants from Tigray and Welo for resettlement in the south-west and west, and their trucks and field hospital were immediately and unquestioningly dispatched in support of resettlement. If they could not offer more, they were at least very compliant.

On 9 February 1985 Mengistu made a dramatic appearance on television, a medium he used only rarely. He declared that the nation was facing a grave crisis as a result of the drought and famine. He proclaimed that his program for resettlement would free Ethiopia from the scourge of recurrent drought and famine. And he called for strict austerity and announced a program of special taxes: all employed persons were to pay one month's salary, firms would pay 2 per cent of gross annual earnings (which meant that the tax would have to be paid regardless of whether the firm made a profit) and peasants were to pay a flat rate of 40 birr. For his speech, Mengistu donned the uniform he had made for himself after returning from North Korea in October 1983: a rough blue cotton jacket, buttoned to the neckline, with large floppy collars, and trousers to match. He had worn it occasionally before but from that moment on it became his standard dress and was decreed to be the only acceptable business and official social attire for government and party officials. Gradually, Western business suits were shed and everybody, first Politburo members, then cabinet officers, then vice-ministers and office directors, changed to the new garb. By late 1985 all government employees salaried at more than $250 per month were required to adopt it. Some donned it with embarrassment, others with bitterness, complaining that after having lost their other freedoms they were now being denied even the freedom to choose how they should dress. Foreign Minister Goshu apparently so disliked it that he frequently reverted for ceremonial occasions to traditional Ethiopian garb.

Armed with orders from on high, the revenue service set out

energetically to collect the new taxes. There was astonishment when it was learned that they were to be applied to the army as well, even to the lower ranks of the soldiery. The considerable discontent that the taxes caused was heightened by an explosion of public exasperation, the product of a kind of psychological delayed timing mechanism, over the regime's profligacy during the previous September and its failure to act promptly on the drought and famine. Why, people asked, should they be told to tighten their belts when their government had spent so lavishly. Criticism of the regime became more open. There were rumors of conspiracies in the army to overthrow Mengistu. At the end of March some 30 middle-grade and junior officers were arrested and several were said to have been shot. Early in April a new set of austerity measures was promulgated: it established severe gasoline rationing, forbade driving on Sunday and restricted the use of government-owned vehicles by personnel below the rank of minister. These steps caused further acute discomfort among the urban middle class that staffed the government and the state enterprises. They must also have aroused discontent within the military, for at the end of April all the Brigadiers General in the Ethiopian army, 15 in number, were promoted to Majors General. Thirty-five Colonels were promoted to Brigadiers General. It was the largest senior promotion ever to take place in the Ethiopian army.

On 8 and 9 April Mengistu convened a plenary meeting of the WPE's central committee. In his speech he praised Soviet humanitarian assistance and called for strengthened relations with the 'socialist states'. He lashed out vehemently at 'American imperialism' and accused the 'imperialists' of aiding Ethiopian insurgent organizations militarily, economically and politically. He made no mention whatsoever of Western humanitarian assistance, though by that time the West had sent over 400,000 tons of grain since late the previous year, the United States approximately half of it. The main speakers after Mengistu were all pro-Soviet hardliners.

Mengistu's extreme rhetoric bred more extreme action. At the end of May Addis Ababa University and all other institutions of higher learning in Ethiopia — Asmara University, the Gondar medical school and the two agricultural colleges, at Alemaya and Jimma — were closed down just a few weeks short of the end of the school year, a timing that prevented the students from finishing course work and that delayed graduation. Students and faculty were packed off to the resettlement areas to build shelters and clear land.

In the days of the imperial regime the university had been a hotbed of dissent. Though the police occasionally entered the campus to arrest an extremist agitator, for the most part both students and faculty freely expressed their opinions, and student demonstrations were common. Now, students and faculty grumbled cautiously among themselves but quietly complied. A small incipient demonstration outside the university's main gate was quickly broken up and the would-be demonstrators hauled off for questioning and jail. A few days before they were bussed off to the resettlement areas, the students were convoked to the Congress Hall for a pep talk. They listened in silence as party officials harangued them. One had the temerity to ask why they were being taken from their studies, just a few weeks before completion of the semester, when there were plenty of unemployed in Addis Ababa. The answer that came from the podium was that the Party wanted the students to go. They were the future elites of Ethiopia. The party wanted them to get close to the people, to teach them and to learn from them.

Notes

1. With the money received from AID, Nathan bought tents and other equipment and arrived in Ethiopia in May with a team of a dozen Israelis. He never made it to Ibnet. The Israelis waited in their hotel rooms in Addis Ababa with mounting impatience while the government of Ethiopia, in full session, deliberated on their case for almost a week. Finally they were told that they could not work in Ibnet but would be welcome elsewhere. No reason was given for this decision. Evidently, however, the Ethiopian government was afraid to let a team of Israelis work in a relief camp that was no great distance from villages inhabited by Falashas. By that time, in any case, the Ethiopians had already decided to close Ibnet a second and last time.

2. This, regrettably, was not the only instance of official harassment of the American Embassy's Ethiopian — or American — staff. Ethiopian employees of the Embassy were frequently arrested and held for months on end without any charges ever being filed. The practice was clearly intended to intimidate the Ethiopian staff and make them more amenable to providing information on the activities of the American staff, but it was also meant to punish those Ethiopians considered to be too close and friendly to the Americans and to make life miserable for all who worked for the US Embassy. In May 1985, one of the Embassy's United States Marine guards was briefly abducted and beaten up by a group of thugs believed to belong to Mengistu's own personal secret security organization. The Embassy vigorously protested the arrests of its Ethiopian staff members and the assault on the Marine guard. For the most part, the Ethiopian government never bothered to reply. It did, however, answer the Embassy's note of protest over the incident in Gondar. It accused the Embassy and Senators DeConcini and Trible of exaggerating what had happened and of interfering in Ethiopia's internal affairs.

3. The Ethiopian capital is seven hours ahead of Washington on daylight saving time.

4. The text of this extraordinary document is reproduced in Appendix I.

THE CHALLENGES TO MENGISTU'S RULE

Whether by design or simply through pragmatic response, Haile Selassie transformed Ethiopia, during his 58 years of rule, from a primitive feudal empire to an incipient modern state. He consolidated central power by depriving regional rulers of their traditional autonomy; no more were they allowed to be kings, only, at most, great servants of the state. He created a standing national army, where before there had been only feudal levies, and a modern governmental structure. Under his rule institutions of higher learning were founded and the basis was laid for mass education. Policies and programs for encouraging economic development were launched. The Emperor's diplomacy made Ethiopia an active and respected player in African and even in world affairs. To a degree, the seeds of his own downfall were embedded in each of these measures, though it is hard to see how he could have hoped to survive nearly so long as he did if he had not taken them. In the end, the political, social and economic system that he brought into being was destroyed because its creator outlived his ability to carry on the task and, like many autocrats, failed to make adequate arrangements for his succession.

Though an absolute monarch almost to the end, Haile Selassie looked basically toward the Western model. His successor, Mengistu Haile Mariam, has, as we have seen, chosen to pursue the task of modernization of state and society in Ethiopia on the Soviet model. He has established state ownership as the norm in the industrial and commercial sectors and proclaimed collectivization to be the goal in the agricultural sector. He has created an enormous standing army, severed Ethiopia's links with the West and aligned it with the East, and set in motion sweeping social and cultural transformations. His vision is one of a unitary, totalitarian state in which regional and ethnic differences will be submerged by political ideology and all activities will be controlled and regulated by the party, the state and their various agencies. This, it hardly needs be said, is an ambitious program, particularly for a country that is among the poorest and most backward in the world and that by history and tradition has been given over to separatism and anarchy.

Since almost all African countries have single-party systems, sole leaders and state enterprises, and since military dictatorship and radical rhetoric are more the rule than the exception, there has been a tendency to classify the Ethiopian experiment as just another variety of 'African socialism' and Mengistu as another Nyerere or Mugabe. The label is a wholly mistaken one; neither Mengistu nor anyone else who could speak for his regime has ever used it, and the Ethiopian government would be the first to object if it were applied to it. The socialism that the Ethiopian regime proclaims is not based on vague notions of brotherhood or communialism and it is not eclectic or pragmatic. Though one cannot rule out that it may eventually develop a specifically Ethiopian twist here or there, the theoretical framework is Marxist–Leninist and strictly orthodox, on the model of the Soviet Union. The WPE declares itself a 'Marxist–Leninist vanguard party'. In his September 1984 speech, Mengistu announced the establishment of the People's Democratic Republic of Ethiopia to be the main and most immediate task of the party. Of this entity he had the following to say:

> The social basis, the organizational structures and the working procedures of the People's Democratic Republic of Ethiopia are based on the fundamentals of marxist–leninist state formation and working procedures . . . democratic centralism, socialist legality, internationalism and the conscious participation of the people are its defining characteristics.[1]

It has been very plainly stated that the criterion for socialism in Ethiopia is not what might work but what should be made to work, not pragmatic experimentation but dogmatic principle.

Can Mengistu succeed in the enterprise that he has embarked upon? The answer will depend on whether he can overcome the two most urgent problems facing Ethiopia, civil war and food production, and on whether the WPE and Marxist—Leninist ideology can be made to take root in Ethiopian soil. A closer look needs to be taken at these three issues and where they stand in the mid-1980s.

Civil War

The picture is a mixed one, on the whole more favorable to the Ethiopian regime than a few years back, but still far from being what could be called, by any stretch of the imagination, one of a problem on its way to assured resolution. It has been reduced to two main areas, Eritrea and Tigray, and to the two organizations that predominate in these areas, the EPLF and the TPLF. The many other 'liberation fronts' that once seemed a threat — the Oromo Liberation Front, the Afars, the Sidamo Liberation, the Somali Abdos, and the WSLF, to name the best known — are now of very little consequence. They blossomed amid the chaos of the 1970s, but none had a base broad or firm enough to assure it a flourishing existence against a government solidly entrenched in Addis Ababa. The WSLF was always mainly a creation of the government of Somalia. It found sympathy and support among ethnic Somalis in Ethiopia but it could not thrive without money, arms and personnel from Mogadishu. The Sidamo and the Somali Abdo liberation fronts were also in large part creations of the Somali government. The Afars, while fierce warriors and very obstreperous, are too small a group to pose a serious threat except in time of crisis at the center of power. The Oromos, of course, comprise the majority of Ethiopia's population, but they are very divided and are spread all around the southern half of Ethiopia. The OLF conducts sporadic hit-and-run operations in Wollega, Sidamo, Bale and even Harerge but its activities are too limited to make it much more than an annoyance. Christian Oromos are heavily represented in the government. To a much greater extent than was commonly realized, this was the case even under Haile Selassie, but revolution has brought Oromos, or persons of mixed Oromo–Amhara blood, to positions of power in large numbers. The overwhelming majority of the Derg was of these extractions. As a broad generalization, it can be said that the government's writ applies throughout the southern two-thirds of the country.

It is in the north that rebellion flourishes, not only in Eritrea, traditionally a fringe area, but in Tigray and large parts of Welo and Gondar, the heartlands of the ancient kingdoms of Ethiopia. The Eritrean and Tigrean rebellions have worked closely together and to a very large extent have reinforced one another; when the one has been under pressure from the Ethiopian army, the other has often come to its aid. Yet the two have very different roots and fundamentally different goals.

The Eritrean insurgency traces its immediate origins to 50 years of Italian colonization from the last decade of the nineteenth century through the defeat of Italian forces at the hands of the British in 1941. Italian colonial rule was often harsh and Italian laws set standards of racism that proponents of apartheid could only admire. Eritreans nonetheless benefited from the industry and commerce and the general level of cultural development that Italy brought to their country. The fruits of Italian colonization made Eritreans think of themselves as superior to their cousins in Ethiopia and, particularly among Muslims, reinforced pre-existing inclinations toward separatism. Eritreans in fact, however, have very little in common. Eritrea has none of the characteristics that ordinarily underpin a claim to self-determination; its population has no common religion, no common language, and no common ethnic origin. It is divided about equally between Christians and Muslims. There is some linguistic unity: Tigrinia and Tigre, semitic languages closely related to one another, are spoken by about three-quarters of the population, but Kunama and Afar count important followings. There is a multiplicity of ethnic and national groups, nine by the official count of the EPLF, the main rebel organization. The cement that binds Eritreans together is a common hatred of governments in Addis Ababa, be they monarchical or Marxist–Leninist, allied with the West or the East. The Eritrean rebellion probably owes more to the brutal and retrograde methods of the monarchy and its Marxist–Leninist successor than to any other one thing.

Cynical exploitation by foreign governments, seeking to promote their own aims, would come a close second. The Eritrean insurgency got its first infusions of foreign arms and money from Arab states, the conservative ones seeking to promote what they conceived to be the cause of Arabism and the radical ones to undermine Haile Selassie's pro-Western regime. This second reason caused the Soviets, the Cubans and the Chinese to join in. Soviet aid to the Eritrean insurgency in the late 1960s and early 1970s was surreptitious, extended through intermediaries, but the Cubans and the Chinese made little effort to disguise their support for Eritrean independence. The Chinese dropped the Eritreans in favor of Haile Selassie just as soon as the Emperor gave them the recognition they sought. The Cubans and the Soviets switched sides after Mengistu seized power. Qadhafi was an ardent supporter of the Eritreans until 1976 when he recognized in Mengistu a revolutionary of his own stripe and changed sides. Since the early 1980s most outside support has come from conservative Arab states, though Syria and Iraq have continued to offer some help to the Muslim Eritrean Liberation Front. The main motivation of the conservatives is now less to promote Arabism than to make life a little more difficult for the Marxist–Leninist regime in Addis Ababa. The EPLF has benefited from, and astutely exploited, a considerable body of public sympathy in Britain and France but in neither country has it got aid from the government. The United States has never given arms or money to the Eritrean insurgents, or entertained any direct contact with them, despite repeated allegations to the contrary by the current Ethiopian regime, though, as reported in the previous chapter, the United States in 1984 and 1985 did give food for famine relief to the ERA via Western private relief agencies.

As we have seen, in 1974 the Eritrean rebellion was on the wane and near to being reduced to hit-and-run operations. It was given a new lease of life by Mengistu and other hard-liners in the Derg who rejected General Aman's conciliatory proposals and sought a solution by force of arms. The turmoil into which the revolution threw Ethiopia's political and social structures offered the insurgents the prospect of victory, though they let it slip, because of inevitable internal divisions. By the early 1980s the Marxist–Leninist, predominantly Christian EPLF had almost eliminated its Muslim and Arab ELF rival. By then, however, the EPLF was on the defensive, though it managed more or less to hold its ground and even to make occasional local gains. Under Mengistu's personal direction, the Ethiopian army undertook yearly campaigns from 1979 through 1983, but the results were disappointing. The large Ethiopian army offensive of 1982 failed in its aim of taking Nacfa, a heavily disputed and by then wholly obliterated village in the northern coastal highlands. In January 1984, the EPLF took the offensive. It seized the town of Tessenai near the Sudanese border and the Ethiopian army garrison there fled to safety in Sudan. Then in battles in the northern coastal area it routed an Ethiopian armored division and took the small port and supply depot of Mersa Tekla. The EPLF hoped that these successes would mark a turning-point, the beginning of a comeback similar to that of the mid-1970s. Despite a spectacular raid on Asmara airport in May of the same year, in which some 15 Ethiopian military aircraft and two Soviet planes were destroyed or damaged, the EPLF's change in fortune has proven only momentary. In August 1985 the Ethiopian army retook Tessenai and Berentu. Then in the following months, having mustered a force of some two hundred thousand men, it launched its largest and most successful offensive since 1978. The army took scores of rebel-held villages, overran the EPLF's key agricultural area in the Baraka valley, and recaptured Mersa Tekla and most of the Red Sea coast. But the offensive foundered short of Nacfa with heavy casualties on the Ethiopian side.

One reason for this Ethiopian success is the change that took place in Khartoum in April 1985 when President Nimeiri was ousted. In Nimeiri's last years the EPLF and the TPLF enjoyed considerable support from the Sudanese government. Nimeiri's successors hoped to improve relations with Ethiopia. One of their first steps was to close the offices of the EPLF and the TPLF in Khartoum and severely restrict their cross-border operations. A second was that, after the attack on Asmara airport, Mengistu appointed a new commander in the north, General Merid Negussie, an officer who combines the functions of Chief Administrator of Eritrea and commander of northern zone military forces. This was an extraordinary step, for until then the two functions were kept in separate hands. It has proved a successful one. General Merid has impressed foreign visitors as intelligent, realistic and pragmatic, and eager to improve the lot of the Eritrean population; his major subordinates have shown much the same spirit. They have encouraged Western relief agencies to set up programs in Eritrea and have co-operated discreetly even with programs that allow people to come from rebel-held areas to collect relief food. On the military side, General Merid has moved quietly and cautiously to consolidate control over the areas held by the Ethiopian government and here and there to expand them.

Whether the Ethiopian government will see its way clear to exploit the favorable conditions created by the change of regime in Sudan and the more enlightened practices of a new civilian administrator-cum-military commander in Eritrea remains to be seen. It will have to overcome the temptation to try to use the southern Sudanese insurgency to make more trouble for the government in Khartoum. If Mengistu cannot bring himself to cut back his support for John Garang, the current Sudanese government, like Nimeiri, will after a while lose hope for an accommodation with Ethiopia and begin again to loosen the reins on the EPLF and the TPLF. The war weariness of the Eritrean population also offers the Ethiopian government opportunities, but there is a limit to what can be expected solely from a more enlightened attitude on the part of the local administration. Asmara is still a tense and very heavily patrolled city, one that looks half emptied of its population. The EPLF is not going to furl its flag just because of a momentarily unfavorable conjuncture of events, and prospects for serious negotiations between the EPLF and the Ethiopian government look no more promising now than in the past. In his September 1984 speech, Mengistu offered 'regional autonomy' within the framework of the People's Democratic Republic that is to be established. Just what this means has not been further defined. A return to genuine autonomy could cut the ground from under the Eritrean insurgency but it would have to be accompanied by serious guarantees. If Mengistu is offering only Soviet-style autonomy — and this is almost certainly what he intends — his proposal is not likely to have more than very limited appeal. In his September 1984 speech he ruled out any role for the EPLF by saying that the WPE 'is the sole organization which represents the aspirations of the working people of all nationalities'. As if to make the point absolutely clear, he added: 'Other than the Workers' Party of Ethiopia . . . there can be no other vanguard organization representing workers in Revolutionary Ethiopia today.'[2]

This uncompromising position, together with the expectation that all the Ethiopian government will have to offer Eritrea is fictional autonomy under tight central government control, makes it easy for the EPLF to justify continuation of the fighting even though prospects for achieving its declared aim of independence are practically nil. The result can only be more pointless destruction and bloodshed. Independence for Eritrea is a chimera. It would be a catastrophe for all concerned, Eritreans, Ethiopians and the peoples of neighboring countries. An independent Eritrea could not be self-sustaining, particularly if, as would seem unavoidable, it were cut off from its Ethiopian hinterland. It would be a pawn in the hands of whatever foreign power or powers cared to underwrite it with arms and money. It would never know peace because no Ethiopian government of any political stripe would ever come to terms with its independence. But unless the government in Addis Ababa can bring itself to offer Eritreans more than it has up to now, it is likely to face continuing civil war in Eritrea for a long time to come.

Fighting in Eritrea has been a mixture of guerrilla warfare and pitched battles. Ethiopian forces hold all the major towns and control the roads, though often only by daylight and even then with traffic moving only in convoy. The EPLF claims total control over the countryside; in fact, this frequently amounts to nothing more than an absence of effective Ethiopian government control. In the western and northern parts of Eritrea, the rebels' control has been nearly absolute and government forces have not entered; or, if they have tried, have had to face battle with EPLF troops armed with artillery and tanks. Elsewhere there is no sharp line delineating areas of insurgent influence from those where the government exercises some authority. The two interpenetrate and authority changes hand from day to night.

Fighting has been very bitter in Eritrea, and from time to time it has been alleged that the Ethiopian army has used poison gas there. There has been some testimony about an engagement in 1981 near Keren in which the Ethiopian army, with the assistance of the Soviet Union, was said to have employed poison gas. The Ethiopian government has angrily denied all such charges. When in a speech in December 1982 then US Deputy Representative to the UN, Kenneth Adelman, mentioned allegations of Ethiopian use of poison gas, the Ethiopian government threatened to break relations with the United States and apparently came close to doing so.

Fighting in Tigray, Eritrea's southern neighbor, is almost exclusively of a guerrilla warfare nature, yet the central government holds less of Tigray than it does of Eritrea. The Tigrean rebellion is a decade more recent than the Eritrean. It sprang up in the mid-1970s, under the impact of the dislocations caused by the revolution. In September 1974 Ras Mangesha Seyoum, Haile Selassie's governor of Tigray, ignored the revolutionary regime's summons to Addis Ababa and took to the Tigrean hills. There he set up an organization that he called the Tigrean Liberation Front and managed to win some support for it. He later brought it into the EDU. Most of the EDU forces that gathered in Sudan and that advanced into Ethiopia in 1977 were Ras Mangesha's Tigreans. After that time, however, his following dwindled and a group of Tigrean students of Marxist inclination, aided and inspired by the EPLF, seized control of the Tigrean insurgency. They proclaimed the Tigrean People's Liberation Front, which they announced to be to the left of the regime in Addis Ababa. The TPLF rapidly asserted control over the countryside, which is to say over more than 90 per cent of Tigray. Its activities spread into Tigrinia-speaking areas of neighboring Welo and into Gondar.

A substantial degree of mystery surrounds the Tigrean insurgency. At first glance it is not quite clear just why it should exist. Tigray is indisputably part of Ethiopia; unlike Eritrea, it has never led a separate existence. In fact, for a great part of Ethiopia's history it was the seat of the empire. The last emperor before Menelik II, Yohannes IV, was Tigrean. The rebellion is often attributed to Tigrean sense of pride and resentment that governance of Ethiopia should have fallen into other hands. This may play some role but it is far from being a satisfying explanation, particularly since Tigreans in the past accepted, albeit at times reluctantly, Amhara domination of the state. Regional particularism is, however, strong in Tigray, and the terrain, mountainous and very broken, is ideal for guerrilla operations. Tigray and the adjoining areas of Welo and Gondar are ecologically the hardest hit in Ethiopia. The substantial population of this once rich farming region can no longer eke a living from its cruelly eroded and deforested soil. Rebellion is a natural outlet in these circumstances.

The TPLF has not publicized itself in the West to anything like the extent of the EPLF. This in part accounts for the uncertainty over just what it represents and wants. It proclaims itself Marxist–Leninist and in the areas it controls it has applied many of the policies adopted by the regime in Addis Ababa. It prides itself on conducting not a rebellion but a 'people's war'. It appears to want autonomy, for it has called for 'the creation of voluntarily integrated nations and nationalities whose relations are based on equality, democracy and mutual advantage'.[3] But it has also threatened that, 'if the existing national oppression continues or is aggravated, then it means the birth of an independent and democratic state of Tigray'.[4] The threat can hardly be taken seriously. One must suppose that what the TPLF wants is to throw out the crowd in power in Addis Ababa and to set itself up as the government of Ethiopia.

It has no chance of achieving that goal but neither, it seems, does the government of Ethiopia have much prospect of bringing the Tigrean rebellion to an early end. The TPLF draws inspiration from the Weyane rebellion of 1942 and 1943, when Tigreans, under a charismatic outlaw leader, Haile Mariam Redda, tried to shake off Haile Selassie's just-restored rule. Haile Mariam made the mistake of confronting the Emperor's army, which was assisted by British artillery and air power, in a pitched battle. He was defeated and the rebellion was crushed. Taking its lesson from this, the TPLF has held rigorously to guerrilla tactics; it follows the guerrilla rule of never engaging a superior or equal force and never fighting at a time and place of the enemy's choosing. Its forces wait until they find a weak spot and then pounce. Its brief occupation, in October 1984, of the ancient town of Lalibela, capital of one of the kingdoms of medieval Ethiopia and site of magnificent churches carved out of the rock mountainsides, was typical of its *modus operandi*. For reasons unknown, the Ethiopian army had pulled its regular army garrison out of the northern Welo town and left it to the care of only a few companies of local militia. The TPLF moved in and quickly overwhelmed the militia. It held the town for several days and systematically looted government offices and supplies. As government forces approached down the only road linking Lalibela to the outside world, the TPLF disappeared into the fastness of the Lasta mountains.

The Ethiopians have resorted to the tactics traditional to armies that cannot find their enemies. They have destroyed crops, domestic animals and dwellings, and they have attacked concentrations of population wherever they could find them. The Ethiopian army has left scorched earth behind it in each of its offensives in Tigray and the Ethiopian airforce has frequently dropped napalm on villages and farmlands. This has caused enormous devastation which drought has compounded; during 1984 several hundred thousand Tigreans fled to Sudan in search of food. But it has also hardened the population of Tigray against the government and reduced practically to zero the chances of early conciliation. Is the government of Ethiopia practicing genocide in Tigray? Enough is known to ask the question but not to answer it definitively. What does seem certain, though, is that one of the major aims of the resettlement program is to empty Tigray as much as possible of its active population.

The Ethiopian government spends, according to reliable estimate, about 45 per cent of its annual budgets on military and security-related activities, one of the highest such levels in the world. This high level of expenditure is not wholly related to the civil war in northern Ethiopia, for Mengistu's regime would want a big army even if rebellion did not exist. So long as it does — and there seems little prospect that it can be brought to an early end — it will be very hard to reduce levels of military spending. Until they are reduced, the sums for investment in development needed to begin to break Ethiopia out of its poverty will simply not be available. The amounts called for in the regime's ten-year plan, which we shall discuss in a moment, will remain fanciful. Beyond this, however the insurgencies have other seriously damaging effects on Mengistu's government. Serious morale problems have been caused to the army by its inability, despite years of effort and massive infusions of Soviet arms, to suppress them. Dissatisfaction among officers and in certain units is a danger to the regime, one that will not go away so long as fighting drags on without prospect of early resolution. The insurgencies also undercut the regime's claim to legitimacy and foster disaffection among the population of the areas that it does control. Ethiopians have no more fondness than any other people for sending their sons off to fight, and possibly to die or be mutilated, in wars that have gone on so long that they seem never ending and, in the end, futile.

Food Production

Among the major projects given to the Ethiopian government's bureaucracy in preparation for the tenth anniversary celebrations was the drawing up of a ten-year development plan, Ethiopia's first ever. The plan itself was never published, but Mengistu announced its main points in his speech to the WPE founding congress. It called for an investment of 41 billion Ethiopian birr, or about $20b. over the ten-year period from 1984 to 1994 and set an overall average growth rate target for the Ethiopian economy of 6.9 per cent per annum. Agricultural production was to grow by 4.3 per cent a year and to have top priority, but a big push was also to be given to industry, which was to grow by 10.8 per cent per annum. The service sector was to advance at the rate of 6.9 per cent yearly.[5] It was a very ambitious plan. It took no account of the drought and famine that had already struck Ethiopia even before Mengistu's September speech. After the regime began to react to the drought and famine, in October, the public was told that this new development would prevent the plan's goals being reached on schedule, but the plan itself does not appear to have been scrapped. The main change was the reinforcement of the priority accorded to agriculture.

Agriculture is estimated to account for about 75 per cent of Ethiopia's gross domestic product, for about 90 per cent of employment and for practically all exports.[6] Until the Second World War, almost all farming was of a subsistence nature. This posed no particular problem, since cities were few and small. After the Second World War, as the urban population grew rapidly, large commercial farms began to come into existence. This caused dislocations, as the peasants who had farmed on lands given over to commercial farming found themselves displaced by machinery and in many cases joined the ranks of the unemployed in the capital. With the coming of the revolution, the commercial farms were nationalized and became state farms. The revolutionary regime took to state farms with great enthusiasm. They became Mengistu's pet project, for they seemed to fill both ideological need and economic necessity. They were seen as supplying the cities and at the same time giving the state an immediate sector in agriculture while awaiting the necessarily slower process of collectivization. The government tripled their area, from 72,000 hectares at the time of nationalization in 1975 to 221,000 hectares nine years later. It poured machinery, fertilizer, pesticides and the best available technology into them. They turned out to be a monumental disappointment, their average per hectare yield being not quite equal to that of peasants farming small plots without machinery or other modern inputs. In his September 1984 address, Mengistu himself acknowledged that 'the productivity of these farms has not been as satisfactory as expected . . .' But he attributed this to 'management weaknesses and various other problems', and insisted that 'their contribution . . . is not to be underestimated'.[7]

The land nationalization decree of 4 March 1975, a central feature of the revolutionary regime's program for destroying the old order, cancelled the peasants' debts and freed them of the requirement to pay rent to a landlord. But it set 10 hectares as the upper limit that a farmer could cultivate and forbade the hiring of labor, the acquisition of additional land or the sale of land. The ban on the hiring of labor set a practical limit of about 7 hectares, since that usually was the most that could be cultivated by traditional methods without hired help. While state farms and collectives were offered higher prices for their crops, individual peasants were made to sell their surplus, or a large part of it, to the state Agricultural Marketing Corporation at a fixed low price, unless they could somehow smuggle it on to the free market. Peasants who had land or who got it as a result of the March 1975 decree became better able to feed themselves and their families but did not become prosperous. They were deprived both of the ability and the incentive to produce a surplus. How could they do so when the rules put such strict limits on them? And why should they want to when they got so little for their crops and when there was so little available to buy with the small amount they could expect to earn? The result, inevitably, was a fall in per capita food production. In 1982 it was estimated to be only 81 per cent of what it had been in 1969–71.[8]

The Derg quite clearly had collectivization in mind when it issued the land nationalization decree in March 1975, for the decree's provisions made sense only if seen as leading in that direction. Still, it was necessary to move with caution. The peasantry had just got rid of the landowners and begun to savor its gains; it did not look gladly to interference by the state. The proclamation establishing agricultural collectives was issued on 26 June 1979. Early efforts to press peasants into collectives brought clashes between them and the authorities. The regime backed off. Collectivization was declared to be absolutely voluntary. Substantial inducements were offered to those who would collectivize: loans, seed, fertilizer and pesticide, and priority for water, electricity and social services. The response, however, was disappointing; the few who came forward were peasants with poor land or very small plots who had little chance of making it on their own. Those who were better off clearly did not like the idea of giving up their land and merging their efforts with those of others. In an effort to ease the peasantry into collectivization, the regime established a three-tiered system: at the bottom, service co-operatives, in which inputs are collectively purchased and outputs collectively sold but land continues to be held and cultivated individually; at the second level, collective ownership of machinery and of some land is added, with the peasant retaining a private holding; and at the third and top level, the producers' co-operative, a fully collectivized organization with all holdings in common. By the mid-1980s, however, only a few hundred producers' co-operatives were in existence. Many of these would not be self-sustaining without the special subsidies and incentives offered by the state.

Undeterred by these problems, Mengistu announced in his September 1984 speech that 'our main strategy will be the organization of the peasantry into producers' co-operatives and, parallel with this, the expansion of state farms'. He decreed that over the following ten years, '53 per cent of the agricultural population will be organized into producers' co-operatives . . .' and that the proportion of the land to be cultivated by producers' co-operatives would rise to 50 per cent. This, he announced, would be accompanied by a rapid infusion of modern technology into agriculture on a large scale that would rapidly increase productivity. Living conditions for the peasantry would be improved and their material and and spiritual life made 'fuller and more comfortable'.[9]

This rosy picture notwithstanding, the World Bank made a very strenuous effort in the second half of 1984 to persuade the Ethiopian government to give more incentive to private agriculture. Its proposals met with relieved agreement from experts in the Ministry of Agriculture, but when they were put to the regime's political level they were rejected. As a result, toward the end of 1984 the Bank shelved its plan to invest heavily in agricultural development in Ethiopia and substituted a more modest program. The EEC was scheduled to make a grant of 230 million ecus for agricultural development in Ethiopia in the spring of 1985. But with deep misgivings about wasting money on projects that would only deepen Ethiopia's dependence on Western food aid, it too tried to persuade the government to allow more scope for private farming. It got the same answer though with a special twist: Ethiopia, stunned EEC officials were told, has a socialist economy in which there will be no monetary incentives for production, only medals and certificates of appreciation. Plainly with the EEC and IBRD and perhaps other Western urgings in mind, Mengistu offered this comment in his September 1985 Revolution Day speech: 'if it is proved that a specific package of foreign aid or loan is incongruous with the country's path of development, welcoming such an aid is tantamount to restoring dependence or neo-colonialism which we had overthrown with a great struggle and sacrifice.'

By common consensus, Ethiopia has the potential not only to feed itself but to export food. Yet, since the revolution, it has fallen short of self-sufficiency even in good crop years. Some international organization experts in Ethiopia, speaking privately, estimate the deficit in food production attributable to bad agricultural policies to be 400,000 tons a year and growing. What is it that has made the Ethiopian leader so determined to pursue agricultural policies that have given such discouraging results in Ethiopia and failed so blatantly in their application in the Soviet Union, in Eastern Europe, and, earlier, in China? The answer is political. Mengistu explained it this way in his September 1984 speech:

> Organizing the peasants in producers' co-operatives helps not only to bring about a socialist economy and a reliable increase in productivity, but also ensures the supremacy of socialism in the political field. Thus there can be no alternative to making unstinting efforts for the growth and development of producers' co-operatives.[10]

And again: 'the socialization of rural production relations is impera-
tive. To think otherwise is to question the whole concept of socialist
construction.'[11] A Western ambassador in Ethiopia, in an off-the-
cuff comment, put it this way: Ethiopia's leaders, having chosen
socialism, do not see how they can have a socialist state with a
private agricultural sector, especially when agriculture occupies
such a large place in the national economy.

The regime knows that private farming, if freed from the
constraints that have bound it since 1975, would soon produce a
class of prosperous peasants. This it is too insecure to tolerate. It
fears also that the success of private farming would call into question
the entire structure of Ethiopia's relatively recent experiment with
state socialism and beyond that possibly even its credentials with the
Soviet Union. No matter how pressing Ethiopia's food problems,
for its government politics clearly comes first. Its agricultural
policies are intended first and foremost to produce not food —
though it is hoped and expected that they will yield food also — but
a specific political result that, depending on one's perspective, could
be called socialism, state socialism or communism. Dependence on
Western food aid is a painful thing for a government that prides
itself on having severed its links with what it calls imperialism. In his
speeches, Mengistu regularly laments this dependence and calls for
greater efforts to achieve self-sufficiency. Yet for political reasons
he rejects changes that could assure that result. So long as the
criterion for agricultural policies remains not what works but what is
politically acceptable and orthodox, it is doubtful that the Ethiopian
government will be able to show a significant measure of success in
food production. Production is in fact likely to decrease if the call in
the ten-year plan for 50 per cent collectivization by 1994 is
enforced.[12] In any event, Ethiopia is almost certain to remain
dependent on the West for food donations for many years to come,
even if it experiences no further droughts.

The Implantation of Marxism–Leninism

Ethiopia would seem a wildly improbably candidate for conversion
to Marxism–Leninism. It is a country with a population that for the
most part is deeply religious and whose intellectual and cultural ties
with the outside were, until the mid-1970s, anchored strongly and
almost exclusively in the West. It is easy to dismiss the idea that the

regime could succeed in implanting its political philosophy in Ethiopia or in winning an important constituency for its alignment with the Soviet Union. After all, the Soviets are widely and deeply unpopular and the regime itself arouses no popular enthusiasm; one has only to witness the apathy of the crowds, obedient but unresponsive, at Revolution Day ceremonies. It imposes itself through fear and coercion. But before drawing sweeping conclusions it would be well to have a closer look. We may find that this is an area where the regime stands not a bad chance of modest success over time.

It might be argued that religion poses an insuperable barrier to Communism in Ethiopia. Neither Christianity nor Islam is a recent import. The Ethiopian Orthodox Church traces its origins back to the fourth century. Ethiopian Christians are on the whole deeply observant, and their government's espousal of Marxism–Leninism seems to have made them more so. (Several of the regime's top figures are said to retain ties to the church and many wives of senior figures — allegedly including Mengistu's — attend church services. Most of those who made the revolution are still relatively young, but those who die invariably have Christian funerals.) For many, reaffirmation of attachment to the traditional faith has become a safe means of quietly affirming one's opposition to the secular order of things. Religious feelings run deep and strong. In May 1985 an angry mob foiled an attempt to desanctify a small church in Addis Ababa. The mob beat to death the priest and the deacon caught removing the arc of the covenant from the church. They thought it was going to be made over into a reading room for Marxist–Leninist propaganda.

Anyone who has been to Addis Ababa in recent years can testify that the streets around the churches are crowded with faithful on Sundays and holy days. But one generally sees very few young men among these crowds. The regime and the Party have mounted an energetic drive toward indoctrination of the young. Indoctrination sessions for youth are frequently held on Sunday mornings. Since the late 1970s the teaching of Marxism–Leninism has been obligatory at the university and secondary school levels. To graduate from high school and university, students are required to show proficiency in expounding Marxist–Leninist doctrine and in interpreting current events according to it. In 1985 the teaching of Marxism–Leninism was extended to elementary education. Clearly, the tactic is to focus on the young while leaving the old to their faith and their ways. Many adult practicing Christian Ethiopians fear that it may be working.

On the whole the regime has been cautious in its dealings with religion. The Derg did not move to depose Haile Selassie until the Ethiopian Orthodox Patriarch, Archbishop Tewoflos, endorsed the revolution. The land nationalization decrees of 1975 stripped the Ethiopian Orthodox Church of its large rural and urban holdings. Tewoflos, judged too independent and headstrong, was arrested in 1976 and has not been heard from since. Subsequently, more malleable figures have headed the Ethiopian Orthodox Church. The Church carefully stays out of politics. It has been given a state subsidy and is kept under close watch, but it has not been harassed. Other Christian sects have not been so fortunate. The Protestant sects — the regime calls them the 'new religions' — were persecuted to one degree or another by the imperial regime. Persecution has continued and become more harsh since the revolution. Several of these sects have wide followings, in particular Makane Yesus (a name that can be roughly translated as 'Camp of Jesus'), a Protestant faith with a native clergy. Makane Yesus developed a wide following in Wollega and in north-eastern areas of Bale and Sidamo. In some districts it has been tolerated but in others — particularly in Wollega — its leaders have been arrested and its churches closed. These sects do not have hierarchies that lend themselves to state control. They do not take subsidies from the Ethiopian state. And they have relations with Protestant churches in the United States and Western Europe, causing them to be viewed as potentially subversive. Makane Yesus has at times been identified with the OLF. For all these reasons, the regime harasses the Protestant sects, but it has stopped short of trying to suppress them.

Islam has been treated more gently even than orthodox christianity by the Marxist–Leninist government of Ethiopia. It suffered discrimination under the monarchy but since the revolution Muslim holy days have been given official recognition and the building of new mosques has been permitted. In part this is simply because the Derg wanted to show itself to be enlightened where its imperial predecessor was obscurantist. It is also in deference to the sensitivities of Libya and South Yemen, Ethiopia's two radical Arab friends, and to avoid giving conservative Arab regimes a pretext to incite Ethiopia's Muslim population. As though in recognition of its good fortune, Islam in Ethiopia has confined itself entirely to the spiritual realm. It is exclusively of the Sunni persuasion and thus not susceptible to the political fervors of Khomeini's Iran. It has shown no interest in politics, though it is keenly aware that it comprises at least half the population and probably more.

Muslims in fact play almost no part in Ethiopia's government. The current Ethiopian leadership is Christian almost to a man, even down to its secondary level; there is only one Muslim in the Cabinet (at the time of this writing, early 1986), Minister of Transportation and Communications Yusuf Ahmad, and only three altogether in the 120-member Central Committee of the WPE. Marxist–Leninist governments have had considerable success in undercutting Christianity in the Soviet Union, Eastern Europe and Cuba. Ethiopian history offers no clear-cut instruction on the matter of whether Ethiopian Orthodox Christianity poses a barrier to the penetration of foreign faiths or ideologies. There is the interesting instance of the seventeenth-century emperor, Susenyos, who was deposed, in 1632, for having gone over to Catholicism in order to obtain arms from the Portuguese to fight a Somali invasion. But history also teaches that Christianity was imposed in Ethiopia largely from the top down, through edict of the ruler.

The Ethiopian Orthodox Church cautiously stays out of politics but it does not abet the regime; it bides its time. It and the various Protestant sects are likely to continue to lead vigorous existences, for the Ethiopian people want and need them. But with the educational system and the mass media under the complete control of a regime dedicated to the propagation of Marxism–Leninism, they cannot be counted on to arrest the progress of the official ideology.

The Workers Party is supposed to play a central role in the regime's effort to implant itself and assure its long-term success. The Party, it is true, is far from being representative. The government has been unusually candid on this point; on the eve of the founding congress, the Ethiopian press reported that 65 per cent of the WPE's membership was drawn from the personnel of government and the military. In his address to the founding congress, Mengistu acknowledged that 'there still are many areas which the party structure has not reached and where party bodies have not been set up'. He attributed this to 'the need to be strict in our recruitment policy' and to avoid 'unnecessary delay'.[13] In fact, recruitment policy has hardly seemed discriminating. Many upper- and mid-level bureaucrats in Addis Ababa joined because they were told that they would lose their jobs if they did not; others in less key positions signed up so as to keep open their prospects for advancement. No figures have been released on the size of the Party. Educated guesses give it between twenty-five and forty thousand members for all of Ethiopia, not a great number when one considers that the country's population is estimated at over forty million. In rural areas the Party apparatus is weak or in places non-existent. But it is well established in all the towns and has taken over large, centrally located buildings in Asmara, Harar, Dire Dawa and Gondar.

It is tempting to dismiss the WPE as a body of very little importance, one created by the regime solely for purposes of symbolism. This would be a mistake. Mengistu has underscored the importance he attaches to it by putting his new title of General Secretary ahead of those of Chairman and Commander in Chief of the Armed Forces; unquestionably he sees its role as that of carrying out his directives. Thanks to the support he has given the Party, its officials have quickly come to exercise considerable power. The regional and district party secretaries have taken precedence over the chief civilian administrators. Western relief workers have found that the local party secretary, not the administrator or his staff, is the one to turn to for getting things done. In Addis Ababa, personnel of the various government departments, among them the Foreign Ministry, were by the fall of 1984 complaining that they could make almost no decision without the Party's approval, a sure sign that it was asserting its authority. A network of political commissars was also set up in the army.

By its very existence the party helps create a bulwark for the regime. Because of the jobs and privileges they derive from Party membership, a whole new category of people has a stake in the system. To a large extent, the same can be said of Ethiopians returning from study in the East bloc. According to official Soviet figures, the Soviet Union provides 'over 500' scholarships a year to Ethiopian students at the undergraduate and postgraduate levels, and the number currently in these programs is nearly 2,500.[14] If shorter technical training programs are included, the number of Ethiopians studying in the Soviet Union must be much higher. Figures for Ethiopians in school elsewhere in the East bloc are not available but East Germany, Bulgaria and Cuba all have large training programs; it is estimated that some twenty thousand young Ethiopians have passed through the Cuban center for indoctrination and technical training on the Isle of Pines. When these students finish their studies, they return to an academic, governmental or state enterprise milieu in which older, Western-trained Ethiopians predominate. Their integration is often difficult and conflicts are frequent; the older Western-trained generation, much of which is disaffected from the regime, considers that those trained in the East have an inferior education. Many Westerners and Western-trained Ethiopians assume that young Ethiopians who study in the Soviet Union will come back disenchanted with the Soviet system. This seems to be the case for some but for others the investment made in learning Russian, and the sense of belonging to a group that is at odds and in competition with Western-educated Ethiopians seems to override whatever reservations they may have about the Soviets, the Ethiopian regime and its alignment with the Soviet Union.

While the number of students going to the East has soared since 1977, the flow to the West has diminished substantially. The regime permits study in the West (though since 1984 military service has been invoked as grounds for denying permission to leave the country), but it allows no money to be taken out of Ethiopia for it. A surprising number of middle-class Ethiopian families still manage to get their children to the United States, and even a few senior officials of the regime have children in the West. Many of those who study in the West, however, will probably not come back. Students going to the East bloc have no choice but to return, and they are beginning to come back in considerable numbers. Western-educated Ethiopians are a major asset for their country and for the West but one that is not being renewed. The face that Ethiopia presents to the outside world will change almost beyond current recognition in the years ahead as the Western-educated leave the scene and are replaced by those trained in the East or in Ethiopia only. This will certainly affect Ethiopian attitudes toward East and West, though just how is hard to gauge. Westerners who know Ethiopia well doubt that the mere fact of an education in Moscow will cause the sons and daughters of this proud and intelligent people to lose either their critical sense or their deep feelings of national identity.

Notes

1. *Central Report Delivered by Mengistu Haile Mariam* (Addis Ababa, September 1984), p. 30.

2. Ibid., p. 45.

3. 'Tigray', document submitted by the Foreign Relations Bureau of the TPLF to the 36th session of the UN General Assembly, September 1983, p. 10, cited by Gebru Tareke in 'Resistance in Tigray, from Weyane to TPLF', *Horn of Africa*, vol. 6, no. 4 (1983–4), p. 25.

4. Ibid.

5. *Central Report Delivered by Mengistu Haile Mariam*, p. 87. In theory at least, higher growth rates could be achieved for industry with investments much smaller than those required to move agriculture up at a slower pace, owing to the small size of industry in the economy and the very large size of agriculture.

6. Ethiopia's major exports are coffee, hides and oil seeds.

7. *Central Report Delivered by Mengistu Haile Mariam*, p. 54.

8. Theodore M. Vestal, 'Ethiopia's Famine: A Many-Dimensioned Crisis', *The World Today*, July 1985, p. 125.

9. *Central Report Delivered by Mengistu Haile Mariam*, pp. 67–8.

10. Ibid., p. 35.

11. Ibid., p. 67.

12. Late in 1985 the Ethiopian regime started a program of 'villagization' under which peasants have been forceably moved off the land they cultivate, obliged to tear down their houses there and set them up again in new specially created centers. The regime says the measure is needed to enable it to provide educational, social and sanitary services to the peasantry. The explanation would be more persuasive if the regime had the means to provide these services or even the serious intention of doing so anytime soon. In fact, 'villagization' aims at strengthening political control over the peasantry and at opening the way for collectivization of agriculture. It will surely set off a decline in agricultural production that will unavoidably be accelerated as collectivization follows. It has already transformed the rich countryside between Addis Ababa and Debre Zeit and in the area around Harar. Amhara farmers in much of Gojjam have resisted — at times violently — and the regime has put the program on hold there.

13. Ibid., p. 144.

14. Anatoly Gromyko, speech before the eighth International Conference of Ethiopian Studies, November 1984, Addis Ababa.

CONCLUSION

The tenth anniversary of the revolution, celebrated in September 1984, was supposed to mark a decisive stage in Ethiopia's development along the new socialist path chosen for it. Unquestionably, a certain symbolic importance attaches to the occasion. It was chosen as the moment for the proclamation of Ethiopia's official vanguard Marxist–Leninist party, itself heralded as the prelude to the coming establishment of the People's Democratic Republic of Ethiopia. To the deep embarrassment of the Ethiopian regime, and as we have seen not wholly by accident, it coincided with Ethiopia's worst famine of the twentieth century.

As Mengistu reminded his audience in the Great Hall of the People on that particular September day, ten years is not a very long time in which to remake a backward society. In fact, a more appropriate ten-year point from which to judge the Ethiopian leader's achievements might be February 1987, the decennium of his seizure of sole power. Before 1977, Mengistu played an enormously important — perhaps decisive — role, but authority was still shared; he was not yet free to give Ethiopia his unique imprint. Had he been supplanted, others would surely have taken Ethiopia in different directions which would very likely also have been more humane. Since 1977, power has been his alone, within the vague natural limits that peoples tolerate the exercise of sole power by dictators.

A balance sheet drawn up for this second and more important ten-year anniversary would have to give Mengistu credit for holding Ethiopia together in 1977 in the face of the onslaught of the Somalis and the Eritreans, a time when a man of less firm resolve might have faltered. But account would also have to be taken of the fact that Mengistu's own policies contributed substantially to the 1977 crises. Conciliation might have worked in Eritrea had the Derg chosen it, instead of confrontation, in 1974. If it had, many tens of thousands of lives would have been spared in Eritrea in the years that followed, and the bloodshed and destruction of the Somali invasion might have been avoided. More clearly on the positive side of the ledger, Mengistu would have to be given credit for the great advances in literacy and education achieved under his rule, and for the social mobility that has come about. Possibly the most heartening sight in

Ethiopia of the 1980s, in many villages as well as in the cities, are the masses of children trooping to and from school, notebooks and pencils in hand. Facilities for elementary, secondary and university education have been expanded enormously. A university education has come within reach of the sons, and to a lesser extent the daughters, of peasant farmers and urban manual laborers. Literacy has advanced from an estimated 6 per cent before the revolution to an officially claimed figure of 60 per cent at the time of the tenth anniversary. All this, of course, has its reverse side. Many of those recorded as literate can hardly do more than read and write their own names, and the enormous expansion of education has inevitably been accompanied by a serious decline in its quality. Still, the achievement is a praiseworthy one, though to recognize it as such is not to say that it justifies the slaughter of the revolution and the red terror or the cruel repression of subsequent years. All could just as well have been done under a more enlightened government.

The balance sheet for the critical areas examined in the last chapter is susceptible of more clear-cut interpretation. In the war in the north, though the regime has no realistic political solution, it has made some military advances. But an end to the fighting is nowhere in sight, in Tigray even less than in Eritrea. Though food production has been declared a major priority, agriculture has been a disastrous failure, not essentially — as the regime claims — because of drought, deforestation or soil exhaustion but because of policies dictated by ideology and designed to achieve political goals more than to produce food. The regime has made some progress toward establishing a power base for itself. But the very great majority of Ethiopians remain estranged from it and will stay that way until their government makes itself less arbitrary and its record on the critical issues of civil war and food production shows substantial improvement.

The regime's accomplishments so far are not the ingredients of success but they are enough for survival. Examples abound of Third World regimes that hang on against all apparent odds. Mengistu's chances have to be rated at least fair. He is in his mid-forties and in good health; rumors that he is seriously ill crop up in Addis Ababa from time to time, apparently the result of wishful thinking, but all seem without foundation. He is alert and quite as ruthless as ever. Though repressive measures have softened somewhat, Mengistu's name alone inspires something like terror among Ethiopians; those who think they might be in earshot of an informer pronounce it in hushed tones of awe. Individuals known to be out of sympathy with the regime are kept under close watch, though they are usually not arrested so long as they stay silent and out of suspicion of trouble. Active opposition, criticism of the regime or dissidence of any kind are grounds for arrest, prolonged detention or execution. Like the people's democracies that the Ethiopian government aspires to imitate, Ethiopia's laws theoretically guarantee a gamut of rights that in practice do not exist. Secret police, arbitrary arrest and the use of informers were all practices of Haile Selassie's regime, but the revolutionary regime has carried them far beyond anything previously known. As a result the public is cowed and visible opposition does not exist. (The reader interested in more detail on human rights problems in Ethiopia is referred to the annual reports issued by Amnesty International and by the Department of State.)

Mengistu's regime faces no threat from a spontaneous outburst of public dissatisfaction like the one that toppled his neighbor Nimeiri early in 1985, at least so long as food supplies for Addis Ababa are assured. People know that any demonstration against the regime, or any demonstration not sponsored by the regime, would be quickly and brutally suppressed. The danger to Mengistu's person and rule, if danger there should be, would most probably come from a lone assassin or from a military coup. The likelihood of the former is essentially unknowable and of the latter unpredictable. As might be expected, Mengistu pays a great deal of attention to the army. He has gone to great lengths to win its loyalty and has dealt with those suspected of disloyalty or found in dereliction of duty with extreme severity. While there is good reason to believe that discontent among officers and troops is in certain cases substantial, the army like the public seems cowed. The sheer size of the military establishment makes a coup difficult. In a small army the commander of a division or even lesser unit might reasonably hope to prevail even if he could not rally others. In a body numbering over three hundred thousand, a successful conspiracy would probably have to involve a large number of senior officers, with the risk of detection growing as the numbers increased. The regime's final bulwark, of course, is the security apparatus. The Ministry of National and Public Security, run by Mengistu's long-time and loyal associate Tesfaye Wolde Selassie, seems generally to be an efficient organization. Mengistu also has his own separate security service, in which Cubans and possibly also Soviets work.

The next move on Mengistu's agenda is the establishment of the

People's Democratic Republic of Ethiopia. This has been long talked about and long delayed, but Mengistu now seems to promise it very soon; in his September 1985 Revolution Day speech the Ethiopian leader declared that 'we are now at he eve of the realization of the PDRE'. This institution is to replace the avowedly provisional apparatus (the Ethiopian Government's formal title since the overthrow of the Emperor has been the Provisional Military Government of Socialist Ethiopia) under which Ethiopia has been ruled since the revolution. The exact form that it will take has not been announced; a commission has been at work drafting a constitution since early 1984. The main question at issue seems to be how closely the constitution and the new institutional arrangements will follow the Soviet model. The Soviets have so far not been ready to give formal recognition to Ethiopia as a fully-fledged 'socialist' state. The most they have been willing to accord it was 'socialist-oriented state' or 'revolutionary democratic state'.[1] If the constitution and structure of government proclaimed for the PDRE follow orthodox Soviet lines, logic would seem to require that the Soviets bestow upon Ethiopia formal membership in the socialist community of nations. This would have the implication of locking Ethiopia even more closely, and perhaps permanently, into Soviet embrace. Presumably it would require the Soviets to shoulder greater responsibility for Ethiopia's economic development than they have been interested in doing so far. The standard Soviet prescription for Ethiopia has been a heavy flow of arms but no great effort on the economic side. There seems to have been tacit understanding between Mengistu and the Soviets that he could turn to the West for whatever he could get in the way of economic aid so long as political and ideological principle were not sacrificed. Formal membership in the bloc would presumably call this policy into question by obliging Ethiopia to join Moscow's Council for Mutual Economic Assistance, a move that it seems hesitant to make.

There could be other implications too. The establishment of Ethiopia as a fully-fledged bloc state would raise the prospect of Soviet military intervention in Ethiopia to quash any upheaval that would threaten to bring about a reversal or even a slackening in its political alignment. Given the distance and the many other obstacles involved, military intervention by the Soviet Union may seem a far-fetched, unreal prospect. The Soviets would surely prefer to avoid it, for it would meet with strong Western and African objections and would risk causing Ethiopians to rally against them; it would be a far more complicated operation than the one they so ill-advisedly plunged into in Afghanistan in December 1979. But the Soviets have an enormous stake in Ethiopia, larger in monetary and probably even in political value than the one the United States had at the beginning of the 1970s. It is hard to believe that they would stand by and allow it to be lost, even if Ethiopia does not assume full membership in the bloc. It is not unthinkable that Moscow might, in certain circumstances, feel itself impelled to intervene to tip an uncertain balance. The example of South Yemen gives reason for concern. There, in January 1986, the Soviets intervened with their aircraft, gunboats and numerous military trainers to back forces that overthrew President Mohammed Ali Nasser, a leader who, while pledged to Moscow, had begun to show disturbing signs of independence.

Part of the reason for the long delay in the proclamation of the PDRE may be difficulty in reaching a decision over how fully integrated Ethiopia is to become into the Soviet system. Mengistu and his coterie give every indication of wanting to strengthen their ties with the Soviet Union, but such a policy enjoys hardly any popular support. The Soviets want to consolidate their position, but they clearly are not eager to take on heavier financial responsibilities. In his September 1985 Revolution Day speech, Mengistu seemed to want to reassure Moscow that he would not expect it to assume added burdens. He put it this way:

> [the] relation between developing and socialist countries is, of course, free from exploitation but is at once a relation in which the developing countries themselves will have to meet the obligation expected of them, i.e. it is not one in which they are permanent beneficiaries, nor can it be so either.

Western governments must wish that the Ethiopian leader would apply the same scruple in his dealings with them.

For the West, Ethiopia's turn eastward was a considerable shock, albeit one that took a while to be felt. It has meant many things. On the global level, it contributed measurably to the West's disillusionment with *détente* and to the subsequent rise in East–West tensions. Regionally, it has meant the loss of an important and strategically located partner and has raised fears that the governments of neighboring countries, some even more important to the

West's security and prosperity, could be put in danger. This threat runs a gamut of gradations. At the low end of the spectrum, it is simply a matter of the indirect impact beyond Ethiopia's borders of the domestic strife into which that country has been plunged by the policies of its government. Ethiopia is the heart of the Horn and its sorry state has infected the whole of the region with instability. Its government's policies have sent hundreds of thousands of its citizens fleeing in refuge to Somalia, Sudan and Djibouti, creating enormous burdens for those countries. An Ethiopia moving forward in moderation and economic development, encouraging its people to produce and trade, could lead the region toward a modest degree of prosperity. An economically successful and politically stable Ethiopia would have many kinds of influence on its neighbors. An Ethiopia in a state of continual economic and political turmoil makes it difficult for any other country in the region to calculate its own course and precludes all the others from effective common effort in the developmental field. Further up in the spectrum is the danger that Ethiopia would try to overthrow neighboring pro-Western governments, either indirectly by under- mining their stability or even conceivably — taking advantage of its overwhelming military superiority — through direct military pressure on them. The Ethiopian government's support for the opponents of the governments of Sudan and Somalia and its fostering and abetting of discontent in those countries is in part tit for tat in response to the low grade subversion that from time to time has been directed against it from Somalia and Sudan. But its military action against Somalia in the summer of 1982 was palpably not just a reprisal for an attack by the WSLF but also a deliberate effort to topple the Somali government. Though it loudly proclaims that it wants only to be left alone to develop its country, quite clearly Mengistu's regime is uncomfortable over being surrounded by governments friendly toward the West. It would welcome having more ideologically and politically compatible neighbors and is ready to do what it can, within the limits of caution, to promote that objective.

   In the years since Ethiopia moved into the Soviet orbit, Western governments have not ceased to hope that it could be coaxed into something like genuine non-alignment. A return to the partnership that existed between Ethiopia and the West before the revolution is patently out of the question, but a more balanced relationship, one in which the West would no longer find its interests in the area threatened, seems a reasonable and realistic goal. There have,

naturally, been differences of opinion among Western governments, mainly between the United States and Western Europe but
also among Europeans, over how to get there. Some in Western
Europe, and a few in the United States, have tried to resolve the
problem by denying that it exists, that is by inventing for the
Ethiopian government a non-alignment that in its more serious
statements even it does not claim for itself. This position, never
really tenable, has been pretty thoroughly demolished by the
Ethiopian regime's actions in recent years.

The mainstream of opinion in Western Europe has favored
offering Ethiopia economic assistance, promoting trade and
extending the hand of friendship even if it is — momentarily only, it
is hoped — spurned. This is the policy practiced to one degree or
another by all Western European governments since the Ethiopian
revolution. It is essentially a waiting policy, one that aims to 'keep a
foot in the door'. The Europeans have in general not undertaken
initiatives specifically aimed at bringing about early changes in
Ethiopian policy. Their approach has been essentially to rely on
time, goodwill, and a large measure of hope, to effect the desired
modifications in Ethiopia's behavior. So far, this approach cannot
be said to have been successful, except in a fairly marginal way. The
development money that Western governments have put into
Ethiopia since 1977, directly or through the EEC, has not brought
Ethiopia closer to non-alignment and has not bought Europe
influence with the Ethiopian government, only that vague and
insubstantial commodity called presence. Western European
officials visiting Addis Ababa get a polite reception, even a warm
one when they come with their check books, but nothing more.
Their aid, when it is properly used, contributes something to the
improvement of living standards, or at least helps keep them from
going too much downhill, but it also bolsters the position of the
Ethiopian government, and by extension that of the Soviet Union in
Ethiopia.

This same general approach guided the Carter administration's
1978 initiative. The latter's failure, and Ethiopia's move closer to
the Soviet Union at the end of the decade, set the stage for the more
ambitious policy of the Reagan administration. This policy was, in
fact if not in design, not totally unlike that of the United States'
European allies. After some internal debate, the Reagan administration agreed in 1983 to allow Boeing to sell two 767 passenger
aircraft to Ethiopian airlines. An educational and cultural affairs

program was re-established at the American Embassy in Addis Ababa beginning in 1983, and it met with an enthusiastic response from the Ethiopian public. As we have seen, when drought and famine struck Ethiopia, the United States became the largest donor of food aid. The Embassy persistently but quietly pushed for compensation for American citizens whose holdings were seized in 1975, and the Ethiopian government finally began to address itself seriously to this issue in June of 1985; the settlement reached in December of that year, although long overdue, removed this unnecessary irritant in US–Ethiopian relations.

Through all these steps the United States sought to show the Ethiopian government and people that it valued its ties with them and that it wanted closer relations. At the same time, the Reagan administration wanted to see an early change in Ethiopia's policies and was not ready simply to wait for that to happen. To that end it pressed for high-level talks with the Ethiopian government. It wisely rejected the idea of trying to bring pressure on Ethiopia through aid to the insurgencies, but it did, albeit with little success, try to encourage its European allies to press Ethiopia more vigorously. The extensive American effort to engage Ethiopia in talks did not succeed in bringing Mengistu's government to the bargaining table, only in exposing its lack of interest in any serious improvement in relations with the United States. But the United States was successful in persuading Mengistu that military pressure on Somalia would not pay.

In the decade since Ethiopia fell into turmoil, Western governments have held frequent consultations on policy toward that country and toward the Horn of Africa generally, but so far these consultations have not led to unity of approach. Western governments going their different ways may have been justified when there seemed grounds for legitimate difference of opinion over the nature of the Ethiopian regime, its domestic developmental policies and its ties with the Soviet Union. An experience of nearly ten years with the government of Mengistu Haile Mariam has disappointed many Western hopes but also dispelled many Western illusions. It is time now for Western governments to come together on this important issue, to give it more attention and to work more closely together to respond to the challenges that the crisis in Ethiopia poses for them.

Note
1. These terms were used by Anatoly Gromyko in 'Socialist Orientation in Africa', *International Affairs*, no. 9 (1979), pp. 95–104.

APPENDIX I: PRESS STATEMENT BY THE MINISTRY OF FOREIGN AFFAIRS OF SOCIALIST ETHIOPIA

The Ministry of Foreign Affairs of Socialist Ethiopia has learned with great outrage the shockingly big lie about the alleged burning of a feeding station at Ibinat in Gondar. While the reported incident never took place, what has been surprising to note has been the audacity of high ranking officials of the Reagan Administration to go berserk once again on their usually familiar anti-Ethiopian campaign of denigration, disinformation and falsification.

To put the record straight, 30,000 able bodied persons left the Ibinat feeding station of their free will. Just before their departure, they were furnished with sufficient food to eat, seeds to plant and farm implements. Assistance continues to be provided for 25,000 drought affected compatriots.

In the light of the above facts, the so-called incident at Ibinat is therefore a clear demonstration that officials of the U.S. Administration will not spare the slightest pretext no matter how detached it might be from reality, in their effort to besmirch, and, if possible, to sabotage the striving of the Ethiopian Government to contain the effects of the debilitating drought affecting the country.

It is the height of folly for officials of the U.S. Administration to hope against hope that the policy of the Ethiopian Government on relief matters, resettlement or any other related issues have to be formulated in Washington. The management of the relief camps in Ibinat was entirely under the hands of the Ethiopian Government and the need to send off able bodied persons home, equipped with food provisions, implements and seeds in time for ploughing was a well thought out measure undertaken on the decision of the Ethiopian Government.

The feeding station was not meant to continue operation in perpetuity. As a feeding and distribution center, it was designed to meet specific problems after which it gradually phases out. At Ibinat where after a limited period of feeding and convalescing 30,000 able bodied persons, who were able to start a new life left the station of their own free will with sufficient food and all other requirements that could take them through to the next harvest.

It is quite obvious that there is nothing wrong with this practice. If Washington was not consulted on the matter, it is because the

184

sovereign decision of Ethiopia is not and will not be subject to the dictate of the U.S. Administration.

The allegation that the feeding station was rased to the ground was the most incredible aspect of the fabulous story. It is inconceivable that the Ethiopian Government, which spends considerable financial outlays to build stores, houses and other infrastructure to contain the effects of drought could be a party to an act of destruction as has been falsely ascribed to it. Leaving aside the utterly groundless insinuation, there has been no burning of dwellings, although what has taken place was the clearance of accumulated dirt for hygienic purposes.

The violent reaction of officials of the U.S. Administration to baseless and highly speculative press reports is more a reflection of their animosity to the Ethiopian Revolution and people than the professed outward expression of concern for the welfare of the drought victims. It has now become common occurrence for officials of the U.S. Administration to cling to any imaginable thing concerning matters relating to Ethiopia in their vain effort to mobilize negative international public opinion against her.

The vociferous reaction of high ranking officials of the U.S. Administration on the alleged incident at Ibinat is more a manifestation of their malicious intentions towards Ethiopia than anything else.

3 May 1985

Appendix II: US EMERGENCY ASSISTANCE FOR ETHIOPIA, 1984–1985

US Emergency Assistance for Ethiopia for US Fiscal Year 1984

Distributor[b]	Commodities (metric tons)	Commodities and transport ($000)
CRS Regular[c]	11,863 (food)	6,035.0
CRS Emergency[d]	11,980 (food)	9,096.2[e]
WFP	12,500 (food)	3,884.6
LWR	5,000 (food)	2,372.3
CRDA	–	700.0 (transport only)
UNICEF	(medicine)	1,000.0
Total	41,343	23,088.1

Notes:

a. 1 October 1983 to 30 September 1984.

b. Names of Distributors.

ADRA	Adventist Relief and Development Association
AJJDC	American Jewish Joint Distribution Committee
CARE	[No longer an acronym]
CDAA	Churches Drought Action Africa
CRS	Catholic Relief Services
	(Regular program — maternal child health)
	(Emergency program)
CRS—North	Catholic Relief Services — Food for the North Initiative
CRS—MC	Catholic Relief Services on behalf of Missionaries of Charity
FFH	Food for the Hungry
ICRC	International Committee of the Red Cross
ICRC/CRDA	International Committee of the Red Cross/Christian Relief and Development Association (Wheat in Exchange for Seeds)
LICROSS	League of International Red Cross Societies
RRC	Ethiopian Relief and Rehabilitation Commission
SAVE	Save the Children, US
UNDRO	United Nations Disaster Relief Organization
WFP/IEFR	World Food Programme's International Emergency Famine Relief
WVRO	World Vision Relief Organization
WVRO—North	World Vision Relief Organization — Food for the North Initiative

c. Catholic Relief Service's regular program is a mother–child feeding program run since the early 1970s for the benefit of poor families in the Addis Ababa and Dire Dawa areas. Its purpose is to assure proper growth and health of infants and to train mothers in nutritional and health practices.

d. CRS' emergency program is designed to feed those in danger of starvation as a result of drought or other catastrophe. All other programs listed above fall also into the emergency category.

e. Includes $3,495,000 for inland transportation.

Source:
USAID, Addis Ababa.

US Emergency Assistance for Ethiopia for US Fiscal Year 1985[a]

Distributor[b]	Food Aid	
	Commodities (metric tons)	Value of metric tons[c] ($000)
CARE	41,527	22,364.3
CDAA	161,194	108,546.0
CRS Emergency	40,558	22,356.6
CRS Regular	11,869	5,369.7
CRS North	9,000	4,763.0
CRS MC	4,654	2,833.8
ICRC	33,870	16,682.0
ICRC/CRDA (Seeds)	5,000	1,350.0
LICROSS	11,610	5,483.9
RRC	50,000	18,833.0
SAVE	17,401	9,340.9
WFP/IEER	9,973	5,165.1
WVRO	35,464	24,137.0
WVRO North	8,100	4,843.8
Subtotal	440,220	252,069.1

Non-Food Aid	
Item	Value of ($US000)
ADRA (Blankets, Medicines, Logistics)	621.1
ADRA (Airfreight)	12.5
Africare (Medical Teams)	300.0
AJJDC (Medical, Shelter Supplies)	350.0
CARE (Food Monitors)	397.6
Concern (Plastic Sheeting)	55.8
FFH (Support for Feeding & Med. Services)	803.9
Heifer Project Int'l (Draft Oxen)	540.0
Helen Keller Int'l (Medical Support)	34.2
ICRC (Air Transport of Trucks)	400.0
Interaction (Support for Flying Tigers)	17.1
RRC (Fuel Costs for Food Airlift)	25.0
RRC (Blankets, Plastic Sheeting)	170.2
Transamerica (Emergency Food Airlifts)	14,994.2
UNDRO (Monitoring/Coordination Support)	65.5

UNICEF (Truck Leasing and Tires)	1,000.0
UNICEF (Water to Displaced Persons)	750.0
UNICEF (Relief Flight from Europe)	53.0
WASH (Water/Sanitation)	150.0
WVRO (Air/Ground Transport, Water, Medicines)	1,597.6
WVRO (Feeding Center Expansion)	3,808.0
WVRO (18,000 blankets)	71.1
WVRO (Operating Costs for Twin Otters)	1,113.0
Subtotal Non-Food Assistance	27,329.8
TOTAL US EMERGENCY ASSISTANCE	279,398.0

Notes:
a. 1 October to 30 September 1985.
b. For names of distributors, see preceding table.
c. Includes commodity, ocean freight and internal freight.

Source:
USAID, ADDIS Ababa.

Appendix III: TOTAL EMERGENCY ASSISTANCE TO ETHIOPIA FOR US FISCAL YEAR 1985

Country	Food Aid ($000)	Non-Food Aid ($000)	Total Aid ($000)
Australia	14,474	8,610	23,084
Austria	1,080	800	1,880
Belgium	3,970	3,109	7,079
Bulgaria	5,219	8,916	14,135
Canada	41,974	10,044	52,018
China	4,082	3,163	7,245
Czechoslovakia	2,375	1,100	3,475
Denmark	514	4,028	4,542
EEC	59,951	22,650	82,601
Finland	2,378	796	3,174
France	23,045	250	23,295
German D.R.	1,353	10,036	11,389
Germany F.R.	17,124	17,219	34,343
Greece	4,801	152	4,953
Hungary	1,624		1,624

Country	Food Aid ($000)	Non-Food Aid ($000)	Total Aid ($000)
Iceland	51		51
India	15,390		15,390
Iran	1,392		1,392
Ireland	1,232		1,232
Italy	6,940	49,344	56,284
Japan	6,169	18,178	24,347
Korean Rep.	150	710	860
Libya	270		270
Netherlands	5,735	2,705	8,440
New Zealand	38		38
Norway	5,611	360	5,971
Pakistan	135		135
Poland	3,480	4,215	7,695
Romania	6,000	7,000	13,000
Spain	3,500	500	4,000
Sweden	3,891	4,014	7,905
Switzerland	3,020	1,455	4,475
USSR		173,000	173,000
United Kingdom	5,469	32,237	37,706
USA	252,069	27,330	279,399
Yugoslavia	5,514	133	5,647
Zimbabwe	3,750		3,750
United Nations Organizations:			
FAO		3,300	3,300
UNDRO		1,520	1,520
UNHCR	7,600	9,700	17,300
UNICEF	6,760	26,396	33,156
WHO		220	220
WFP	13,994	3,418	17,412
TOTAL	542,124	456,608	998,732

Source:
Figures compiled by the office of UN/Assistant Secretary General Kurt Jansson.

SELECT BIBLIOGRAPHY

Bereket Habte Selassie, *Conflict and Intervention in the Horn of Africa* (Monthly Review Press, New York and London, 1980)

Brzezinski, Zbigniew, *Power and Principle* (Farar Straus Giroux, New York, 1983)

Central Report Delivered by Mengistu Haile Mariam (Government of Ethiopia, Addis Ababa, September 1984)

Erlich, Haggai, *The Struggle over Eritrea, 1962–1978* (Hoover Institution, Stanford, 1983)

Firebrace James, *Never Kneel Down* (Bertrand Russell House, London, 1984)

Garthoff, Raymond L., *Detente and Confrontation—American–Soviet Relations from Nixon to Reagan* (Brookings, 1985)

Gromyko, Anatoly, 'Soviet–Ethiopian Relations Today', paper presented to the Eighth International Conference of Ethiopian Studies, November 1984

Halliday, Fred and Molyneux, Maxine, *The Ethiopian Revolution* (Verso Editions, London, 1981)

Henze, Paul, 'Getting a Grip on the Horn' in Walter Laqueur (ed.), *The Pattern of Soviet Conduct in the Third World* (Praeger, New York, 1983)

—— 'Arming the Horn 1960–1980', paper presented to the seventh International Conference of Ethiopian Studies

—— 'Russians and the Horn', European–American Institute for Security Research Paper, Summer 1983

—— 'Communist Ethiopia — Is it Succeeding?', The Rand Paper Series, January 1985

—— 'Marxism–Leninism in Ethiopia: Political Impasse and Economic Degradation', paper prepared for symposium on African revolutions in the Marxist–Leninist mode, June 1985

—— 'Dilemmas in the Horn', *The National Interest* (September 1985)

Hess, Robert L., *Ethiopia, The Modernization of Autocracy* (Cornell University Press, Ithaca, 1970)

Kapuscinski, Ryszard, *The Emperor, Downfall of an Autocrat* (Harcourt Brace, New York, 1983)

Lefort, Rene, *Ethiopia, An Heretical Revolution?* (Zed Press,

London, 1983)

Legum, Colin, 'Angola and the Horn' in Stephen S. Kaplan (ed.), *Diplomacy of Power* (Brookings Institution, 1981)

Marcus, Harold G., *Ethiopia, Great Britain and the United States, 1941–1974* (University of California Press, 1983)

Mesfin Wolde Mariam, *Rural Vulnerability to Famine in Ethiopia: 1958–1977* (Vikas Publishing House, New Delhi, 1984)

Ottaway, David and Marina, *Ethiopia — Empire in Revolution* (Africana, New York, 1978)

—— and —— *Afrocommunism* (Holmes and Meier, New York, 1981

Ottaway, Marina, *Soviet and American Influence in the Horn of Africa* (Praeger, New York, 1982)

Petrides, S. Pierre, *The Boundary Question Between Ethiopia and Somalia* (People's Publishing House, New Delhi, 1983)

Petterson, Donald K., 'Ethiopia Abandoned? An American Perspective', unpublished article

—— 'Somalia and the United States, 1977–1983: The New Relationship', forthcoming

Porter, Bruce D., *The USSR in Third World Conflicts* (Cambridge University Press, 1984)

Remnek, Richard B., 'Soviet Policy in the Horn of Africa: The Decision to Intervene' in Robert H. Donaldson (ed.), *The Soviet Union in the Third World* (Croom Helm, London, 1981)

Sherman, Richard, *Eritrea — The Unfinished Revolution* (Praeger, New York, 1980)

Spencer, John, *Ethiopia at Bay: A Personal Account of the Haile Selassie Years* (Reference Publications, Algonac, Michigan, 1984)

Survival International, *Ethiopia's Bitter Medicine* (Calvert's Press, London, 1986)

Tarabrin, E.A. *USSR and Countries of Africa* (Progress Publishers, Moscow, 1980)

Tubiana, Joseph (ed.), *Modern Ethiopia from the Accession of Menelik II to the Present* (Rotterdam, Balkema, 1980)

Vance, Cyrus, *Hard Choices* (Simon and Schuster, New York, 1983)

INDEX

Aaron, David 44, 49–51, 74
Adair, Ross 8
Addou, Somali Ambassador 33
Adelman, Kenneth 162
Afars 157
Afghanistan 54, 74, 100–1, 180
African Development Bank
  (ADB) 53, 71n
Agency for International
  Development (AID), US
  125–6, 133–6, 143–7
agriculture 165–9 *see also*
  collectivization
Ahmad, Samir 79
Ahmad, Yusuf, Minister 172
Aklilu Habte Wold 5
Alemayehu Haile 24–6
Alemu Abebe, advisor 151
All Ehtiopia Socialist Movement
  (MEISON) 19, 24–5, 49, 90–1,
  97
Aman Andom, General 6–7,
  9–11, 23, 30, 105, 111–12
Amanuel Amde-Michael 9
Amin, Idi 38, 66
Amin, Mohammed 125
Andreev, Gennadi 100
Andropov, Yuri A. 69
arms supplies to Ehtiopia
  Soviet 17–19, 27, 29, 39, 41–2,
    91, 102
  US 2–3, 8, 14–16, 19–21, 27,
    39–40, 51, 90
army 5–6, 18, 91, 108–9, 153, 164,
  178
  see also Derg
Asfa Wossen, Crown Prince 5
Ashwood, Carol 140–1
Asmara 1, 9, 15, 28, 73
assistance for Ethiopia
  development *see* development
  humanitarian *see* famine
  military *see* arms supplies

Atnafu Abate 10, 13, 27, 106–7,
  112
Ayalew Mandefro, Ambassador
  49–50

Balenbale 78–9
Berhanu Bayih, Politburo 135–6,
  147
Bonkers, Don, Congressman 64–5
Brezhnev, L.I. 39, 94
Brown, Harold 44
Brzezinski, Zbigniew 34–5, 42–4,
  50
Bulgaria 93, 131, 173

Cahill, Kevin, Dr 36
Canada 130–1
Carter, Jimmy, President 31,
  33–7, 49–51, 74
  administration 13, 23, 26, 31–2,
    34–7, 40–1, 48–9, 54–5, 74–5,
    182
Castro, Fidel 29–31, 94, 97, 113
Catholic Relief Service (CRS)
  118, 124, 132–4, 186–7
Chad 114–15
Chapin, Frederick 51–5
China, People's Republic of 3,
  18–19, 54, 100, 158
cholera 148–9
Christianity 83, 170–2
Clark, Dick, Senator 20
collectivization 167–9
  and resettlement 127–9
Commission for the Organization
  of the Party of the Workers of
  Ethiopia (COPWE) 54–5, 60,
  98–100
Compensation for nationalized
  US property 13, 51–3, 71n, 183
Crocker, Chester 61–3, 125, 127,
  150
Cuba 41–4, 93–5, 158, 173

193